DECLARING WAR

Declaring War directly challenges the two-hundred-year-old belief that the Congress can and should declare war. By offering a detailed analysis of the declarations of 1812 and 1898 and the War Powers Resolution of 1973, the book demonstrates the extent of the organizational and moral incapacity of the Congress to declare war. This book invokes Carl von Clausewitz's dictum that "war is policy" to explain why declarations of war are an integral part of war and proposes two possible remedies – a constitutional amendment or, alternatively, a significant reorganization of Congress. It offers a comprehensive historical, legal, constitutional, moral, and philosophical analysis of why Congress has failed to check an imperial presidency. The book draws on Roman history and international law to clarify the form, function, and language of declarations of war, and on John Austin's speech act theory to investigate why and how a "public announcement" is essential for the social construction of both war and the rule of law.

Brien Hallett is an Associate Professor at the Matsunaga Institute for Peace at the University of Hawai'i-Manoa, where he teaches courses in peace and conflict resolution, with a special interest in the thought of Gandhi, Martin Luther King, and Vaclav Havel. His primary research interest is the declaration of war and the historical, legal, constitutional, moral, and philosophical issues that surround it. Hallett is the author of *The Lost Art of Declaring War* (1998) and several encyclopedia articles.

DECLARING WAR

CONGRESS,
THE PRESIDENT, AND
WHAT THE CONSTITUTION
DOES NOT SAY

BRIEN HALLETT

University of Hawai'i-Manoa,
Matsunaga Institute of Peace

CAMBRIDGE UNIVERSITY PRESS
Cambridge, New York, Melbourne, Madrid, Cape Town,
Singapore, São Paulo, Delhi, Mexico City

Cambridge University Press
32 Avenue of the Americas, New York, NY 10013-2473, USA

www.cambridge.org
Information on this title: www.cambridge.org/9781107608573

First published 2012

Printed in the United States of America

A catalog record for this publication is available from the British Library.

Library of Congress Cataloging in Publication data
Hallett, Brien.
  Declaring war : Congress, the president, and what the Constitution
  does not say / Brien Hallett.
     pages   cm
  Includes bibliographical references and index.
  ISBN 978-1-107-02692-6 (hardback) – ISBN 978-1-107-60857-3 (paperback)
  1. War, Declaration of – United States.   2. War and emergency powers – United States.
  I. Title.
  KF4941.H35   2012
  342.73'062–dc23   2012012603

ISBN 978-1-107-02692-6 Hardback
ISBN 978-1-107-60857-3 Paperback

For Peter T. Manicas, PhD
Teacher

21. Second proposition: It is essential for a just war that an exceedingly careful examination be made of the justice and causes of the war and that the reasons of those who on grounds of equity oppose it be listened to. For (as the comic poet [Terence] says) "A wise man must make trial of everything by words before resorting to force"....

24. Again, a king is not by himself capable of examining into the causes of a war and the possibility of a mistake on his part is not unlikely and such a mistake would bring great evil and ruin to multitudes. Therefore, war ought not to be made on the sole judgment of the king, nor, indeed, on the judgment of a few, but in that of many, and they wise and up right men.

Francisco de Vitoria
(1934 (1532), lvii)

Tzu-lu asked Confucius, "If the Lord of Wei was waiting for you to bring order to his state, to what would you give your first priority?"

Confucius replied, "Without question it would be to order names properly."

"Would you be as impractical as that?" Tzu-lu responded. "What is there to order?"

[Confucius] How can you be so coarse! An exemplary person (*chün tzu*) remains silent about things that he does not understand! When names are not properly ordered, what is said is not attuned; when what is said is not attuned, things will not be done successfully; when things are not done successfully, the use of ritual action and music will not prevail; when the use of ritual action and music does not prevail, the application of laws and punishments will not be on the mark; and when laws and punishments are not on the mark, the people will not know what to do with themselves. Thus, when the exemplary person (*chün tzu*) puts a name to something, it can certainly be spoken, and when spoken it can certainly be done. There is nothing careless in the attitude of the exemplary person (*chün tzu*) toward what he says.

(13/3. Cited in Hall and Ames 1987, 269–70)

Contents

Figures

Acknowledgments

During the many years I have been working on this book, I have benefited from the encouragement and comments of many colleagues. My earliest notes were read and discussed with Svante Karlsson, who saw some potential and encouraged further effort. Bob Mann read an early draft and most honestly pointed out that it was a very early draft. A little farther along Ken Moss combined gracious hospitality and stimulating conversation with generous comments and suggestions. Jeffrey Peake introduced me to the work of the New Institutionalism and his own study of executive agreements, which confirmed important parts of my thinking.

The four years I participated in the War and Peace Workshop at The Graduate University for Advanced Studies (Sokendai) in Hayama, Japan, both were stimulating and provided ample time for research and writing. The encouragement and support of Sugawara Hirotaka, Shimizu Yoshimitsu, Sharon Traweek, and the other participants were invaluable.

As the project neared completion, Dustin Howes contributed his probing intellect, his infectious enthusiasm, and his groundbreaking work on Hannah Arendt and intersubjectivity. Nisha Fazal's reading was central to transforming the late drafts into final drafts. George Simson provided his usual enthusiastic support and generous suggestions. Barbara Polk shaped the early chapters with her no-nonsense and practical perspective. And, finally, Peter Manicas was my sharpest critic and most helpful commentator. He insisted on sound logic and clear expression. The remaining lapses in either logic or obtuseness of style, naturally, reflect only the stubbornness of the author.

Prologue

> The Congress shall have power ... to declare war, grant letters of marque and reprisal, and make rules concerning captures on land and water ...
>
> (article I, section 8, clause 11)

This book is about the power to declare war: who should possess the authority, how they should exercise it, what purposes a declaration serves, and why. This book is, consequently, about the relationships among conflict resolution, speech acts, and the rule of law. This consequence follows from the fact that declarations of war are speech acts. They are public "announcements" of official decisions. As public "announcements," they can be motivated by either one of two antithetical attitudes: One can declare war as an act of anger and vengeance seeking "victory" over one's enemy, or one can declare war as the initial step in resolving a serious conflict with one's conflict partner. In the former case, conflict resolution is irrelevant. A desire for "victory" over one's enemy turns both speech and the rule of law into obstructions and hindrances. Why would anyone want to speak to the enemy? What could one possibly have to say to an enemy? Since the object is to destroy the enemy, why would anyone submit to the constraints of law? "Bomb them back to the Stone Age," as General Curtis LaMay used to say. In the latter case, "victory" is irrelevant. A desire for resolution with one's conflict partner turns both speech and the rule of law into aides and facilitators. Speech facilitates negotiations of the grievances and remedies, and law aids in reducing the necessities of war by restraining intemperate actions.

The tension in this book is that both speech act theory and, especially, conflict resolution theory are overwhelmed by concern for the rule of law. This occurs because the starting point for this book is the two-hundred-year-old congressional failure to discharge its constitutional responsibility "to declare war." There is so much that has to be said about this congressional failure that rule of law pushes speech act and conflict resolution theory very far into the background. A need, therefore, exists to underline the foundational roles of both at the very beginning.

The conflict-resolution theory that underpins this book is based loosely on Louis Kriesberg's *Constructive Conflict: From Escalation to Resolution* (1998). All conflicts begin as vague and ambiguous unconscious feelings of discomfort. For one reason or another, most of these unconscious feelings never develop into conscious feelings. When they do, the most frequent and natural response is to ignore them, denying, suppressing, or avoiding them in the hope that the conflict will go away. Yet, some conflicts simply will not go away. Moreover, some conflicts neither can nor should be avoided. They demand resolution. But how? One's conflict partner is not a mind reader. He may have the same feeling of discomfort for his own reasons, but he cannot possibly know why you are upset. He cannot possibly know what your reasons are as long as they remain locked up inside your head. The indispensible first step in resolving any conflict, then, is to make the conflict manifest.

A number of ways exist to do this. What ties all of these methods together is that they are all what John Austin (1975) called speech acts. Here, "speech act" is taken to mean any languagelike medium of communication. For example, one can roll one's eyes or squirm in one's chair to manifest the existence of a conflict. A sharp jab to the jaw or a carrier-based air attack on Pearl Harbor is also an unmistakable way to manifest the existence of a conflict. While these "physical" speech acts are excellent ways to manifest a conflict and to confirm the worst fears of an enemy, they are less than optimal ways to initiate the resolution of a conflict. A more effective way is a simple natural language declaration, "I am upset." Still more effective is to articulate both the grievances perceived to have caused the conflict and one's preferred remedies, "I am upset because.... My proposed remedy is...." This gives the conflict partner something substantive to respond to, to negotiate over. Even more effective is to articulate one's perceived grievances and preferred remedies in a tentative and conditional manner. If one's conflict partner responds in like manner, tentatively, with a conditional declaration of his own perceived grievances and preferred remedies, negotiations can begin in earnest with a view to finding a just settlement. A declaration of war, therefore, is not best thought of as a trigger, as the official announcement that the bombing is to commence because a friend is now an enemy to be destroyed. Rather, a declaration of war is best understood as the instrument by which a socially authorized declarer speaks to transform a latent into a manifest conflict. If well spoken, especially if the grievances and remedies are spoken conditionally, a declaration of war becomes the necessary first step to resolving the conflict in hand. Peace, not war, is the objective of a well-written declaration of war; war, not peace, is the objective of a poorly written declaration.

But if this book is ultimately about the relationships among conflict resolution, speech acts, and the rule of law, the foreground story is a troubling tale of tyranny, of dictatorship, and of men ruling in defiance of the law. For the Constitution of the United States strongly implies that the U.S. Congress is the socially authorized speaker who articulates and makes manifest the nation's grievances and peace terms. And the Congress could have done so, had it followed the example of the Second Continental Congress. Over the past two centuries, the U.S. Congress could have declared its perceived grievances and preferred remedies conditionally to foster negotiations, before declaring them absolutely, after negotiation had failed, as the Second Continental Congress did in 1775 and 1776. But the example of the Second Continental Congress was not followed; the Declaration of Independence did not become the congressional model for the declaring of war, and the rule of law was overturned by the tyranny of presidential war making.

DECLARING WAR

1   A Constitutional Tyranny and Presidential Dictatorship

All legislative Powers herein granted shall be vested in a Congress of the United States, which shall consist of a Senate and House of Representatives. ...

> (article I, section 1, clause 1)

The Congress shall have power ... to declare war, grant letters of marque and reprisal, and make rules concerning captures on land and water.

> (article I, section 8, clause 11)

The executive Power shall be vested in a President of the United States of America.

> (article II, section 1, clause 1)

The President shall be commander in chief of the army and navy of the United States, and of the militia of the several states, when called into the actual service of the United States.

> (article II, section 2, clause 1)

For more than two hundred years, we Americans have prided ourselves on our republican Constitution and our democratic politics. We have stood tall and told ourselves and the world that America is "the home of the free." No tyrants live here. Tyrants live and oppress their people elsewhere, across the sea in distant lands, in Cuba, in Haiti, in Nicaragua, in Nazi Germany and Imperial Japan, in North Korea, in North Vietnam, in Grenada, in the Dominican Republic, in Panama, in Bosnia and Kosovo, or in Iraq and Afghanistan. But tyrants in America, never.

Yet, when the dark clouds of discord appear on the horizon and the dogs of war howl and strain at their leashes, what happens in "the land of the

1

free"? Our Constitution is ignored; our democratic politics is circumvented, and smiling tyrants fill the vacuum. For example, what happened during the decades-long tragedy that was the war in Vietnam? Our Constitution mandates that the Congress shall "declare war." But during those decades of war, who paid the least attention to the Constitution? Which member demanded that the Congress stand up, exercise its constitutional responsibility, and "declare war"? Likewise, our democratic politics mandates that the voice of the people be heard. But during those decades of war, who paid the least attention to the voice of the people? The voice of the people was shouted in the streets but was not heard in the halls of power. Not, that is, until the tragedy in Vietnam and the tyranny at home had surpassed all endurance.

In place of our republican Constitution and democratic politics during those decades of war, five presidents acted, not like the chief executives of a republic, but like elected kings. From Harry Truman's initial decision to increase support for the French reconquest of Indochina in June 1950 through Richard Nixon's "Vietnamization" policy in 1969–72, these "presidents" operated as kings and emperors have always done. They decided when and where to bomb, when and where to invade, and when to escalate or deescalate. Like the hereditary kings of old, they decided these vital questions in private for their own best motives and then imposed their decisions on an increasingly skeptical and reluctant Congress and public. In a word, the republic's chief executives were oblivious to the rule of law and the Constitution. They had metamorphized into tyrants.

At its heart, after all, tyranny is not about beating, torturing, or imprisoning innocent people. When law rules, innocent people are not beaten, tortured, or imprisoned. Unnecessary wars are not fought in Vietnam or elsewhere. Strictly speaking, tyranny is about violating the rule of law. The essence of tyranny lies in powerful individuals' acting against the law and imposing their will upon the people. To neuter tyrants, law, not men, must rule. But this most common of common sense has never become common practice. Instead, for more than two hundred years, the president has commanded the armed forces, in accordance with the law. Yet at the same time, he has violated both law and common sense. Repeatedly, he has initiated war in manifest violation of the Constitution and the congressional responsibility to decide the question of war or peace and, on the basis of its answer, to declare or not declare war. In sum, our republican Constitution has failed us when it is most needed, our democratic politics have withered when it is most needed, and tyranny has flourished under the cloak of national security and defense.

Yet, is the matter so simple and straightforward? Is the president simply a tyrant? Many will point out that the president is elected by the people. He serves at their pleasure. As proof, protests against the war in Vietnam forced

Lyndon Johnson out of office, forced him not to seek a second term. True enough, but an elected tyrant is still a tyrant. For tyranny is not a personal characteristic; it is instead a pattern of egregious violations of the law. For example, the Second Continental Congress did not indict George III of tyranny because he was a bad man, because he beat, tortured, or imprisoned innocent colonists. No, the Second Continental Congress indicted him because "The History of the present King of Great Britain is a History of repeated injuries and Usurpations, all having in direct Object the Establishment of an absolute Tyranny over these States." And what were these "repeated injuries and Usurpations"? They were twenty-seven in number that ranged from "He has refused his Assent to Laws, the most wholesome and necessary for the public Good" through "For depriving us, in many Cases, of the Benefits of Trial by Jury" and ending with "He has excited domestic Insurrections amongst us, ... " Twenty-seven specific illegal acts are what made George III a tyrant, not whether he was elected or unelected, not whether he was a nice guy or a bad guy.

And what are the "repeated injuries and Usurpations" of the presidents? Repeatedly, over the two hundred and more years of the American Republic, president after president has begun one war after another without so much as a nod to the Constitution. As with George III so with our wartime presidents, who are tyrants "for depriving the Congress and the people, in all but four cases, of the Benefits of article I, section 8, clause 11 of the Constitution, the congressional power to declare war." Such egregious, repeated violations of the Constitution deserve one and only one label – tyranny. No longer, at the beginning of the twenty-first century, is it acceptable for scholars to describe our Constitution and politics with respect to war as "executive initiative, congressional acquiesce, and judicial tolerance" (Yoo 2005, 13). For, beyond question, our unconstitutional wartime tyranny was not meant to be.

All agree that the question of war or peace is the single most consequential, most controversial, most difficult decision made by any human community. Deciding when or whether the people's blood will be shed, the nation's treasure will be expended, and the state's very existence will be hazarded certainly requires special consideration and special procedures. Understanding this, the Framers of the Constitution thought that they had provided the new Republic with precisely the special procedures that would foster special consideration. Unlike in all the kingdoms, empires, and tyrannies of history, the Framers had the audacity to separate and divide the king's inherent power as the nation's war leader. The president was to command the nation's armed forces; the Congress was "to declare war," as Alexander Hamilton explained in *Federalist No. 69*:

> The President is to be commander-in-chief of the army and navy of the United States. In this respect his authority would be nominally the same with that of the

king of Great Britain, but in substance much inferior to it. It would amount to nothing more than the supreme command and direction of the military and naval forces, as first General and admiral of the Confederacy; while that of the British king extends to the DECLARING of war and to the RAISING and REGULATING of fleets and armies, all which, by the Constitution under consideration, would appertain to the legislature.

This unheard of division and separation of the king's divine right powers was unprecedented. Its aim was to drive a stake into the heart of tyranny. Its hope was that a powerful individual would no longer decide when, or if, the people's blood would be shed; the nation's treasure would be expended, and the state's very existence would be hazarded. Instead, a representative body of the people would make this most significant of decisions.

Such were the hopes of the Framers of the Constitution. But history is not built upon hopes. It is built upon the fulfillment or the lack of fulfillment of hopes. Contrary to the Framers' hopes, a stake was not driven into the heart of tyranny. Tyranny lived on, nourished by a fatally impractical division of the sovereign's war powers, which are three, and not two. Before declaring war, before commanding the diplomatic, economic, and military means, the decision must be taken. The question of war or peace must be asked and answered. The most reasonable democratic and republican assumption in 1787 was that the Congress would, first, decide and, then, declare, before the president commanded. The tyrannical reality, however, has always been that the president decides and commands, while the congressional declaration is an optional extra, an infrequent afterthought.

CATCH 22: CONGRESSIONAL INCAPACITY AND A DICTATORIAL PRESIDENT

Still, is the matter so simple? The president is a tyrant, end of discussion. Instead of warning of an *Imperial Presidency* (1973), Arthur Schlesinger Jr. got it wrong. He should have warned of a *Tyrannical Presidency*. For what else is one to call a powerful individual acting against the law to impose his wars upon a republican government and a democratic people? The situation appears to be very much more complicated than a straightforward case of presidential tyranny.

As a first step, is it not strange that the president is only a part-time tyrant? How can a real tyrant be both elected and only a part-timer? He is a part-time tyrant because he is the very picture of a republican and democratic "chief executive" during times of peace. And why? Because the Congress upholds its part of the constitutional bargain during times of peace. It can and does exercise its peacetime "legislative Powers." It regularly makes laws for the president to administer. Only when the dark clouds of war gather on the horizon and administering peace changes to waging war does the president become a tyrant. If the Congress were exercising its wartime duty "to declare war," then the number of congressional declarations of war would equal the number of America's wars. But, however one counts, America's wars are several times more numerous than the four declarations made by the Congress – those for the War of 1812, for the Spanish-American War, for the First World War, and for the Second World War. As a result, part of the time the president is tyrannical; part of the time he is not.

As a second step, what is the cause of this effect? Why is it even possible for the president step in and do what the Congress is constitutionally mandated to do? All the Framers of the Constitution ever asked the Congress to do was 1) to recognize the gathering clouds of war; 2) to seize the initiative and draft a declaration of war, preferably a conditional declaration, in response to those ominous clouds; 3) to debate the draft declaration; 4) to amend it, if needed; and 5) to vote it up or down. That is all. Painfully though, the bicameral Congress has been and continues to be totally incapable of following this simple procedure. Specifically, it has been unable to get the procedure started. It has been unable either to recognize the initial signs of war or to seize the initiative and start the process. Instead, it has conceded the initiative to the president, waiting patiently for him to decide the question of war and peace. Of the greatest significance for remedying this constitutional contradiction is the contrast with the Second Continental Congress. In 1776 the unicameral Second Continental Congress did, in point of fact, recognize the issue, initiate action, draft a declaration, debate it, amend it, and vote on it.

The essential problem, therefore, has never been presidential tyranny, much less an "imperial presidency." Rather, a failure of the Federal Convention to anticipate soon-to-occur changes in the size, organization, and functioning of the new Congress has led to a complete lack of congressional initiative. Hence, the president is not "simply" a tyrant. For the congressional inability to uphold its part of the constitutional bargain during time of war has forced the president into a very nasty Catch 22: If the Congress were able both to decide on and to declare war, as the Constitution implies, then presidential tyranny would be impossible in time of war as it is in time of peace. But, as the next three chapters prove, the Congress has not, cannot, and will not in the future either decide on or declare war. Hence, Catch 22, the president is caught on the horns of a very sharp dilemma. Speaking to the right-hand horn, if he waits on the Congress to do what it cannot and will not do on its own initiative, he abides by the Constitution but risks losing the nation. An example of this horn is the refusal of the Congress to act upon the clear and present dangers posed by Nazi Germany in Europe and Imperial Japan in Asia until after the bombing of Pearl Harbor. Speaking to the left-hand horn, if the president ignores the Congress so as to defend the nation on his own authority in time of danger, he violates the Constitution, but saves the nation. An example of this horn of the dilemma is Abraham Lincoln's decision not to recall the Thirty-seventh Congress "to declare war" after the 12 April 1861 bombardment and surrender of Fort Sumter. Instead, he made the undoubtedly wise decision to wage the Civil War on the authority of his oath of office to "preserve, protect, and defend the Constitution of the United States."

The president, then, finds himself caught in a Catch 22. As a result, the previous indictment of tyranny does not ring true. The president has not deprived "the *Congress* and the people of the Benefits of article I, section 8, clause 11 of the Constitution, the congressional power to declare war." Instead, it is congressional incapacity that has deprived "the *president* and the people of the Benefits" of a republican division of the sovereign's war powers. Think how much easier the president's job would be if he only had to command the armed forces, as Commander in Chief George Washington did in 1776.

But if benevolent dictatorships always end in malevolent tyranny, then our republican government and democratic politics have teetered on the edge of a precipice for more than two hundred years. That we have not fallen over the edge into the abyss of tyranny is due only to the Roman virtues of our presidents. They have so far relinquished their extraordinary power when peace resumed. But dreaming that the virtuous examples of Cincinnatus and George Washington will protect us from the likes of Julius Caesar and Adolph Hitler is unwise in the extreme.

Therefore, the single most urgent issue confronting both our republican government and our democratic politics is how to drive a stake once and for all into the heart of the Constitution's incipient tyranny. How does one amend the Constitution to eliminate its Catch 22? How does one correct the fatally impractical division of the sovereign's war powers at the root of our presidential dictatorship? How does one overcome an incapacitated Congress so as to establish the rule of law in time of war as well as in time of peace? To answer these questions, this book explores four different approaches.

ORGANIZATION OF THE BOOK

In Part I, history is consulted to understand how and why the ever-larger bicameral Congress is incapable of exercising its constitutional responsibility to decide on and to declare war. The three chapters of this part tell the stories of how the Congress lost forever the power to decide the question of war or peace in 1812. How the Fifty-fifth Congress was determined to play politics instead of declaring war against Spain over Cuba in 1898. And how the War Powers Resolution of 1973 gave the president the legal authority to ignore the Congress.

In Part II, a variety of sources are consulted to answer the question, *How?* These three chapters identify the compositional elements of a declaration of war, the principal functions of a declaration of war, and the six possible procedures for declaring war. Along the way, the full range of presidential and congressional declarations are cataloged and analyzed. The most significant results derived from Part II are 1) the critical difference for the rule of law between procedurally perfect and procedurally imperfect declarations of war and 2) the four principal functions of well-written declarations of war, such as the Declaration of Independence. These four principal functions consist of two pairs of two linked functions each:

I. Recognition and response:
   a) A declaration manifests, transforms, and defines a contentious conflict as this specific "war."
   b) An open and determined declaration is a necessary first step in a conflict resolution process, especially when a conditional declaration of war precedes an absolute declaration.

II. Decision and deployment:
   a) A declaration establishes coherence between the political ends sought and the diplomatic, economic, or military means employed.
   b) An open and determined declaration is a necessary first step in creating a proper coordinate relationship between the declarer of war and the commander of the nation's diplomatic, economic, or military means.

In Part III, the insights gleaned in Parts I and II are put to use to propose two possible solutions. As already noted, the large, bicameral U.S. Congress is entirely incapable of declaring war. Given this fact and assuming that continued tyranny is unacceptable, any solution must begin by proposing a new, small, unicameral, independent entity modeled on the Second Continental Congress to exercise what John Locke called the fœderative powers, including the power to treat of peace, to decide the question of war or peace, and to declare war in an open and determinate manner. The first proposal, therefore, suggests a constitutional amendment to achieve this objective. The second proposal suggests a significant internal reorganization of the Congress to achieve the same objective in a less than satisfactory manner. In fine, both proposals acknowledge the obvious fact that any statutory solution, such as an amended War Powers Resolution, is no solution at all. The incapacity of the large, bicameral Congress cannot be remedied with a bandage; major constitutional surgery is needed.

In Part IV, attention shifts from the concrete and practical to the abstract and theoretical. As is made clear in Parts II and III, the baseline issue is the

degree of procedural perfection with which both the decision and the declaration are made: Whenever war is declared in accordance with recognized
constitutional procedures, rule of law prevails and the declaration has traditionally been termed "perfect." Whenever war is declared as an exception to
recognized constitutional procedures, rule of law is betrayed, tyranny has tri-
umphed, and the declaration has traditionally been termed "imperfect." On
the assumption that the United States is a nation ruled by law and not tyrants,
it therefore follows that imperfect declarations of war are always illegal and
illegitimate. To substantiate the claim that the rule of law is superior to the
rule of men, the penultimate chapter explores the pragmatic value that both
early republican Rome and modern bureaucracies have discovered in adher-
ing to proper procedures. In the final chapter, a philosophical analysis of the
speech act foundations of declarations of war is undertaken. Illuminating the
foundations should answer several unanswered questions that the previous
pages may have raised in the reader's mind.

Two appendixes are also found at the end of this book. The first repro-
duces all the legally recognized congressional declarations of war in American
history, beginning with the Declaration of Independence. These texts constitute textual data for concluding that the Congress of the United States cannot possibly fulfill its constitutional responsibility to decide on and to declare
war. The second appendix is a short comment on the declaring of war in
parliamentary governments. Since the declaring of war is a universal issue and
since parliamentary regimes possess a different structure from presidential
regimes, the principles articulated in this study need to be applied somewhat
differently to parliamentary governments.

In conclusion, this book is based upon the two complementary assump-
tions, that tyranny has no place in our republican and democratic nation
and that the rule of law is superior to the rule of tyrants, even during time
of war. For more than five thousand years, kings, emperors, and dictatorial presidents have declared war on their personal authority as the nation's
war leader. In 1787, a group of delegates meeting in Philadelphia attempted
unsuccessfully to change the course of that history. They rejected the traditional consolidation of the power to decide the question of war or peace, the
power to declare war, and the power to command the armed forces in the
hands of a single individual. Instead, they attempted unsuccessfully to separate these three powers. Their experiment was both radical and noble, but a
complete failure. By focusing narrowly on the complexity hidden within the
infinitive phrase "to declare war," it is hoped that the experiment begun in
Philadelphia in 1787 might finally reach a successful conclusion during the
twenty-first century.

PART I

WHAT IS THE HISTORY?

2 How the President Declares War

The War of 1812

The Congress shall have power ... to declare war, grant letters of marque and reprisal, and make rules concerning captures on land and water.

(article I, section 8, clause 11)

He [Pierce Butler of South Carolina] was for vesting the power [to make war] in the President, who will have all the requisite qualities, and will not make war but when the Nation will support it.

Friday, 17 August 1787
Federal Convention, Philadelphia

The congressional declaration of 1812 is the first and most important example of how the president declares war. With it, President James Madison established the enduring precedents, procedures, and excuses. By 1812, it was well understood, if not widely accepted, that presidential decision making and leadership were essential elements for overcoming the organizational paralysis of the Congress. Since 1789, the size of the House had more than doubled, and its original committee-of-the-whole system had early on broken down in that chamber as a result of an ever-increasing workload. In its place, the modern standing-committee system slowly evolved by fits and starts. But war is not peace. Were presidential decision making and leadership also necessary for the declaring of war? Might it be possible for the Congress to decide the question of war or peace independently of the president? If so, then the hopes of the Federal Convention would be realized. If not, then the American republic would differ little from all the tyrannous kingdoms and empires of history, at least with respect to war.

With the shrewd assistance of the newly elected Speaker, Henry Clay, President Madison was able to answer the question. As in peace, so in war, the congressional power to declare war could not be exercised without strong and insistent presidential leadership and decision making. To overcome congressional paralysis on this issue as well as all other issues, the power to declare war would be exercised only after a presidential decision and only with presidential leadership. Not incidentally, the newly evolving standing-committee system in the House greatly facilitated President Madison's task.

In more concrete terms, since the beginning of the wars of the French Revolution and Empire, 1792–1815, the Congress had assiduously sidestepped French and British aggression on neutral American rights and interests. But how long could the United States ignore this aggression? How long could the nation remain aloof and neutral from this world war? During August 1811, President Madison decided that eighteen years was too long. The United States could no longer avoid open belligerency. With this decision, he established his first consequential precedent. The president would trouble the Congress to discharge its constitutional responsibility "to declare war" only for the largest wars, for world wars. To understand just how enduring this precedent is, one has only to recall that all four open and determined congressional declarations of war are for world wars, the War of 1812, the Spanish-American War, and the First and Second World Wars. President Madison well understood that anything smaller than a world war simply does not warrant the president's time and trouble to force congressional involvement.

AN ABSURD WAR

Answering the question of when, however, still leaves open the question of how. How was President Madison to push a very reluctant Congress "to declare war"? What procedures could he put in place to accomplish the task? Before answering this question, one must first appreciate how absurd it was for the United States to fight the War of 1812. In the first place, the war was declared against Great Britain on 18 June 1812, four days before Napoleon launched his fateful invasion of Russia. Had President James Madison maintained President Thomas Jefferson's policy of "peaceful coercion" for a year or so more, Napoleon's downfall would have been evident, and his eventual abdication on 6 April 1814 would have obviated any need for America to enter this world war at all. As already noted, previous American participation had been minimal and marginal. It consisted of the Quasi-War against France, 1798–1800, during the Adams administration, and antipiracy operations along the North African coast, 1801–5, during the first Jefferson administration. During the second Jefferson administration, a policy of "peaceful coercion" was followed, embracing embargoes, non-importation acts, and other American diplomatic and economic sanctions. These sanctions were in response to the depredations of the Napoleon's Continental System, begun in 1806, and the British response of 1807, the Orders in Council. Because of these two dueling policies, violations of American seaborne commerce multiplied, despite its nonbelligerent status as a neutral power.

In the second place, the rescinding of the British Orders in Council was Madison's ostensive objective for the War of 1812. The French Continental System was less effective and, hence, caused less disruption to American trade, commerce, and shipping. Yet, because of the speed a ship could sail in 1812, the war was "won" the day it began. With the assassination of Prime Minister Spencer Perceval as he entered the House of Commons on 11 May 1812, the principal defender of the Orders was removed from the scene. This allowed the new government, under Lord Liverpool, to revoke the Orders in Council on 17 June 1812, the very same day that the Senate voted on the declaration of war against Great Britain. The next day, the House voted the declaration, which Madison approved that afternoon (Adams 1896–1904, 6:284–8). But not only was the war "won" before it began, its most famous "victory" occurred after peace had been restored. General Sir Edward Packenham, commanding the British forces before New Orleans, was defeated by Andrew Jackson on 8 January 1815, two weeks after the peace treaty had been signed in Ghent, on 24 December 1814. But, again, the communications technology of the day prevented the news from Ghent reaching New Orleans in time. In between "winning" and "victory," the war was one military disaster after another for the Americans. The British raided up and down the coast at will; Washington was burned. The American invasions of Canada, the conquest of which was much anticipated, could hardly summon the energy to get across the border, much less conquer. Only the naval victories on the Great Lakes of Erie and Ontario and on Lake Champlain prevented a British invasion from Canada.

A large part of the explanation for the military disasters was Jefferson's neglect of the army and the navy. The army had an authorized strength of ten thousand, but, in January 1812, six months before the declaration of war, it mustered fewer than three thousand five hundred officers and men, mostly scattered across the frontier to ward off attacks by Indians (Ketcham 1971, 521–2). The navy was in even worst shape. It possessed sixteen ships, ranging from three heavy frigates rated at forty-four guns to four brigs rated at twelve and fourteen guns. This fleet, however, was outnumbered fifty to one by the Royal Navy. It was but a sixth the size of the fleet that the Royal Navy regularly stationed in American waters during peacetime, and none of the American ships could begin to match the Royal Navy's ships of the line rated at seventy-two guns. Moreover, only four were ready to sail when war was declared, the rest were in various stages of disrepair (Adams 1896–1904, 6:362–3; Ketcham 1971, 522, 535). To enter a world war with a force of this size against one of the larger and better equipped belligerents made little sense.

Or, consider the economic logic of the war. In a letter to Speaker Henry Clay dated 21 January 1812, Secretary of the Treasury Albert Gallatin reported that exports for the previous fiscal year had totaled $45,294,000. Of this total, $38,500,000 had been exported to Great Britain and its allies Spain and Portugal and $1,194,000 had been exported to France and its allies (Brant 1941–61, 5:403). But, of course, Great Britain was not just an excellent export market; it was also America's principal supplier of imports. Or, at least, it was when British imports were not barred by the Non-importation Act of 1806. This fact created a truly tantalizing fiscal scheme for financing the war against Great Britain, the convoluted complexities of which are best described by quoting Henry Adams's perplexing summary:

> The Non-importation Act stopped importations from England. If war should be considered as taking the place of non-importation, it would have the curious result of restoring trade with England [and thereby greatly increasing custom revenues].... Thus, two paths lay open. Congress might admit British goods, and by doing so dispense with internal [war] taxes, relieve the commercial States [i.e., New England], and offend France; or might shut out British goods, disgust the commercial States, double the burden of the war [taxes] on America, but distress England and please Napoleon. (Adams 1896–1904, 6:230–1)

Equally unaccounted for were the principal domestic consequences of the war. Against all expectations, this most divisive of wars ushered in the Era of Good Feelings, 1817–25. Before any good feelings were possible, however, the "disgust" of the commercial states over the war boiled over into sedition and threats of secession. As the war dragged on, the discontented New England Federalists drew themselves up and convened the Hartford Convention, 15 December 1814 to 5 January 1815. At the convention, twenty-six disgruntled delegates from Connecticut, Massachusetts, and Rhode Island proposed, according to the convention secretary, Harrison Gray Otis, "to lay the foundation for a radical reform in the national compact" (Brant 1941–61, 6:342). The convention eventually approved a report calling for a grab bag of constitutional amendments (*ibid.*, 6:361). Upon approval by the three state legislatures, Harrison Gray Otis, the opium trader Thomas H. Pickins, and William Sullivan traveled to Washington as commissioners for the convention to present its demands to the Congress and president. Unfortunately, they arrived during the first weeks of February 1815 in the midst of the joyous celebrations over the end of the war. News of Andrew Jackson's 8 January 1814 victory at New Orleans had reached Washington on Saturday, 4 February 1815, and was followed two weeks later with the news that a peace treaty had been signed in Ghent on 24 December 1814. Pickins and Sullivan attended the president at his regular

Wednesday evening *levée*, but only to pay their respects. Otis stayed in his boarding house, grousing to his wife that he would not go where "all was tinsel and vulgarity." And, moreover, he had "received no [dinner] invitation from Mr. Madison. What a mean and contemptible little blackguard" (*ibid.*, 6:370). Thus, if the Hartford Convention with its sedition and threat of secession marked the apogee of partisan bickering, its sudden demise into irrelevance also signaled the death of the Federalist Party and the ushering in of the Era of Good Feelings with the election of James Monroe, Madison's secretary of state, as the fifth president in 1817. In the final accounting of this most absurd and divisive of wars, the domestic balance sheet showed a positive gain in stable and productive politics.

A NEW RHETORIC OF DIABOLISM

Yet, war was declared. In order to accomplish this, three factors were necessary: a new rhetoric, a new Congress, and a new president. A new rhetoric was essential to inducing the Twelfth Congress to vote a declaration of war, since the old rhetoric obviously did not work. What was needed was to shift the debate away from the concrete negotiable grievances of defending American rights at sea as a neutral nonbelligerent to a new set of nonnegotiable "psychic grievances." Continued efforts to resolve the conflict, of course, had to be taken off the agenda if war was to be had.

In public relations terms, the old concrete negotiable demands were real, but emotionally sterile. Outside New England shipowners, who cared whether the rights of neutral ships were systematically violated? By repackaging the depredations of a very real world war as a putative "second revolutionary war," Madison and the War Hawks were able to "nationalize" the war and to argue that it was necessary to prevent the "indignity," the "dishonor," the "humiliation" of "recolonization" by Great Britain. Ronald Hatzenbuehler and Robert Ivie have described this as a process of "superimposition," the placing of a new, more appealing rhetoric of nonnegotiable emotional demands on top of the actual, negotiable demands:

> The significance of Republican rhetoric [in 1812] is more readily understood when compared with the failure of [John Adams and the] Federalists to justify [a general] war [against revolutionary France] in 1798 [instead of the Quasi-War actually fought]. Whereas Federalists had defined their crisis with France narrowly as an attack on commercial interests, Republicans universalized the threat by associating similar attacks on American commerce with affronts to national honor and rights and by interpreting such affronts as sure signs of a fixed and determined hostility toward the sovereignty of the United States [i.e., a design to "recolonize" America].... The crisis with France in 1798, therefore, was not a threat to the survival of the republic or republicanism. A rhetoric of diabolism [that ascribed to Britain an evil intention to "recolonize" America] had not [in 1798] evolved

to release the force of political ideology as a unifying motive for war [as it had by 1812]. (1983, 134–5)

This new, compelling rhetoric was needed for two reasons: first, to engage the general public, to get them emotionally involved, as the old rhetoric of negotiable demands had failed to do; second, and more to the point, to persuade the "Old Republican" opposition within the Republican Party to change their votes, since the Federalists were going to vote against the war on purely partisan grounds. Once a new rhetoric was deployed, the Old Republicans eventually felt they had sufficient political cover to assuage their consciences and face the voters. They, therefore, had little option but to maintain party loyalty and vote the new party line (Hatzenbuehler and Ivie 1983, 39–40).

By way of a passing observation, the Scylla and Charybdis of the power to declare war are found in the division of justificatory rhetoric into the two types identified by Hatzenbuehler and Ivie. The problem, of course, is that the two types work at cross-purposes to each other. On the one hand, wars can be justified by an appeal to negotiable demands that are actually relevant to the eventual settlement of the conflict. On the other hand, wars can also be justified by an appeal to nonnegotiable, emotional demands that are irrelevant to the eventual settlement of the conflict but that are exceptionally relevant to stirring up domestic support for a war, as in 1812. As a result of this justificatory contradiction, should the declarer of war go for the maximum public relations impact by personalizing and demonizing the conflict, or should the declarer go for the maximum conflict resolution impact? For example, should President George H. W. Bush accuse Saddam Hussein of being worse than Hitler, as he did on Thursday, 1 November 1990, or should he limit himself to the more restrained negotiable demands of the Security Council resolutions ordering Iraq to leave Kuwait (Nelson 1990)?

Striking the balance between emotion and conflict resolution is, to restate the obvious, very difficult. In this regard, however, official statements, such as the Declaration of Independence or Security Council resolutions, tend to emphasize the relevant negotiable demands, while political speeches, such as those given by George H. W. Bush during November 1990 at Mashpee, Massachusetts, or Orlando, Florida, tend to emphasize the emotional "Saddam is Hitler" trope (*ibid.*).

A NEW CONGRESS FOR YOUNG AMERICA

In addition to a new rhetoric, a new Congress was required. Unlike previous Congresses, the Twelfth Congress bristled with the energy and impatience of Young America, as a new generation arrived in the nation's capital from the South and the newly admitted western states. It counted seventy new members in a House of one hundred and forty-three and marked the first great generational shift in American politics (Adams 1896–1904, 6:158). Until November 1811, Congress had been the preserve of mature men who had been born as British subjects and fought the Revolutionary War; now, it was dominated by the energy of brash young men younger than forty who knew only the enthusiasm and optimism of an independent and expanding America; as Henry Adams summarized:

> Hardly one third of the members of [the Twelfth] Congress [1811–13] believed war to be their best policy. Almost another third were Federalists, who wished to overthrow the [Madison] Administration; the rest were honest and perhaps shrewd men, brought up in the school of Virginia and Pennsylvania politics, who saw more clearly the evils that war would bring than the good it might cause, and who dreaded the reaction upon constituents. They could not understand the need of carrying into every detail a revolution in their favorite system of [peaceful] government. Clay, Calhoun, Cheves and Lowndes [the main War Hawks] asked them to do in a single session what required half a century or more of time and experience, – to create a new government, and invest it with the attributes of old-world sovereignty under pretext of the war power. The older [Jeffersonian] Republicans had no liking for such statesmanship, and would gladly have set the young Southerners in their right places.
>
> By force of will and intellect the group of war members held their own, and dragged [the Twelfth] Congress forward in spite of itself, but the movement was slow and the waste of energy exhausting. (Adams 1896–1904, 6:170–1)

The first sign of this new generational shift was the election of the thirty-four-year-old freshman representative from Kentucky, Henry Clay, as Speaker of the House, to the astonishment of the Old Republicans. From this position, Clay would dominate the session, pack the key committees, lead the War Hawks, and, on Sunday, 15 March 1812, transmute the unique congressional power to declare war into a "divided, but shared power." Then, once "divided, but shared," the president would rule, and not law, because the Congress would have lost forever its ability to resist a president determined to war.

A NEW PRESIDENT OR AN OLD REPUBLICAN?

A new emotionally satisfying rhetoric deployed by a new energetic Congress still needs mature leadership. With greater coincidence than irony, the War of 1812 was declared under the aegis of James Madison, coauthor with Elbridge Gerry of the precise wording of the Declare War Clause. If anyone should have known the original intent of the Founding Fathers, it was he. And, indeed, Madison did seize the opportunity to turn one of his own interpretations of article I, section 8, into precedent: In his second *Letter of Helvidius*, he had interpreted the clause as meaning that, in time of war, "the executive has no other discretion than to convene and give information to the legislature"

(1900–10, 6:160). And this is exactly what he did. He convened the Twelfth
Congress a month early to deal with the "crisis," and he gave it "information" in the form most especially of his Annual Message of 5 November
1811 and a special secret message of 1 June 1812 specifically requesting a
declaration against Great Britain. Notably, but with restraint, both messages
were framed in the new rhetoric of defending the nation's honor. Conflict
enhancement, not conflict resolution, was the order of the day.

Still, one might ask, surely "convening" cannot transform a unique congressional power to declare war into a "divided, but shared power," any more than
"giving information" can. Unfortunately, though, "convening" and "giving
information" interject the king directly into Parliament. It shifts the point of
decision and initiative away from the Congress to the president. The decision
has shifted because the specific "information" given is that I, President James
Madison, have decided that war with Britain is no longer avoidable, that it has
now become a necessity to protect the national honor. Initiative has shifted
because a cooperative congressional leadership coordinates closely with the
president, obediently following his lead, as will be seen shortly.

And, indeed, Madison's readiness to contemplate war was new "information." It was most out of character for the president, who was as Old
a Republican as there was. From 1793 on, Madison had long supported
Jefferson's policy of "peaceful coercion." Still, Madison had been slowly moving away from that policy since 1809. Barely three weeks before his inauguration as president in March 1809, while still serving as Jefferson's secretary
of state, Madison outlined his thinking in confidential instructions dated 10
February 1809 to William Pinkney, the American minister to London:

> It is equally to be presumed that if the resumed exercise of our rights of navigation
> on the high seas [after the repeal of the Embargo of 1807] should be followed by
> the depredations threatened by an adherence of the belligerents to their respec-
> tive Edicts, the next resort on the part of the United States will be, to an assertion
> of those rights by force of Arms, against the persevering aggressor or aggressors.
> (1900–10, 8:43)

War was, of course, not desirable because it was repugnant, a "savage and
brutal manner of settling disputes among nations" (Ketcham 1971, 530;
Brant 1941–61, 5:479). Yet, submission was not acceptable either, because
it would besmirch the national honor and dignity and destroy the national
identity, as the new rhetoric held. Whether "force of Arms" would be applied
to Britain or to France or to both in what was called at the time a "triangular
war" would depend on which "preservered" in its aggression.

A year later, on 20 January 1810, when now President Madison renewed
his instructions to Minister Pinkney in London, the dilemma remained the
same:

You will find that the perplexity of our situation is amply displayed by the diversity of opinions and prolixity of discussion in Congress. Few are desirious of war; and few are reconciled to submission; yet the frustration of intermediate courses seems to have left scarce an escape from that dilemma. (Madison 1900–10, 8:90–1)

The "perplexity" was resolved in Madison's mind eighteen months later on 23 July 1811. On that date, after more fruitless talks, Augustus Foster, the British minister to the United States, confirmed that his latest instructions from the foreign minister, Lord Wellesley, indeed contemplated continued "perseverance in the orders in Council." Unable to accept "submission" and national dishonor, faced with an opponent unable to see his own self-interest, Madison resigned himself to the inevitable, as Edward Coles, his personal secretary, recalled:

[This proof of obdurance] closed the door to peace in Mr. Madison's opinion … [and] irrevocably fixed on war as the only course left to us. (cited in Brant 1941–61, 5:479; cf. Ketcham 1971, 530)

Or, as Madison explained more fully in his letter of 26 and 27 February 1827 to Henry Wheaton:

that the orders in Council, to which we had declared we would not submit, would not be repealed, without repeal of internal measures of France, which not violating any neutral rights of the U.S. they had no right to call on France to repeal, … With this formal notice [on 23 July 1811], no choice remained but between war and degradation, a degradation inviting fresh provocations & rendering war sooner or later inevitable. (Madison 1900–10, 9:272–3; Adams 1896–1904, 6:220–1; Brant 1941–61, 5:479)

The final decision, however, appears not to have been made until the next month, in August 1811. Escaping from the heat and humidity of Washington to his home in Montpelier, Madison conferred with his new secretary of state, James Monroe. As Monroe wrote to John Taylor in 13 June 1812:

Nothing would satisfy the present ministry in England, short of unconditional submission, which it was impossible to make. This fact being completely ascertained, the only remaining alternative, was to get ready for fighting, and to begin as soon as we were ready. This was the plan of the administration, when [the Twelfth] Congress met in November last; the President's message announced it; and every step taken by the administration since has led to it. (James Monroe Papers 1960)

Before he could take on the Twelfth Congress, however, Madison had to get his own cabinet into fighting trim. This he accomplished by enlisting James Monroe as secretary of state in place of Robert Smith.

THE WAR CABINET

The story of how President Madison prepared for war, therefore, begins on 3 March 1811 as the indecisive Eleventh Congress adjourned and its members journeyed home to face the coming elections. So factious had been the politics of Madison's first term in office that his own cabinet had been infected by it, leading many to believe that internecine division would destroy his administration as it had John Adams's before (Brant 1941–61, 5:277). The focal point of faction within the cabinet was Robert Smith, Madison's secretary of state. Smith was troublesome on three counts: He was incompetent; he quarreled continually with Albert Gallatin, Madison's extraordinarily competent secretary of the treasury; and he opposed many of Madison's policies. Madison, however, was willing to endure all of Smith's shortcomings for the sake of party unity. Then, during the winter of 1811, as the unproductive Eleventh Congress was wrapping up its business, Smith went too far, even for Madison. He opposed Madison's Jeffersonian policy of nonintercourse, as did many, and, abandoning all pretense of loyalty to the president, conspired actively to undermine it. He encouraged opposition in the Congress and conferred indiscreetly with the British chargé, John Philip Morier. Madison was unable to respond to Smith's sabotage immediately (*ibid.* 5:275–6). Among other constraints, Robert Smith's brother, Samuel, was a leading senator, whose influence was great enough to scuttle the amendments to the nonintercourse act that Madison desired and to block the confirmation of any successor to his brother that Madison might have proposed. Madison, therefore, bided his time.

On either 19 or 20 March 1811 (Madison's memoranda are not clear), two weeks after the Eleventh Congress adjourned, Madison asked for Smith's resignation, offering him the post of minister to St. Petersburg to soften the blow. Simultaneously, on 20 March 1811, Madison wrote to James Monroe requesting that he take on the duties of secretary of state. Elected governor of Virginia, on 16 January 1811, only three months beforehand, Monroe hesitated. Then, after consulting several colleagues, he accepted and began his new duties on 1 April 1811. Madison now had a competent and loyal Secretary of State, who, in addition, would have nine months without congressional interference before he faced Senate confirmation. While Monroe's arrival much improved the workings of the cabinet, the situation was still unstable. Monroe had entered the cabinet with the understanding that he considered Madison's current pro-French policy wrong. Madison's Jeffersonian policy of nonintercourse harmed Britain more than France. In its place, Monroe planned to work for reconciliation with Great Britain and the ending of economic sanctions against the nation. However, three months later, during July 1811, as already noted, dispatches arrived from London in which the British foreign minister, Lord Wellesley, advised his minister in Washington, Augustus Foster, yet again, that the Orders in Council would not be rescinded (Brant 1941–61, 5:478–9). This was too much for both Madison and Monroe. Monroe, like Madison, now saw Great Britain's continued intransigence as an insufferable attack upon the national honor. Later that summer, in August, during Monroe's visit to Madison's home at Montpelier, the two agreed that war was inevitable unless Britain made some gesture acknowledging the seriousness of American complaints against the Orders in Council by the end of the year (Ammon 1990, 299). In line with this decision, Madison called the newly elected Twelfth Congress into session a month early.

THE WAR HAWKS

With Henry Clay as the newly elected Speaker firmly in charge of the House, Young America awaited Madison's Annual Message of 5 November 1811. The message was less than a clarion call for war, but it was enough. Its most warlike passages was the following:

> With this evidence of hostile inflexibility [on the part of Great Britain] in trampling on rights which no independent nation can relinquish, Congress will feel the duty of putting the United States into an armor and an attitude demanded by the crisis, and corresponding with the national spirit and expectations. (1900–10, 8:162)

Responding to "the national spirit and expectations," Clay immediately seized the initiative and packed the war committees with young War Hawks, assigning John C. Calhoun of South Carolina, Felix Grundy of Tennessee, and Peter Buell Porter of New York to the House Select Committee on Foreign Relations; David R. Williams of South Carolina to the Select Committee on Military Affairs; Langdon Cheves of South Carolina as chair of the Select Committee on Naval Affairs; and Ezekiel Bacon of Massachusetts and Langdon Cheves of South Carolina to the Standing Committee on Ways and Means (Adams 1896–1904, 6:124). Appreciating the value of these newly elected members, Madison quickly opened a direct line of communication to them. At his direction, Monroe became a regular visitor at the "War Mess." This was the name given to the boarding house where Speaker Clay and the principal War Hawks stayed.

As the committees deliberated, a rather sensational and useful piece of news reached Washington. The sensational part was that the governor of Indiana Territory, William Harrison, at the head of a force of approximately eight hundred had been attacked by young braves from the village of Tippecanoe in the early morning hours of 8 November 1812 and had suffered sixty-one killed and one hundred and twenty-seven wounded, against thirty-eight

Indian dead left on the field (*ibid.* 6:104). The useful part was the way in which this incident could be used to inflame anti-British sentiments further. For example, Representative Grundy went so far as to assert that "war is not to commence by land or sea; it is already begun [at Tippecanoe]" (cited in *ibid.* 6:140). Unfortunately, though, the British had had nothing to do with the incident at Tippecanoe. Rather, it had been provoked by Governor Harrison's unauthorized invasion of Indian Territory. Still, Tippecanoe was useful grist for the young and enthusiastic War Hawks' mill. Twenty years of attacks upon American ships on the high seas had failed to provoke the nation into a declared war; perhaps, falsely attributing Tippecanoe to the British would do the trick.

Three weeks after receiving President Madison's November message, on 29 November 1811, Representative Peter Porter brought forward the Select Committee on Foreign Relation's report. Echoing the president, the report concluded, "The period has arrived when in the opinion of your committee it is the sacred duty of Congress to call forth the patriotism and resources of the country" (cited in *ibid.* 6:136). It further recommended an increase in the regular army, the enlistment of fifty thousand volunteers, the outfitting of those naval ships then laid up, and the arming of merchantmen. Two weeks of debate on the committee's report followed.

What made this debate so different from a hundred similar debates over the previous twenty years was the change in its rhetoric. Now, as Representative Porter made clear, the issue was not "pacific coercion," but active arms to expunge the stain upon America's honor:

> The period has arrived when in the opinion of your committee it is the sacred duty of Congress to call forth the patriotism and resources of the country. By aid of these, and with the blessing of God, we confidently trust we shall be enabled to produce the redress which has been sought by justice, by remonstrance, and for-bearance in vain. (cited in *ibid.* 6:136)

High patriotism and the blessing of God were, of course, all well and good, but "remuneration" is better as Representative Porter also made clear early in the debate that followed his report:

> It was the determination of the committee to recommend open and determined war, – a war as vigorous and effective as the resources of the country and the relative situation of ourselves and our enemy would enable us to prosecute.... By carrying on such a war at public expense on land [to conquer Canada], and by individual enterprise at sea [i.e., by the commissioning of privateers], we should be able in a short time to remunerate ourselves ten-fold for all the spoliations she [Britain] had committed on our commerce. (cited in *ibid.* 6:136–7)

The Young America War Hawks desired war and were supremely confi-dent. Their confidence was not, of course, based upon any sure knowledge or appreciation of "the relative situation of ourselves and our enemy"; rather, it was spontaneous, the result of their youthful enthusiasm and optimism. But, even more than the youthful impetuosity of the War Hawks, the clamoring for war resulted from the burgeoning nationalism of Young America, especially in the South and Southwest. This renewed spirit of national pride desired to transcend the passive and pastoral precepts of the self-contained Jeffersonianism that animated the Old Republicans but no longer fired the imagination of Young America.

SPRING ARRIVES

As February turned to March, an auspicious scandal occurred. Providentially, John Henry and Count Edward de Crillon had arrived in Washington from London toward the end of January 1812. After securing an interview with Secretary of State Monroe, Crillon revealed that he was acting for Henry, a British spy dissatisfied with the payment he had received from His Majesty's government. Henry, Carillon continued, possessed papers proving that he had been engaged by the governor of Lower Canada, Sir James Craig, to stir up sedition in New England during the years 1808–9. Against a consideration of $125,000 and a promise not to publish the papers until Henry had left the United States safely, Crillon would turn the papers over to Monroe. Monroe eventually bargained Crillon down to $50,000, the money was paid out of the department's contingency fund, and Henry left for New York to await the sloop-of-war, *Wasp*, bound for France.

News of Henry's departure arrived in Washington on a weekend, so that his papers could not be sent to the Twelfth Congress until the following Monday, 9 March 1812. There, they caused an immediate stir because of the implication that the Federalists were colluding with the British government. However, upon closer inspection, it was discovered that the papers had been sanitized. Names had been deleted, and Henry's activities described only the most general terms, which greatly weakened their value as propaganda. It was also learned that Henry had already left the country and, hence, was not available for questioning and that the administration had paid $50,000 for the papers. Incensed by the price, the Federalists were soon crying foul. Later, in May, it was learned that the count de Crillon had been arrested by the French authorities upon his arrival in Bayonne and that he was in reality a gambler named Paul Emile Soubiron. The only bright spot was that Soubiron had not swindled Monroe – the Henry papers were real enough – but he had swindled Henry, who touched very little of the $50,000 paid by Monroe to Crillon/Soubiron (*ibid.* 6:185; Brant 1941–61, 5:417).

A DICTATORIAL PRESIDENT ENTERS CONGRESS

With the Henry scandal swirling, on the morning of Sunday, 15 March 1812, Secretary of State Monroe met with Speaker Clay at the "War Mess." The purpose of the meeting was to plan future legislative strategy. Since November 1811, Monroe and Clay had had many similar meetings, and they would have many more subsequently. However, their 15 March 1812 meeting was different, unusual, and momentous for two reasons: First, Monroe and Clay reached a final agreement on the endgame. The decision for war was now all but sealed. If the sloop-of-war *Hornet* carried a favorable response from the British cabinet repealing the Orders in Council when it returned later in the spring, the momentum for war could still have been halted. But this was unlikely. Two months later, on Tuesday, 19 May 1812, the *Hornet* docked in New York, and its dispatches arrived in Washington three days later. The news was negative, as expected. Second, Clay, with neither malice nor forethought, handed the congressional war powers over to the president. Instead of preserving the decision for the Twelfth Congress, he severed the decision from the declaration. Madison would make the decision; the Twelfth Congress would publish and declare the president's decision. That is, Clay violated the distinction that separates war from peace, assimilating the Congress's wartime duty to its peacetime procedures.

Clay did this with the best of hearts in the most natural way. Since their arrival in Washington the previous November, the War Hawks had been in close liaison with the president by means of Secretary of State Monroe's frequent visits to their War Mess. Like journalists who become too close with their sources, this association posed distinct dangers of co-option. At their 15 March meeting, the line was crossed, and Speaker Clay and the War Hawks were co-opted. Ironically, the specific mechanism by which they were was Monroe and Clay's concern over co-option. In order to prevent the appearance of executive infringement upon a congressional prerogative, Monroe and Clay agreed that Clay should prepare an aide-mémoire of their meeting addressed to Monroe requesting that Madison "consider" three "propositions." The three "propositions" were innocuous enough; they simply summarized what had been agreed upon at the meeting. It was the attitude that Clay adopted in the letter and the postscript that he penned along the left-hand margin that caused all of the trouble:

Wash. 15th Mar. 1812

Dr Sir

Since I had the pleasure of conversing with you this morning, I have concluded, in writing, to ask a consideration of the following propositions:

That the President recommend an Embargo to last say 30 days, by confidential message:

That the termination of the Embargo be followed by War: and,

That he also recommend provision for the acceptance of 10.000 Volunteers for a short period [a year or two], whose officers are to be commissioned by the president.

The objection to an embargo is, that it will impede sales. The advantages are, that it is a measure of some vigor upon the heels of Henry's disclosure – that it will give tone to public sentiment – operate as a notification, repressing indiscreet speculation and enabling the prudent to look to the probable period of the commencement of hostilities and thus put under shelter before the storm. It will above all powerfully accelerate preparations for the War.

By the expiration of the Embargo the Hornet will have returned with good or bad news, and of course the question of War may then be fairly decided.

The acceptance of such a Corps of Volunteers as is descried will get rid of all constitutional embarrassments, furnish a force in itself highly useful and leave a certain quarter of the Country disposed to fly off without even a pretext for dereliction. Yr Friend

H. Clay

[Endorsement in margin (by Clay)]

Altho' the power of declaring War belongs to Congress, I do not see that it less falls within the scope of the President's constitutional duty to recommend such measures as he shall judge necessary and expedient than any other which, being suggested by him, they alone can adopt. (Clay 1959-84; 1:637; see also Monroe 1960)

In fine, the three "propositions" formed a well-thought-out legislative strategy for easing the Twelfth Congress into an open and determined declaration of war. Inasmuch as both Madison and the War Hawks desired war, this was undoubtedly the best way for them to obtain it. In raw political terms, all that Speaker Clay was asking was for the president to provide sufficient political cover for the Old Republicans to vote for a declaration of war that they opposed on solid Jeffersonian principles. The problem, therefore, lay, not in the "propositions." Rather, it lay in the acceptance of presidential initiative and leadership for declaring war in the same way it had already been accepted for peacetime legislation. Now, in both peace and war, congressional power was "divided, but shared."

How did Clay's aide-mémoire do this? In two ways. First, in his marginal endorsement, he stretched *Helvidius*'s "convene and give information" into "the President's constitutional duty to recommend such measures as he shall judge necessary and expedient." Clay's "constitutional duty to recommend," in effect, makes of the president not just a full partner with the Congress, but the lead partner as well. The president is now the dictatorial partner who takes the decision for war or peace and then "recommends" it to the Congress so that it might "adopt" his decision by declaring (or "authorizing") it. In this manner, with this aide-mémoire, Clay separated the decision from the declaration, thereby transforming a unique congressional power "to declare war" into a "divided, but shared power." Unfortunately, though, the minute the decision is separated from the declaration, all power is drained from the power "to declare war."

Second, and more important, in the body of his aide-mémoire, Clay created a viciously self-reflexive loop: The Speaker of the House of Representatives "asked" the president to "consider" three "propositions" already agreed to by the president so that, should the president find these most agreeable "propositions" worthy, he could propose them to the Congress, which would take them up. Under no circumstance would the House take the initiative to exercise its unique power to declare war. One hundred and sixty-one years later, Speaker Clay's aide-mémoire was codified as the War Powers Resolution of 1973, with two important changes to erase the Congress and highlight the president. Instead of presidential co-option taking place over congenial dinners with the secretary of state at a congressional War Mess, the president is now to "consult" the Congress in a more abstract, undefined way. Instead of the Speaker of the House's "asking" the president to "consider" three propositions, the president is now to "report" his decision to the whole Congress within forty-eight hours. Unchanged, of course, is the final step, the "adoption" of the president's decision by the Congress.

To clarify, consider the counterfactual: Yes, in the partisan political atmosphere of 1812, when the War Hawks numbered no more than a third of the Congress, as a matter of practical politics, war would occur if and only if President Madison took the lead. In practical terms, this meant very close liaison with the War Hawks, including providing them with a solid legislative strategy. This was an absolute political necessity at that time to accomplish that objective. What was not necessary was for the Speaker of the House to appeal to the president to initiate congressional action. Instead of entreating the president, Speaker Clay could have listened to Madison's endgame, accepted it, and, then, adopted it as his own. For example, Speaker Clay could just as easily have gone upstairs to his room at the War Mess that Sunday afternoon and begun his aide-mémoire by writing:

Wash. 15th Mar. 1812

Dr Sir

Since I had the pleasure of conversing with you this morning, I have concluded, in writing, that the House will take up the following three propositions on or about April 1st:....

That an Embargo be imposed to last say 30 days:

That the termination of the Embargo be followed by War: and,

That provision be made for the acceptance of 10.000 Volunteers for a short period [a year or two], whose officers are to be commissioned by the president....

The practical politics of declaring war would not have changed, but the tone and the attitude would have. Instead of "asking" the president to "consider" three self-reflexive "propositions," the Speaker would now be telling the president what the House would do. More important, this changed attitude would have made it completely unnecessary for Clay to pen his constitutional dictum in the left-hand margin. But Speaker Clay did not tell President Madison what the House would do; instead, he supplicated the president to tell the House what to do, as any good parliament supplicates its king. Consequently, the most devastating result of Clay's aide-mémoire was that the Congress would now become passive and reactive, waiting patiently to "adopt" the president's "recommendation," unable to exercise its war powers on its own initiative. In fine, Clay's aide-mémoire created a "shared power" with the president as the lead shareholder.

Or, take a different perspective. Shift one's view from the traditional relationship between the president and the Congress to the relationship between the president and the Supreme Court. If applied to the Supreme Court the intense system of consultation developed by Monroe and the War Hawks would amount to presidential control of the judiciary. Imagine the consequences if the attorney general dined regularly with the justices to discuss how upcoming cases should be handled. Once mutual agreement had been reached, the chief justice would then compose an aide-mémoire "asking" the president to "consider" the proposed rulings and to "recommend" them to the Court in an official message from him. The justices would then "adopt" the mutually agreed upon decisions "recommended" to them by the president. Such a system is entirely acceptable in a tyranny, if not in all types of monarchy, according to Montesquieu. But howsoever the judicial power may be interpreted, such a "consultative" system effectively destroys the judicial power and its independence, just as surely as Speaker Clay's aide-mémoire destroyed the unique congressional power to declare war. Neither the judicial power nor the power to declare war is a "shared power." Both are "unshared," unique powers.

"Shared powers" are both perfectly acceptable and undoubtedly necessary for peacetime legislation. Without presidential initiative and agenda setting, the Congress would never overcome its organizational paralysis. But war is not peace, and the ways of war are not the ways of peace. One wishes that the experience of the thirty-four-year-old Speaker from Kentucky had not been entirely with peace.

THE WAITING GAME

Once Speaker Clay had invited President Madison to direct the affairs of the Twelfth Congress, on Sunday, 15 March 1812, the time had come to put the president's plan into action. Two weeks later, on Monday, 30 March 1812, the House Select Committee on Foreign Relations informed Monroe in the appropriately suppliant posture that it was ready to proceed as planned. The committee would "be happy to be informed when, in the opinion of the Executive, the measures of preparation [for war] will be in such forwardness as to justify the step contemplated" (cited in Brant 1941–61, 5:427). The next day, in a secret session before the House Select Committee on Foreign Relations, Monroe made three points: First, he reaffirmed that Madison's position had not changed, "that without an accommodation with Great Britain Congress ought to declare war before adjourning." Second, he reviewed the current situation, emphasizing how greatly Madison and he had been disappointed by Foster's recent instructions from London and the need to await the arrival of the *Hornet* later in the spring so as to learn more precisely both Britain's and Napoleon's attitude toward the United States. Should France's attitude turn hostile, it would be necessary to "resort to measures against her also," the so-called triangular war. And, finally, he proposed in a somewhat modified form two of the measures that Clay and he had agreed upon two weeks before: To remedy problems in recruiting, he suggested that the Twelfth Congress authorize the president to accept fifteen thousand of the twenty-five thousand troops authorized for the regular army on eighteen-month enlistments; and, to retain maximum flexibility, he suggested that "no immediate declaration of war being contemplated [by President Madison], an embargo of sixty days, within which time the *Hornet* must return, will leave the ultimate policy of the government in our hands" (cited in *ibid.*).

As agreed, the committee accepted Monroe's proposals, reassuring him that the Twelfth Congress would pass the embargo as soon as the president forwarded his request to them. The next day, 1 April 1812, Madison "gave information" to the Congress in a confidential message to the House requesting a sixty-day embargo, which passed the House that same evening on a vote of seventy to forty-one. A decisive step for war had been taken. Or had it? Shipowners up and down the coast were voting against both the embargo and the war by sending their ships to sea, fearing the loss of profits more than capture by either the French or British (Adams 1896–1904, 6:201). In addition, a closer look at the House vote showed that less than half of the full House had voted with the majority (*ibid.* 6:202). This lack of a solid majority did not inspire confidence. In the Senate, with the generous partisanship that characterized all Senate actions in those years, the embargo was amended, lengthening it from sixty to ninety days, a change that had the effect of turning a decisive war measure into an indecisive negotiating ploy. Confusion, not decision, reigned, as Madison reported to Jefferson on 24 April 1812:

> You will have noticed that the Embargo as recommended to Cong^s was limited to 60 days. Its extension to 90 proceeded from the united votes of those who wished to make it a negotiating instead of a war measure, of those who wished to put off the day of war as long as possible, if ultimately to be met, & of those whose mercantile constituents had ships abroad which would be favored in their chance of getting safely home. Some also who wished & hoped to anticipate the expiration of the terms, calculated on the ostensible postponement of the war question as a ruse agst the Enemy. (1900–10, 8:188)

As always, the sources of this disruptive partisan confusion were the same:

> The measure of the Embargo was made a difficult one, both as to its duration & its date, by the conflict of opinions here, and of local interests elsewhere; and to these causes are to be added, that invariable opposition, open with some & covert with others, which have perplexed & impeded the whole course of our public measures. (*ibid.*)

In fine, five months after proposing war to the Twelfth Congress, neither unity nor consensus had been achieved – only partisanship and confusion. All was still unsettled in the eyes of the Twelfth Congress, as Madison explained to Jefferson:

> At present great differences of opinion exist, as to the time & form of entering into hostilities; whether at a very early or later day, or not before the end of the 90 days, and whether by a general declaration, or by a commencement with letters of M.[arque] & Reprisal. (*ibid.*)

Notwithstanding the way in which it "perplexed & impeded the whole course of our public measures," the House accepted the Senate's amendment of the embargo from sixty to ninety days, and Madison approved the measure three days after he had sent it to the Twelfth Congress. In Madison's mind, at least, the dice were cast, and war was now inevitable. Having lengthened the embargo by thirty days, the Twelfth Congress condemned itself to staying in Washington an extra month as the summer heat grew more and more uncomfortable. But what would it do in the interim? Not much. It passed a bill, which Madison approved on 10 April 1812, authorizing the president to call up one hundred thousand militia for six months. Then the Senate recessed until 8 June 1812. The House was about to follow, but, after vigorous efforts by the administration, it stayed in town. Still, many members returned home to attend to private business, planning to return by June (Adams 1896–1904, 6:204).

As a measure of New England's aversion to the war, during May, Secretary of the Treasury Albert Gallatin attempted to place the $11,000,000 loan that the Twelfth Congress had authorized at 6 percent. New England refused to participate, and so the placement failed, and only $6,000,000 was taken up (*ibid.* 6:207). War taxes now took on a greater urgency and importance than they previously had. But, still, the Twelfth Congress refused even to consider war taxes. The bills remained quietly hidden in the Standing Committee on Ways and Means. On 18 May 1812, Madison was also renominated by the Republican caucus for a second term, to which he would be reelected in November. The next day the sloop-of-war *Hornet* arrived in New York and forwarded its long delayed dispatches to Washington, where they arrived three days later (*ibid.* 6:215).

The dispatches were disheartening. Those from England carried the news that Lord Wellesley had been replaced as foreign minister by Lord Castlereagh. Although the new foreign minister pointedly refused to consider repealing the Orders in Council, he did plead earnestly against war, indicating that the British government was having second thoughts on its policy toward America. Six months earlier, Madison would have seized upon such sentiments as a welcomed excuse for further negotiations. Now, he brushed them aside without ceremony (*ibid.* 6:216; Brant 1941–61, 5:466–9). The dispatches from France were even more disheartening. They contained no solid evidence that Napoleon had actually relaxed his restrictions on American commerce. Indeed, Joel Barlow, Madison's minister to France, reported that he had been unsuccessful not just in obtaining a long-awaited commercial treaty but also in obtaining any acknowledgment that Napoleon had truly revoked his Berlin and Milan Degrees. The twin pillars of Madison's policy were crumbling around him: "Perfidious" Britain no longer appeared determined to "recolonize" America by destroying American commerce, while Napoleon appeared even more determined to punish American commerce for trading with Great Britain. On the eve of his request to the Twelfth Congress for a declaration of war, much of the justification for a war against Great Britain appeared to evaporate, while the casus belli against Napoleon multiplied. Cries for a "triangular war" increased.

As the logic of his policy drained away, Madison did all that he could do under the circumstances. He ignored the facts and clung tenaciously to his original plan. On 30 May 1812, two days before he was to send his war message to the Twelfth Congress, Madison published an editorial in the *National Intelligencer* in which he acknowledged the deficiencies in Napoleon's conduct toward America but argued that this did not excuse the depredations done by Great Britain. Because a "triangular war" was impractical, the prudent course was to deal with each power seriatim, declaring open and determined war against Great Britain now and, then, deciding upon the appropriate measures to be undertaken with regard to France in due time (Brant 1941–61, 5:469–70). And so, having given fair notice of his reasons and his determination, Madison ignored the Senate's unhelpful extension of the embargo to ninety days, kept to his own schedule, and sent his war message to the Twelfth Congress on 1 June 1812, sixty days after he had requested the embargo.

THE ENDGAME

After the clerk had finished reading the president's message behind closed doors, it was referred to the House Select Committee on Foreign Relations, which brought forward a report in the form of a manifesto and the text of an unreasoned absolute declaration of war three days later. The two texts are of particular interest on three counts: First, they were not written by John Calhoun, the acting chairman of the committee, as was believed at the time. Rather, they were drafted by Secretary of State Monroe during the previous month (Brant 1941–61, 5:472–3; cf. Madison 1900–10, 8:192, note 1). The passivity of the Twelfth Congress was now nearly total. Not only did the War Hawks look to the president to take the actual decision for war or peace; not only did they look to the president for their legislative strategy; they also depended upon him, or his lieutenants, to furnish the text. Since the composition of the text is the heart and soul of the power to declare war, subcontracting this task to the president effectively tore the heart out of the congressional war powers.

Second, the manifesto and declaration were presented to the House behind closed doors. This resort to secrecy is not disturbing because critical decisions such as this should be made publicly. The Second Continental Congress had also deliberated in secret. Rather, it is disturbing because it illustrates how much "Henry Clay and his friends were weary of debate and afraid of defeat" (Adams 1896–1904, 6:227). Speaker Clay's manipulation of the House rules to achieve a preordained result merely highlights the need for an entirely different set of wartime procedures to govern the declaring of war, procedures that are less influenced by the congressional leadership, the president, or the mood swings of public opinion.

Whatever these procedures might be, Clay and the War Hawks had every reason to fear defeat. Opposition to the war was clearly strong, if not sufficient to prevent it. In the House, the declaration passed in a secret session without debate by a seventy-nine to forty-nine vote on 4 June 1812. The Federalists were joined in opposition by twenty-one House Republicans. In the Senate, efforts to cripple the war effort occupied the next two weeks. Meeting behind closed doors, several motions were made and defeated by the narrowest of margins to limit the war to naval reprisals and privateering, namely, to fight another Quasi-War, this time against Great Britain. An all-naval war made considerable sense, and it had been supported by Secretary of State Monroe. But Madison opposed this limitation and was able to rally sufficient support to extinguish it. Then, finally, on 17 June 1812 the Senate voted nineteen to thirteen for war, with only three Republicans voting with the Federalists in opposition. Party discipline had been maintained. The next day the House accepted the minor amendments made by the Senate and Madison approved the absolute unreasoned declaration that afternoon. Open and determined war had been declared against Great Britain to the amazement of all (Brant 1941–61, 5:472–7).

With the open and determined declaration of war on 18 June 1812, the delicate issue of war taxes could no longer be avoided. Or could it? On 19 June, Langdon Cheves introduced, from the Standing Committee on Ways and Means, a bill partially suspending the Non-importation Act. He supported his motion by a letter from Gallatin, accepting this bill as an alternative to the tax bills. On the same day news arrived of more American vessels burned by French frigates. Chaos seemed beyond control. War with England was about to restore commerce with the enemy; peace with France meant continued depredations on American shipping. Responding to this topsy-turvy world and summoning all its courage, the House reported the necessary tax bills out of committee the next day, 26 June 1812. In no time, though, it voted seventy-six to forty-two to postpone consideration of the tax bills until the next session in November 1812. Fortunately, the Senate possessed greater courage. It passed a bill authorizing an issue of $5,000,000 in treasury notes, a bill doubling the duties on imports, and other urgently need bills. The House dutifully concurred, and the first session of the Twelfth Congress adjourned in haste on 6 July 1812 (Adams 1896–1904, 6:235).

Open and determined war had been declared. It was Madison's greatest triumph, leading by the end of the fighting to the demise of the Federalist Party and ushering in the Era of Good Feelings. As John Adams observed at the end of a letter to Jefferson dated 2 February 1817, "notwithstand[ing] a thousand Faults and blunders, his Administration has acquired more glory, and established more Union, than all his three Predecessors, Washington Adams and Jefferson, put together" (Cappon 1959, 2:508). While that is certainly true, yet, the subtle and persistent leadership of President Madison in 1812 destroyed the best intentions of delegate Madison, who, on Friday, 17 August 1787, at the Federal Convention in Philadelphia, had proposed that the power of the Congress "to make war" be changed to power "to declare war." In the end, Pierce Butler of South Carolina was the more astute political philosopher, for he was entirely correct. Undoubtedly, it is true that, like a king, "the President ... will have all the requisite qualities, and will not make war but when the Nation will support it."

But President Madison could never have succeeded without acquiescence of the Twelfth Congress, under Speaker Clay's energetic leadership. For only Speaker Clay could submit the Congress to the president's better judgment, hollowing out the congressional power to declare war, draining it of all meaning and substance, and transferring it to the president in the twisted form of a "divided, but shared power." In doing so, he turned over the responsibility both to decide and to draft the declaration of war to the president. With the heat of summer rising from the Potomac, it was time for the members of the Twelfth Congress to get out of town. Their work was complete.

ANALYSIS

Such is the story of the precedent setting declaration of 1812. As is cataloged in Chapter 6, presidents have been exceptionally parsimonious in their use of Madison's precedents. They have "convened and given information" to the Congress on only three other occasions – the Spanish-American War and the First and Second World Wars. Notably, the Spanish-American War is the only time the Congress has, in a manner of speaking, drafted its own declaration of war, as is told in the next chapter. Normally, of course, presidents do not bother to "convene" the Congress. They seldom find it either wise or practical to do so. Still, they always "give information." This eagerness of presidents to "give information" to the Congress is central to the political bargain of the War Powers Resolution of 1973, as is highlighted in Chapter 4. An initial analysis of Madison's precedents, therefore, needs to emphasize four issues: the logically absurd consequences of the Constitution's fatally impractical division of the sovereign's war powers, how the resulting organizational incapacity exacerbates the effects of these absurd consequences, the role of performative speech acts, and a word on the rule of law as a concept.

The Absurd Consequences: A Unique Power or a "Divided, but Shared" Power?

As already noted, with regard to the power "to declare war," the most fundamental question turns on who shall decide the question of war or peace – the president or the Congress. The dilemma arises because the Federal Convention clearly and unambiguously stated that the power to command the armed forces rested with the president as commander in chief. The convention also clearly and unambiguously stated that the power to declare war rested with the Congress. Unfortunately, the convention did not say clearly and unambiguously where the power to decide the question of war or peace lay. This oversight is the natural source of more than two hundred years of contention.

To be sure, every president since George Washington has claimed the power to decide. Since Sunday, 15 March 1812, every Congress has agreed. Hence, no Congress has ever made the counterclaim, as the War Powers Resolution of 1973 makes abundantly clear. Still, it makes little sense not to make the counterclaim; one reason is that when one divides and separates the power to decide from the power to make the public announcement, the result is a reductio ad absurdum: If the power to declare war consists only and solely of the power to make the public announcement, then the declarer of war is no more than the president's town crier. In this case, why would anyone care whether the president bypasses his town crier? If, however, the power to declare war consists of both the power to decide and the power to make the public announcement, then the declarer of war is very much more than a town crier. In this case, everyone should care whenever a dictatorial president bypasses the constitutionally mandated declarer of war.

To sort through this dilemma, the initial problem is not to decide whether the power to decide resides in the president or the declarer of war. Rather, as has already been said, the initial problem is to decide whether the power to declare war is a unique, "undivided and unshared" power or whether it is a "divided, but shared" power meant somehow to "check and balance" the president's power as commander in chief.

Speaking broadly, the Federal Convention most certainly "divided and shared out" the totality of the sovereign's power so as to create a system of "checks and balances." This is not in doubt. However, within this totality, many of the specific powers enumerated are unique to one branch or the other. For example, judicial review is a unique power of the judiciary. Commanding the armed forces is a unique power of the president as commander in chief. But, reductio ad absurdum, if the power to declare war is a "divided, but shared" power, then most certainly the declarer of war "shares" his power with the president in accordance with Speaker Clay's dictum. In this case, the president's "share" is to decide the question of war or peace, which leaves only the public announcement to the Congress, now functioning as his town crier. If, however, the power to declare war is truly unique, an "undivided and unshared" power, then the declarer of war does not "share" its power with the president. Not incidentally, this means that the power to declare war does not "check and balance" the president's power as commander in chief. Instead, the two powers are unique, each operating in a different way to accomplish a different objective, just like the Supreme Court's unique power of judicial review. They are of course related in a complementary and coordinate manner, but they are clearly not "divided, but shared." They unequivocally do not "check and balance" each other. This complementary and coordinate relationship is explored more fully in Chapter 5.

The Role of Performative Speech Acts

Still, absurdity is not an explanation. For an explanation, one must acknow-ledge the role of speech in constituting or creating the state and condition of war. One must recognize that any explanation of the sovereign's war powers begins with the tautology that neither can war be declared nor can commands be given until after the question of war or peace has been decided. It follows, therefore, that no commander, including no commander in chief, can speak and "order" his forces to deploy before the question of war or peace has been decided either by him or by others. President George H. W. Bush did not order American forces to invade Panama on Wednesday, 20 December 1989, and then decide the question of war or peace. His "order" necessarily and unavoidably occurred sometime after he had decided on war and against peace. In the same tautological manner, no war can be declared before the question of war or peace has been decided. Focusing on the declaring of war only, the tautology is needed to put the power "to declare war" in its proper temporal frame of reference:

1) The Decision: This element raises as yet unanswered questions about who decides – whether an individual or a corporate body – and, hence, how the decision is made.
2) The Purpose: This element specifies that it is, in fact, the performative speech that enacts, institutes, or constitutes war as "war," and not as a "tea party" or some other social phenomenon. That is, "to declare war" is to announce publicly one's decision:
   a) to transform the material condition of peace into the material con-dition of war, and
   b) to transform the collective state of amity into the collective state of enmity.
3) The Text: This element specifies the form and content of a "declaration of war." It specifies which words will and which words will not enact, establish, and constitute the new social reality – "war." For example, the request "Please, come to my tea party" does not enact war. The Declaration of Independence does.

Viewed in this tautological and temporal manner, one discovers, as an ini-tial approximation only, that the performative speech acts that constitute an instance of "declaring" war exist in a minimum of four different modes. These four modes are summarized in Figure 1. In one mode, the royal mode, a single individual, a constitutionally recognized king, both decides and declares. In this mode, the king, first, performs the mental act of deciding for war and against peace. Then, after an interval of time, he performs a public speech act, thereby making a constitutionally recognized royal "declaration"

	Question of War or Peace		Public Announcement		
	Who decides?	How?	Who speaks?	How?	
Mode One (Royal Declarations)	King	Mental Act	King	Constitutional Procedures	**Rule of Men**, Governed by Law
Mode Two (Tyrannical Declarations)	Kingly President	Mental Act	Kingly President	Un-constitutional Procedures	**Rule of Men**, Not Governed by Law
Mode Three (Tyrannical Decisions)	Kingly President	Mental Act	Corporate Body	Constitutional Procedures	**Rule of Men**, Not Governed by Law
Mode Four (Lawful Declarations)	Corporate Body	Collective-Speech Act	Corporate Body	Constitutional Procedures	**Rule of Law**, Governed by Law

Figure 1. Four Modes of Declaring War.

of war. After another interval of time, the king "orders" his forces into battle. In sum, the purpose of his royal declaration is to allow him to impose his best judgment on a society ruled by men, yet governed by its own peculiar laws and customs, as Montesquieu might say.

In a second mode, which is the most frequently used mode in American history, a single individual, a constitutionally unrecognized dictatorial president, both decides and declares. In this mode, the dictatorial president, first, performs the mental act of deciding for war and against peace. Then, after an interval of time, he performs a public speech act, thereby making a constitutionally unrecognized tyrannical "declaration" of war. After another interval of time, the dictatorial president "orders" his forces into battle, as President George H. W. Bush did on Wednesday, 20 December 1989, for his invasion of Panama. In sum, the purpose of his dictatorial declaration is to allow a dictatorial president to impose his best judgment on a society ruled by men, and not yet governed by law.

In a third mode, which has been used only three times in American history, a single individual, a constitutionally unrecognized dictatorial president, decides but does not declare. In this mode, following James Madison's precedents, the dictatorial president again performs the mental act of deciding for war and against peace. Then, after an interval of time, he "convenes and gives information" to a corporate body, usually his legislative assembly. After another interval of time, the assembly performs a series of collective speech acts, producing thereby a procedurally perfect "declaration" of war superficially in accordance with the Constitution and laws of the land. Critically, however, the apparent constitutional perfection of the procedure is more of an act of complaisance, and less an act of conformity to the law. For, the corporate body "declared war" only to comply with the desires of the constitutionally unrecognized dictatorial president. Then, after a further interval of time, the dictatorial president performs another mental act, deciding exactly when to "order" his forces into battle, as President James Madison did in 1812. In sum, not only is this procedure vastly more complicated; this mode is no more legitimate than the second mode. In effect, the collective declaration only cloaks in apparently constitutional procedures the dictatorial president's tyrannical decision to impose his best judgment on a society. The third mode is still rule by men, and not yet governed by law.

In a fourth mode, a corporate body both decides and declares. Examples of this mode are the declarations of war made by the Athenian Ecclesia, the Senate of early republican Rome, or a revolutionary assembly, such as the English Long Parliament, the American Second Continental Congress, the French National Assembly. In this mode, a constitutionally recognized corporate body performs a series of collective speech acts that begin when it resolves a resolution containing the question of war or peace. For example, when the body resolves "that these United Colonies are, and of Right ought to be, Free and Independent States, that they are absolved from all allegiance to the British Crown, and that all Political connection between them and the State of Great Britain is, and ought to be, totally dissolved."

Then, after an interval of time, the corporate body next writes a draft declaration, debates it, amends it, and votes on it, thereby "declaring" war. In doing so, it also produces a procedurally perfect "declaration" of war, for example, the Declaration of Independence, which is reproduced in Appendix I. With the culminating performative speech act, the "vote," the entire process has been collective and social; at no point in time has a single decision maker's mental acts monopolized the procedure.

The decision and the declaration having been made collectively in accordance with law, after a further interval of time, the commander in chief enters the picture and, in accordance with law, performs a mental act, deciding exactly when to "order" his forces into battle, as General George Washington did after 4 July 1776. In sum, the lawful purpose of the collective decision and declaration is to allow a legitimately constituted and recognized corporate body to articulate its best judgment for a society both ruled and governed through its constitutional procedures by law, and not men.

Organizational Incapacity

The organizational incapacity of the Congress is only an incidental exacerbating factor, as will become clearer in succeeding chapters. In brief, though, the organizational realities that generate this incapacity are quite simple. Without strong leadership and agenda setting, gridlock is the fate of any large majority-rule institution because of the cumulative effects of 1) high transaction costs, 2) difficulties in coordinating shared interests, and 3) extensive collective action problems among the members. Under the Constitution, only the president possesses the carrots and the sticks required to lead and to set the agenda of an otherwise gridlocked Congress.

The principal reasons that the Second Continental Congress was able to declare war, while the U.S. Congress is not, must, therefore, be attributable to the vast organizational and circumstantial differences between the two. The Second Continental Congress, of course, suffered from all the aliments of any majority-ruled institution – high transaction costs, difficulties in coordinating shared interests, and extensive collective action problems among the members (Jillson and Wilson 1994). However, it was a small, single focus, unicameral institution, and not a large, endlessly distracted, bicameral institution. Whatever its problems, they pale in comparison with those of the U.S. Congress. In the first place, the relatively small size of the Second Continental Congress greatly reduced the problem of coordinating the shared interests among the fifty-six delegates and, hence, greatly enhanced its ability to seize the initiative and act decisively. Initiative was not smothered because it did not have to coordinate the interests of five hundred and thirty-five members divided unevenly into two competing chambers focused primarily on raising $10,000 a week for their reelection campaigns. Instead, it had fifty-six members, not all of whom were in attendance on any given day, and none of whom had to raise money to be reappointed.

In the second place, the collective action problems of the Second Continental Congress were minimal. It dealt with one and only one issue – the management of the war that had broken out with Great Britain during the spring of 1775. It did not have to deal with the endless peacetime problems of a modern industrial and postmodern society. It did not have to deal with the scandal of appropriating funds to build "a bridge to nowhere."

In the third place, the Second Continental Congress was a unicameral body. To be sure, the bicameral structure of the U.S. Congress does facilitate a full and complete airing of all the positive and negative aspects of peacetime legislation. However, the extremely high transaction costs of multiple committee hearings and multiple floor debates in two competing chambers make the declaring of war completely impossible, unless the president, first, makes the decision on his own authority and, then, "convenes and gives information" to the Congress. Consider the issue by analogy with the Supreme Court: Imagine that the Constitution mandated a bicameral Supreme Court. How would that work? Each of the two Courts would select its own docket, each would hear its own cases, and each would reach its own decisions. Then, before the end of each term, the two Supreme Courts would meet in conference to iron out all of the differences in their dockets and decisions. Just outlining the procedures proves that such a bicameral Supreme Court would be incapable of discharging its judicial functions. In exactly the same manner, the bicameral U.S. Congress is entirely incapable of discharging its primary wartime duty "to declare war." This fact is further documented in the next chapter. In 1898 for the Spanish-American War, each chamber worked at cross-purposes to the other. This made for very exciting journalism and politics but frustrated any effort "to declare war" in a responsible manner.

In the end, then, despite its own organizational problems, the radically smaller and more tightly focused, unicameral Second Continental Congress was not *as* paralyzed as is the large, bicameral U.S. Congress. It could and did operate without presidential leadership and agenda setting, as the U.S. Congress cannot possibly do.

A further critical contrast is that the Second Continental Congress was organized under a committee-of-the-whole system, and not under a modern standing-committee system. Perhaps surprisingly, the committee-of-the-whole system is one of the essential requirements for wresting the power to declare war away from the president, as will be emphasized later.

And, finally of critical importance, majority-rule corporate bodies, such as legislatures, the Supreme Court, regulatory commissions, and Parent-Teacher Associations, cannot perform mental acts. This reduces their potential for tyranny enormously. This is the case because the speech of majority-rule corporate bodies is constrained by the dictates of procedural justice. Their enactments must always conform to the prescriptions of an authorizing law, Robert's Rules of Order, or hallowed custom. Such majority-ruled bodies can only enact their decisions by means of a collective performative speech act, for example, a "vote" on a motion to call the question. An excellent example of this is the Second Continental Congress's Declaration of Independence of 1776. Consequently, the rule of law, and not men, proceeds very much more naturally from the collective speech of majority-ruled institutions than it does from the free-form mental acts of executive officers, such as presidents. To be sure, the content of collective speech acts can be hurtful and unjust, as were the Nazi Racial Laws or the various Jim Crow laws in the American South. But the requirement for a collective speech act in accordance with well-established and recognized procedures, rules, and laws significantly reduces the occurrence of substantive injustice.

Rule of Law

A few words may be appropriate to explain the conceptual role that "rule of law" plays in framing the present investigation of the power "to declare war."

As is well known, the term is very difficult to pin down and define. For this reason, no attempt is made to do so. Rather, its many facets are exploited to maximum advantage depending upon the topic under consideration. Of necessity, however, a formalistic or "thin" conception of the rule of law dominates. Under this approach, the rule of law is achieved whenever procedural justice is assured. This "thin" view is unavoidable because, while the Constitution is basically a manual of procedures, the Framers neglected to specify any of the procedures needed to make the Declare War Clause work. For example, had the Framers specified that a resolution containing the question of war or peace had to be introduced, debated at length, and voted on before the appointment of an ad hoc drafting committee from among the members, as in 1776, then the probability of presidential usurpation would have diminished greatly. But they did not do so. Most naturally, in the absence of clear procedures, the Congress floundered and flailed about until President Madison took the matter in hand and developed the dictatorial procedures used ever since.

While the issues surrounding the Declare War Clause are overwhelmingly questions of procedural perfection, the other aspects of rule of law are also part of the picture. In Chapter 6 especially, a substantive or "thick" conception comes to the fore. There, the vital importance of the text of a declaration – how the text of the Declaration of Independence possessed substance, whereas all four open and determined congressional declarations are vacuous and without substance – is seen as a vital part of the solution. Under this "thick" approach, the rule of law requires careful attention to safeguarding human rights and substantive justice, and not just providing formal or "thin" procedural safeguards.

In addition to "thin" and "thick" conceptions, a functional conception will also be used. In functional terms, the importance of who speaks is critical. Under this functional approach, King John's 1215 Magna Carta is recalled. On the field at Runnymede, the barons and prelates dramatically stood the imperial *rex lex* (The king is law) on its head to produce the republican *lex rex* (The law is king). This functional concept emphasizes how a dictatorial presidential decision and declaration lead to tyranny.

In the end, by paying close attention 1) to who declares war, 2) to the substantive content of the declaration, and 3) to the lawful perfection of the procedures used, one hopes that a comprehensive rule of law perspective will lead to a clearer understanding of the tangle of issues that surround the power "to declare war."

CONCLUSION

With this hope in mind, the pole star of any discussion of the power "to declare war" is the example set by the Second Continental Congress and its declaration. The small, unicameral Second Continental Congress did what the large, bicameral U.S. Congress has never done: it both decided on and declared war. It did not masquerade as a dictatorial president's town crier. Consequently, whenever a question about the power "to declare war" arises, the answer can usually be found by examining closely either the organization or the procedures of the Second Continental Congress or the text of the Declaration of Independence.

In contrast, the declaration of 1812 established the necessary dictatorial precedents for overcoming the incompetence and incapacity of the U.S. Congress "to declare war." In the next chapter, the declaration of 1898 against Spain over Cuba confirms and reinforces this congressional incompetence and incapacity beyond all doubt. In particular, because President William McKinley opposed war against Spain, he created an opportunity for the Fifty-fifth Congress to demonstrate its potential for initiative, seriousness, and competence. Had the Fifty-fifth Congress seized that opportunity, it would have done much to redeem past and future congressional failures. Naturally, the Fifty-fifth Congress could neither see nor seize the opportunity. Instead, it was consumed by the glittering prospect of obtaining partisan advantage in the upcoming midterm elections. Consequently, the conditional declaration it wrote and passed on 19 April 1898 had less to do with enacting war against Spain than with inflicting maximum embarrassment on President McKinley and the Republican Party. After all, what is more important to the members of the Congress? Getting reelected or exercising their constitutional responsibility to declare war?

3 Why the Congress Ought Not Declare War

The Spanish-American War, 1898

The Congress shall have power ... to declare war, grant letters of marque and reprisal, and make rules concerning captures on land and water.

> (article I, section 8, clause 11)

"only Congress itself can prevent power from slipping through its fingers.

> (*Youngstown Co. v. Sawyer*, 343 U.S. 579, 654 (1952))

In thinking about the congressional power to declare war in its historical context, one has to come to terms with the modal verbs "can," "ought," and "will." The previous chapter dealt with "can." It recalled the enduring precedents set by President Madison and Speaker Clay. These precedents established that, yes, the Congress *can* declare war, but it *cannot* decide the question of war and peace. Or, more precisely, it "can" declare war, but only in the minimally technical sense of speaking as the president's town crier. The next chapter deals with "will." It discusses the War Powers Resolution of 1973, which codifies the 1812 precedents. Nominally, the resolution authorizes the president to wage war on his own authority for only sixty days, but, in reality, the statutory authorization is open-ended. Once the war has begun, all the Congress can do is whine and appropriate the needed funds. As a result, the resolution makes it virtually impossible to imagine that the Congress will ever again declare war, even in the minimalist sense of acting as the president's town crier. This chapter deals with "ought." It tells the troubling story of how the Fifty-fifth Congress both decided, in a manner of speaking, and declared war against Spain over Cuba in April 1898.

In 1898, for the first and only time in American history, a jingoistic yellow press and the Fifty-fifth Congress ardently wanted war. Standing athwart this popular cry were Presidents Grover Cleveland and William McKinley, who both opposed war with Spain. The situation was literally unprecedented. President Madison had developed procedures to allow a dictatorial president to impose his will to war upon an indifferent or reluctant Congress. Obviously, the Madisonian precedents were irrelevant in a situation where the president wanted to prevent a war, not to initiate one.

After his election, President McKinley maintained President Cleveland's policy of blocking any congressional declaration. However, as the midterm elections approached and the clamor for war could no longer be held back, he gave in to the inevitable. He "convened and gave information" to the Fifty-fifth Congress, in accordance with Madison's precedent. But, then, President McKinley did the unimaginable. He did not have the State Department draft a declaration, and he did not request a declaration. Instead, he asked the Fifty-fifth Congress to draft the declaration, concluding his message by saying, "Prepared to execute every obligation imposed upon me by the Constitution and the law, I await your action" (*Cong. Rec.*: 1898, 3702). With these words, he appeared to step aside while the Fifty-fifth Congress drafted, debated, and voted two declarations of war, a conditional followed by an absolute declaration. For the first and only time in American history, the U.S. Congress, and not the president, actually wrote the declaration and certainly created the appearance of having made the decision. In doing so, the Fifty-fifth Congress demonstrated beyond doubt that no Congress ought ever "to declare war."

THE PEARL OF THE ANTILLES

Cuba had attracted American interest since the 1820s. Before the Civil War, the greater part of this interest was from southerners, who looked upon Cuba with its plantation economy as a natural area for the expansion of slavery. After the Civil War, interest continued. The richness of Cuba's soil and its proximity attracted many investors, despite its foreign people, language, customs, and laws. Still, American interest in Cuba was never strong enough to overcome a certain reluctance to acquire "the Pearl of the Antilles" outright. By the end of the nineteenth century, however, Cuba had become an integral part of America's trading area. Cuban sugar was sold primarily into the American market. This all changed with the protectionist tariff of 1894, which imposed a 40 percent tariff upon Cuban sugar. Thus excluded from the American market, the Cuban economy was immediately devastated. Crippled economically and shackled politically by inept Spanish rule, on 25 February 1895, during the second year of President Grover Cleveland's second term, a group of Cuban dissidents raised the *grito de Baíre* (the cry of Baíre), a denunciation of Spanish misdeeds and a call for an independent Cuba.

With this "cry," the Second Cuban Revolution began, initially under the leadership of the poet José Martí. However, with Martí's death in an ambush in April 1895, the commander in chief of the insurgent forces, the Dominican-born Máximo Gómez, took control and fixed upon a scorched-earth policy as the best strategy to secure Cuban independence from Spain. In line with this policy, the insurgents burned crops and wrought devastation across the island. The results of this destruction were immediate. The Cuban sugar yield was reduced from more than a million long tons, worth $62 million, in 1895 to 220,000 long tons worth $13 million, in 1896 (Trask 1981, 2–3). In response, Governor General Valeriano Weyler y Nicolau instituted a policy of *reconcentrado*, herding the peasants off the land and into concentration camps in an effort to end their support for the insurgents. By December 1897, the death toll from famine and disease in these concentration camps had reached into the hundreds of thousands. In the United States, General Gómez's systematic destruction of property and General Weyler's systematic destruction of people created an enormous wave of revulsion, which William Randolph Hearst's *New York Journal* and Joseph Pulitzer's *New York World* systematically roiled. Cries for American intervention to stop these horrors mounted with each new report.

Blocking intervention, however, were Presidents Grover Cleveland and William McKinley. President Cleveland's opposition during the last two years of his second term, 1895–6, took the form of an ineffective diplomacy and an effective enforcement of American neutrality. The ineffectiveness of his diplomacy can be seen in the fact that Spain spurned all of his suggestions for instituting reforms in Cuba, which meant that the Cuban crisis only grew deeper. The effectiveness of this enforcement effort can be seen in the fact that the U.S. Navy captured thirty-one of the seventy-one gunrunners and filibusters who sailed for Cuba. The Royal Spanish Navy captured one filibuster; the Royal British Navy, two; while storms frustrated four more (Trask 1981, 5). More important, though, Cleveland rebuffed every congressional attempt to interfere or intervene in Cuba. Cleveland's attitude is illustrated in a fascinating, but perhaps apocryphal, anecdote:

> "I was with the President at Woodley, near Washington, one Sunday afternoon," says Mr. A. B. Farquhar [a friend], "when some members of Congress came in and said, 'Mr. President, we wish to see you on an important matter.' I got up, but he motioned me to keep my seat. They said, 'We have about decided to declare war against Spain over the Cuban question. Conditions are intolerable.'
>
> "Mr. Cleveland drew himself up and said, 'There will be no war with Spain over Cuba while I am President.'
>
> "One of the members flushed up and said angrily, 'Mr. President, you seem to forget that the Constitution of the United States gives Congress the right to declare war.'

> "He answered, 'Yes, but it also makes me Commander-in-Chief, and I will not mobilize the army. I happen to know that we can buy the Island of Cuba from Spain for $100,000,000, and war will cost vastly more than that and will entail another long list of pensioners. It would be an outrage to declare war.'" (McElroy 1923, 2:249–50; Farquhar 1908, 15)

The apocryphal part of this anecdote is the idea that Cleveland ever considered the purchase of Cuba a serious, viable option. He certainly toyed with the idea, thinking of it perhaps as the magic-wand solution to this intractable problem, but he knew that neither Spain nor the Congress would accept it. The uncontested part is that Cleveland considered a declaration of war an outrage and that he would not countenance it. The fascinating part, however, is the way in which he used his powers as president to trump the assertion of a congressional power to declare war. This last returns us to the heart of the two-hundred-year-old debate over article I, section 8. However, the matter is more complicated than the anecdote suggests. For, it is not the president's threat to refuse to mobilize the army that trumps the Congress, but rather the fact that the Congress cannot act without presidential leadership, or, at a minimum, presidential permission. The Congress simply cannot resist the urge to wash its hands of complex and politically dangerous matters such as the question of war or peace. As Gray Gables, another friend of Cleveland's recalled:

> Monday night, the 3rd (of August), had an interesting talk, especially about Cuba. He [President Cleveland] told me of the visit of the sub-committee of the Senate Committee on Foreign Relations. He asked them why they did not acknowledge the belligerency of the insurgents if they thought it wise; the Congress had the power to bring about war – it would be the duty of the Executive to obey [or face impeachment]. Oh, no, they did not wish that. Then he explained how the Executive had pushed the American demands as to damages, treatment of prisoners claiming American protection, etc. He thought they went away content, after seeing the actual difficulties, to let the matter remain in the hands of the Executive. (Nevins 1934, 716)

Henry Clay would have heartily approved of the senator's discretion. Without presidential leadership, how could war possibly be declared?

After his election in 1896, neither McKinley's attitude nor his policy was substantially different from Cleveland's. With respect to his attitude, after dinner at the White House on the evening before his inauguration, 3 March 1897, McKinley told Cleveland:

> "Mr. President, if I can only go out of office, at the end of my term, with the knowledge that I have done what lay in my power to avert this terrible calamity [of war with Spain], with the success that has crowned your patience and persistence, I shall be the happiest man in the world." (Gould 1982, 1)

McKinley's reluctance to war drew from two sources: First, he had been elected to establish sound money based upon the gold standard, to balance the budget, and, thereby, to restore prosperity, which had not yet recovered fully from the Panic of 1893. Clearly, war would put into jeopardy all of this. Second, he knew combat:

> "I shall never get into a war until I am sure that God and man approve. I have been through one war [McKinley had been a major in the Civil War], I have seen the dead piled up; and I do not want to see another." (Trask 1981, 58)

When war began, it seems unlikely that McKinley believed that God approved, although there was no doubt in his mind that the majority of the members of the Congress did. Nevertheless, the depth of his antiwar sentiments can be measured quite precisely by the fact that he made an anonymous donation of $5,000 to the Cuban relief fund, which, at his instigation, the State Department established on 24 December 1897 (Leech 1959, 150).

With respect to policy, McKinley followed the same contradictory path that Cleveland had: He attempted to induce the Spanish Government to institute reforms in Cuba, while attempting to restrain the Fifty-fifth Congress and the American public from forcing intervention. Needless to say, his domestic restrain undercut his foreign initiatives. His efforts to threaten the Spanish government with intervention unless it instituted reforms in Cuba sounded more than hollow when he did everything in his power to prevent the Congress from precipitating intervention. The contradictions of American policy, however, were not the principal cause of the war. For that, one must look to the Spanish dilemma.

THE RESTORATION MONARCHY

In Spain, the Second Cuban Revolution created a situation in which the fragile restoration monarchy believed that its continued existence depended upon its ability to preserve the last remnants of Spain's once-vast empire. For the queen regent, María Cristina of Austria, acceding to American demands, much less granting Cuba independence, was unthinkable. It would mean revolution in Spain. The two prime ministers involved agreed. In March 1895 at the beginning of the Cuban insurrection, the Conservative prime minister, Antonio Cánovas del Castillo, stated the matter unequivocally: "The Spanish nation is disposed to sacrifice to the last *peseta* of its treasure and to the last drop of the last Spaniard before consenting that anyone snatch from it one piece of its sacred territory" (Trask 1981, 6). After Cánovas was assassinated by an Italian anarchist, Miguel Angioillo, on 8 August 1897, his eventual replacement, the Liberal prime minister Mateo Práxedes Sagata, steadfastly maintained Cánovas's policy. Spain's dignity and honor could survive losing a war with America, even if that meant that America took Cuba, Puerto Rico,

Guam, and the Philippines from Spain by right of conquest. The one thing the restoration monarchy could not survive was the thought of Spain's giving independence to the scattered islands of its vestigial empire. The empire was Spain's history, Spain's essence, God's gift to Spain for expelling the Moors during the fifteenth century. Upon this rock, all of Presidents Cleveland and McKinley's efforts to avoid war finally broke. The fear of provoking revolution at home was greater than the fear of losing a war overseas.

And so confronted with delay and inaction in Madrid, with continuing atrocities in Cuba, and with mounting pressure to intervene in America, in April 1898, McKinley finally had to admit that it did not lie in his power "to avert this terrible calamity." The Fifty-fifth Congress was about to break its leash. The signs of this impending disaster were everywhere – in the press, in the unhopeful diplomatic correspondence, and in the Fifty-fifth Congress. For example, Jennie Hobart, the wife of Vice President Garrett A. Hobart, recalled the following exchange between her husband and President McKinley:

> "Mr. President, I can no longer hold back the Senate. They will act without you if you do not act at once." "Do you mean that the Senate will declare war on its own motion?" (cited in Trask 1981, 56)

Vice President Hobart answered, yes, and President McKinley knew that dramatic action was required.

"TO CONVENE AND GIVE INFORMATION"

McKinley's first move was to do what presidents have always done. He "convened" the Fifty-fifth Congress and "gave it information." However, the anomaly of his message must be stressed. In terms of historical precedent and in the hopes of both the yellow press and the Fifty-fifth Congress, McKinley's message should have been a full-blooded call for war, like similar messages from Presidents Madison, Wilson, and Roosevelt. But unlike Madison, Wilson, and Roosevelt, McKinley did not want the Congress to declare war. He wanted to avert it, although he now knew that this was all but impossible. Consequently, his message was not a call for war, which disappointed the yellow press and the Fifty-fifth Congress, but not the Spanish government, which greeted it with great satisfaction (*New York Times* 12 April 1898, 2:4).

Before not calling for war, McKinley played for more time. His message was initially scheduled to be sent to the Capitol on Monday, 4 April 1898. However, he decided to postpone its delivery two days, until Wednesday, 6 April 1898. Then, on the advice of Consul General Fitzhugh Lee in Havana, he postponed its delivery another five days, in order to allow for the evacuation of American citizens from Cuba. If these delays disappointed the ten thousand spectators who had gathered in and around the Capitol to hear the message read on 6 April 1898, they infuriated the members of the Fifty-fifth

Congress and the press. Then, finally, at noon on Monday, 11 April 1898, a week late, President McKinley's message arrived and was read by clerks in both Houses. Both the members of the Congress and the enormous crowds that filled the galleries and overflowed into the stairs and halls listened attentively. Much to their disappointment, the message was not what they wanted to hear. They wanted to hear a clarion call for war and Cuban independence. Instead, they got a dry legal brief, a tiresome *tour d'horizon*, which had been drafted by Attorney General John W. Griggs because of his expertise in international law. In the words of the *New York Times* headlines the next day, McKinley's message had provoked "AN ANGRY CONGRESS." Indeed, the subhead continued, "Message Causes Surprise. Feeling in Congress That the President Has Clouded the Situation Rather Than Cleared It" (1:5). And, in truth, from the perspective of the Fifty-fifth Congress, looking for someone to decide and to lead them into war with Spain, McKinley's message was very disappointing and did becloud the situation. However, for a president seeking to avoid war and regain control over an unruly Congress, a cloudy situation that led to congressional indecision was precisely what was needed.

THE MESSAGE

McKinley's message beclouded the situation in three ways: First, it was excessively legalistic. For example, it quoted long passages from Presidents Andrew Jackson, Ulysses S. Grant, and Grover Cleveland, and William McKinley's own annual message of December 1897. Second, it was excessively long and detailed, as can perhaps be seen by repeating just the subheads inserted by the *New York Times* to break up the text:

> Half Century of Revolutions, Spain Refuses Mediation, Reconcentration Policy Adopted, A Policy of Extermination, Home Rule Promised, Our Aid to the Starving, An Armistice Suggested, Spain's Reply Thereto, Recognition of Belligerence Useless, As to Independence, Danger of Recognition, Reasons for Forcible Intervention, Destruction of the Main, Not a Matter for Arbitration, Views of Presidents Grant and Cleveland, Fair Notice to Spain, The War in Cuba Must Stop, Asks for Power to Act, Spain's Last Step. (12 April 1898, 1:7; 2:1–4)

But third, and most important of all, McKinley's message did not ask for a declaration of war. Indeed, it did not ask for anything, except an appropriation for relief supplies for the suffering Cubans. What McKinley did was to provide the Fifty-fifth Congress with a realistic analysis of the Cuban crisis. He listed the four options open to America once diplomacy had failed, narrowed this field to two, and, then, let the Fifty-fifth Congress draw its own conclusions. This process began about halfway through his message when he recycled a passage from his annual message of December 1897:

Of the untried measures there remain only: Recognition of the insurgents as belligerents; recognition of the independence of Cuba; neutral intervention, to end the
war by imposing a rational compromise between the contestants, and intervention
in favor of one or the other party. I speak not of forcible annexation, for that cannot
be though of. That by our code of morality would be criminal aggression. (*ibid.*;
Cong. Rec.: 1898, 3699–702)

Next McKinley argued that the first two options were contrary both to
American interests and to well-established policy. In defense of this latter point,
he quoted long passages from President Andrew Jackson's 21 December 1836
message refusing recognition of the independence of the Republic of Texas.
Having rejected both types of recognition, he then argued in favor of "forcible intervention." His arguments were strong but lacked a conclusion, which
certainly beclouded the situation. Thus, in the concluding passage where presidents have traditionally asked the Congress for a declaration of war, McKinley
balked. He refused to commit himself to either a neutral or an interested
intervention or any intervention at all, committing himself only to the very
ambiguous goal of "full and final termination of the hostilities." Having successfully "beclouded" the issue, McKinley concluded with a bombshell:

In the name of humanity, in the name of civilization, in behalf of endangered
American interests which give us the right and the duty to speak and to act, the war
in Cuba must stop.

In view of these facts and of these considerations, I ask the Congress to authorize
and empower the President to take measures to secure a full and final termination
of the hostilities between the Government of Spain and the people of Cuba, and to
secure in the island the establishment of a stable Government capable of maintaining order and observing its international obligations, insuring peace and tranquility,
and the security of its citizens as well as our own, and to use the military and naval
forces of the United States as may be necessary for these purposes.

And in the interest of humanity and to aid in preserving the lives of the starving
people of the island, I recommend that the distribution of food and supplies be
continued, and that an appropriation be made out of the Public Treasury to sup-
plement the charity of our citizens.

The issue is now with the Congress. It is a solemn responsibility. I have exhausted
every effort to relieve the intolerable conditions of affairs which is at our doors.
Prepared to execute every obligation imposed upon me by the Constitution and
the law, I await your action. (*ibid.*, 3702)

"I [the President!] await your [the Congress's!!] action." Speaker Henry
Clay would not have understood. President James Madison would not have
understood. No other president, save Grover Cleveland, has ever imagined
saying such. McKinley's anti-Madisonian, nondecision accomplished three
objectives. It ruled out recognition for Cuban independence, provided all of
the reasons for intervention in Cuba, but sidestepped the ultimate question

of whether or not actually to do so. It requested "statutory authority" to use the armed forces but did not indicate whether or how McKinley might use them. Moreover, the strength of McKinley's resolve actually to employ the army and navy was questionable, as his only concrete suggestion was for an appropriation for relief assistance. This is strange in the extreme, since waging war against Spain is rather different from distributing relief assistance to the Cubans. And, finally, President McKinley says that he "awaits" congressional action, as if to say that he has finally bowed to the will of the people and the Fifty-fifth Congress for war and will now sit passively on the sidelines until he receives his orders. Needless to say, he did nothing of the sort, taking an active, if behind the scenes, role in shaping the resolutions that were eventually passed. In particular, he was adamant on the "recognition" issue. Intervention was possible, but not recognition of Cuban independence.

A BICAMERAL CONGRESS AND ELECTORAL POLITICS

Angered and dismayed though they were, the members of the Fifty-fifth Congress could console themselves with the fact that the president had stated clearly and unambiguously, "The issue is now with the Congress." No longer, it appeared, would the president stand in the way of a declaration of war, as President Cleveland had. Now, therefore, was the time to act. But how? The situation was unprecedented. Lacking both precedence and guidance, the members of the Fifty-fifth Congress naturally fell back upon what they knew – upon the rules and procedures they used to pass peacetime legislation. That the ways of peace are not the ways of war did not occur to the members. Consequently, taking McKinley's message under consideration, the members of the Senate Committee on Foreign Relations and of the House Committee on Foreign Affairs met separately and prepared separate reports for their respective chambers, including different draft resolutions declaring war against Spain. These reports were ready two days later on Wednesday, 13 April 1898, and read on the floors of the respective chambers. The House acted with dispatch and passed its resolution late that same evening. The Senate, accustomed to a slower pace, delayed its vote until Saturday, 16 April 1898. Reconciling the two different resolutions occupied three more days, so that the compromise declaration was not passed until Tuesday, 19 April 1898.

But notice the problem: The U.S. Congress is not a unicameral legislature. It does not have a single "Committee on Foreign Policy." Instead, it is a bicameral legislature. It has two independent committees, one on foreign affairs and another on foreign relations. To vet peacetime legislation, this is a most excellent arrangement. It allows for the fullest possible evaluation of the president's peacetime foreign policies. It requires that the president's foreign policies be inspected from two different perspectives, first, from the perspective of the nation's foreign relations but also from the perspective of the nation's foreign affairs. Yet, peace is not war. The ways of peace are not the ways of war. Hence, despite the fact that the president's own party, the Republican Party, held a majority in both chambers, competition, not thoughtful deliberation, characterized proceedings.

In sharp contrast to the debates in the unicameral Second Continental Congress, what transpired during the seven days between Wednesday, 13 April 1898, and Tuesday, 19 April 1898, was not a solemn debate over whether to war with Spain – that was already a forgone conclusion – rather, what transpired was, in the words of the *New York Times*, "a great game of politics" (19 April 1898, 1:7). To appreciate the "game," one must know that the midterm congressional elections were only six months away. With these elections looming, none of the congressional Republicans was very happy at the prospect of being saddled with a president openly defying the popular sentiment for war. Indeed, few Republicans could imagine winning the election if the Democrats could campaign on a "Free Silver and Free Cuba" platform. Realizing this, McKinley had changed course and submitted his message of 11 April 1898. Consequently, in order to enjoy the "great game" one must know the party affiliations of the major players.

McKinley was, of course, a Republican, elected to office in 1896. The House also possessed a Republican majority of two hundred and six. It was led by Speaker Thomas Brackett Reed, Republican of Maine, a vehement opponent of both the war and all thought of American expansion, which would be the inevitable result of a war with Spain. The Senate, however, was more complex. The Republicans held the majority with forty-four Republicans against thirty-four Democrats, but they did not control the Senate. They had to accommodate five Silver Republicans, five Populists, and the two Silver Party senators from Nevada. The "game" on the Senate side produced the proverbial "strange bedfellows." The forty-six Democratic, Populist, and Silver Party senators had an obvious interest in embarrassing McKinley and the Republicans just before the midterm elections. To do this, they had to insert a clause recognizing the independence of the Cuban Republic in defiance of McKinley's policy of no recognition. They could not succeed, however, without support from some Republicans. Fortunately, many of the Senate Republicans believed that they would lose the coming election unless Cuban independence was recognized: hence the "strange bedfellows" and strong sentiment in the Senate for recognition. On the House side, the game consisted in seeing whether McKinley and Reed could maintain Republican solidarity in the House and, thereby, block any Senate initiative on recognition. Any serious debate of whether or why the war itself was justified was of course irrelevant to scoring political advantage in the elections. The example of the Second Continental Congress would not be consulted.

LET THE "GAMES" BEGIN

As already noted, the Republican-controlled House was first off the mark. The day began quietly enough, the House occupying itself with routine matters until three o'clock, when the Acting Chairman of the Committee on Foreign Affairs Robert Adams, Republican of Pennsylvania, entered the chamber to deliver the committee's report, including the following resolution, which the *New York Times* reported "were not as ringing as the spectators [in the House gallery] had expected":

> Joint resolution (H. Res. 233) authorizing and directing the President of the United States to intervene to stop the war in Cuba, and for the purpose of establishing a stable and independent government of the people therein.
>
> Whereas the Government of Spain for three years past has been waging war on the Island of Cuba against a revolution by the inhabitants thereof without making any substantial progress towards the suppression of said revolution, and has conducted the warfare in a manner contrary to the laws of nations by methods inhuman and uncivilized, causing the death by starvation of more than 200,000 innocent noncombatants, the victims being for the most part helpless women and children, inflicting intolerable injury to the commercial interests of the United States, involving the destruction of the lives and property of many of our citizens, entailing the expenditure of millions of money in patrolling our coasts and policing the high seas in order to maintain our neutrality; and
>
> Whereas this long series of losses, injuries, and burdens for which Spain is responsible has culminated in the destruction of the United States battle ship Maine in the harbor of Havana and the death of 260 of our seamen;
>
> *Resolved by the Senate and the House of Representatives of the United States of America in Congress assembled,* That the President is hereby authorized and directed to intervene at once to stop the war in Cuba to the end and with the purpose of securing permanent peace and order there and establishing by the free action of the people thereof a stable and independent government of their own in the Island of Cuba; and the President is hereby authorized and empowered to use the land and naval forces of the United States to execute the purpose of this resolution. (*Cong. Rec.*: 1898, 4041; *New York Times,* 14 April 1898, 1:7)

The resolution did not contain a clause recognizing Cuban independence and, thus, conformed to President McKinley's policy. However, this occurred not as a matter of conviction, but rather of politics, as the *New York Times* reported:

> The [Republican] majority of the committee [on Foreign Affairs] was opposed to recognition, not because they were adverse to recognition, but in order to be able to act in harmony with the President. (14 April 1898, 1:5)

Having avoided embarrassment in committee, the next hurdle for the Republican leadership was to secure passage of the committee's resolution on the floor of the House, which was accomplished, but not without much "tumult" and "mortification."

As soon as Acting Chairman Adams had finished his report, Representative Joseph W. Bailey, Democrat from Texas, the Minority Leader, rose to object to Mr. Adams's request for immediate and unanimous consent to the committee's resolution. Pandemonium now broke out, as the *New York Times* reported:

> Half the members of the Democratic side were on their feet, shouting against what they called the unfairness of the Republican programme. At the height of the tumult Mr. Brumm of Pennsylvania denounced a statement by Mr. Bartlett of Georgia as a lie, whereupon that gentlemen hurled a book at the Pennsylvanian's head and rushed down the aisle with the evident intention of following up the book with blows of the fist ... while an excited mob closed round the two men, ... the Speaker sent the mace to bring calm. ... This riot quelled, there was another personal spat between Mr. Bailey and Mr. Quigg. ...
>
> Mr. Johnson of Indiana supplied the next sensation by interrupting Mr. Henderson of Iowa with a denunciation of his fellow Republicans for forcing the resolutions for what he pronounced a useless war through the House without opportunity for fair debate. Mr. Johnson continued his speech in spite of the Speaker's call to order, and only subsided when confronted by the symbol of the House's authority [the mace], waved aloft by the Sergeant at Arms. For three hours the furor of debate raged, with crimination and recrimination hurled from side to side of the Chamber, until at 6 o'clock the vote was taken and Republicans and Democrats came together and voted for the majority resolution [322 to 19]. (14 April 1898, 1:7)

Whatever the solemnity of its responsibility, the House was clearly unable to conduct its business in anything resembling proper decorum; partisan politics and sharp parliamentary maneuvering took precedence over deliberate debate, in contrast to the conduct of the Second Continental Congress. The shortcomings of the day's performance were, of course, noted at the time:

> Some mortification is expressed by members of both houses because of the turbulence of the House at one stage of the proceedings this afternoon. This incident, together with the fact that the two houses did not agree beforehand upon the terms of a resolution is regarded as certain to invite harsh criticism of the Congress, and the suggestion that it was unfortunate to transfer the direction of the controversy from the President to the legislative branch of the Government. (*New York Times* 14 April 1898, 1:7)

"Mortification" and "turbulence" in the Congress! The members of Congress maneuvering for electoral advantage! As President Madison and Speaker Clay well knew, this maneuvering was built into the modern standing-committee organization of the Congress. By stepping back and awaiting congressional action, President McKinley failed to provide the needed leadership to curb the members' natural instincts.

Meanwhile, in the Senate, Senator Cushman K. Davis, Republican from Minnesota, chairman of the Committee on Foreign Relations, handed the committee's report to the clerk at nearly one o'clock in the afternoon of the same day, Wednesday, 13 April 1898. After it was read, Senator George F. Hoar, Republican from Massachusetts, requested that, under the rule, the resolution lie over a day before it should be considered. Before Vice President Hobart could rule, Senator Joseph Benson Foraker, Republican from Ohio, took the floor but immediately yielded to Senator David Turpie, Democrat from Indiana, who submitted the report of the four dissenting members of the Committee on Foreign Relations. The minority report also offered an amendment to the majority resolution calling for the recognition of the existence of the Cuban Republic. Vice President Hobart accepted Senator Turpie's report and ordered both it and the majority report sent to the printers. He then ruled favorably on Senator Hoar's request for the matter to lie over for a day. These parliamentary questions decided, the Senate spent the next four hours making "Stirring Speeches for Intervention and Recognition," ending the day at 5:25 pm after having spent the last few minutes passing private pension bills; extending the time for the Gainsville, McAllister and St. Louis Railroad Company to construct a railroad through the Indian Territory; and extending the time allotted for the construction of a bridge across the Yazoo River at Greenwood, Mississippi (*New York Times* 14 April 1898, 3–4).

THE "GAMES" CONTINUE IN THE SENATE

And so ended the first day of the congressional games – with tumult and mortification in the House and business as usual in the Senate. President McKinley and Speaker Reed had held the line in the House, but the initial maneuvers to force "recognition" had been made in the Senate with the introduction of the minority report by Senator Turpie. The games were far from over. In the Senate, the trouble centered on the first resolved clause of Senate Joint Resolution 149. For the Republicans, the trouble was that the "... are, and ..." phrase introduced either a factual or a logical inconsistency into the clause. For the Democrats, the trouble was that the first resolved clause did not include language specifically "recognizing" the Republic of Cuba:

> Joint Resolution for the independence of the people of Cuba, demanding that the Government of Spain relinquish its authority and government in the Island of Cuba, and withdraw its land and naval forces from Cuba and Cuban waters, and directing the President of the United States to use the land and naval forces of the United States to carry these resolutions into effect.
>
> Whereas the abhorrent conditions which have existed for more than three years in the Island of Cuba, so near our own borders, have shocked the moral sense

of the people of the United States, have been a disgrace to Christian civilization, culminating, as they have, in the destruction of a United States battleship, with two hundred and sixty of its officers and crew, while on a friendly visit in the Harbor of Havana, and cannot longer be endured, as has been set forth by the President of the United States in his message to Congress of April eleventh, eighteen hundred and ninety-eight, upon which the action of Congress was invited: therefore,

Resolved, First. That the people of the Island of Cuba are, and of right ought to be free and independent.

Second. That it is the duty of the United States to demand, and the Government of the United States does hereby demand, that the Government of Spain at once relinquish its authority and government in the Island of Cuba, and withdraw its land and naval forces from Cuba and Cuban waters.

Third. That the President of the United States be, and he hereby is, directed and empowered to use the entire land and naval forces of the United States, and to call into the actual service of the United States the militia of the several States to such extent as may be necessary to carry these resolutions into effect. (*New York Times* 14 April 1898, 3:6)

During Thursday, Friday, and Saturday, the Senate discussed many issues, both great and small, relevant and irrelevant, for eight to ten hours a day before overflowing crowds. On Saturday, however, the debate came to a head when the so-called Turpie and Teller amendments were approved and sent to the House. The Teller amendment was uncontroversial. It added the following fourth resolved to Senate Joint Resolution 149:

Fourth. That the United States hereby disclaims any disposition or intention to exercise sovereignty, jurisdiction, or control over said island except for the pacification thereof, and asserts its determination, when that is accomplished, to leave the government and control of the island to its people.

It was agreed to without dissention, or even much comment, in both the Senate and the House and, hence, survived into the final resolution. At the time, it appeared to reiterate the obvious. No one in either chamber championed the annexation of Cuba, and President McKinley had stated clearly in both his annual message and his message of 11 April 1898 that "forcible annexation" could not be thought of because "by our code of morality [that] would be criminal aggression." In contrast, the Turpie amendment was extremely controversial. Indeed, it was the heart and soul of the game. Although it did not survive into the final resolution, it established the vortex around which everyone swirled. The amendment added the following "recognition" clause to the first resolved:

That the people of the Island of Cuba are, and of right ought to be free and independent and that the Government of the United States hereby recognizes the Republic of Cuba as the true and lawful Government of that island.

As the *New York Times* reported, after the exhausting debate:

The vote came as a welcome relief from a state of extreme tension at the close of a session which had lasted for eleven hours and which had been rendered notable by the addresses of some thirty Senators [from ten in the morning until shortly after seven in the evening], ... The galleries retained their "standing room only" status all day long, many of the spectators remaining in their seats from the opening of the session until its end, sending out after sandwiches to sustain life, consuming luncheon providentially brought with them. (17 April 1898, 1:7)

The first vote was on the Turpie amendment, which passed fifty-one to thirty-seven. Next, Senator Davis offered the Teller amendment, which passed without a calling of the yeas and nays. The Senate had declared itself firmly in favor of recognition and by a surprisingly large majority, which included many Republicans. With passage of these two amendments, the deadly serious games really began, a classic ballet of parliamentary maneuvering.

Next, in defense of McKinley's policy of nonrecognition, Senator William P. Frye, Republican from Maine, rose to propose that "are, and" be struck from the first resolved. In response, to sustain Democratic momentum, Senator Davis moved to lay the amendment on the table, a motion that was accepted fifty-five to thirty-three. Senator John T. Morgan, Democrat from Alabama, then proposed a substitute resolution, which was also challenged by Senator Davis, who moved that it should lie upon the table. The motion to table Senator Morgan's substitute was sustained, eighty-three to five. Senator Davis, then, moved that the Senate take up House Joint Resolution 233 from the table. In terms of the "great game of politics," this was the crucial maneuver of the evening. As Senator Davis explained, his purpose in taking up the House resolution was not to consider it but rather to substitute the amended Senate resolution for it. Although unstated, the purpose of this substitution was to gain a parliamentary advantage when the resolution was returned to the House. If Senator Davis's motion for substitution were successful, then the House would be forced to consider the amended Senate resolution, as its own resolution had been shunted aside. Since the Senate resolution now contained the Turpie amendment on recognition, this meant that the members of the House would be forced to declare themselves for or against recognition. It was a vote they had artfully avoided in their own resolution. Senator Davis was planning to maximize pressure upon the members of the House to vote against President McKinley's policy of nonrecognition in the hope of gaining the maximum advantage for the Democrats at the midterm elections. This type of baldly political maneuver was possible only in a bicameral legislature. No delegate to the unicameral Second Continental Congress could ever have imagined such.

Needless to say, the importance of the motion for substitution was not lost upon his colleagues. A short debate ensued, but, in the end, Senator Davis's motion to take up House Joint Resolution 233 from the table so as "to strike out all after the resolving clause and to insert in lieu of what is stricken out the Senate joint resolution as it has been amended" was approved sixty to twenty-eight (*Cong. Rec.*: 1898, 3989). Having substituted all after the resolving clause, Senator Davis, next, moved "to strike out the preamble of House joint resolution 233 and insert the preamble of Senate joint resolution 149 in lieu thereof" (*Cong. Rec.*: 1898, 3992). However, Senator Hoar now raised a point of order, noting that a preamble could not be amended until after a vote had been taken to pass a bill or resolution. His point sustained by Vice President Hobart, Senator Hoar took the opportunity to make a short, but extremely cogent, speech on why he opposed the resolution:

> Mr. President, I can not give my vote for this resolution upon its final passage for several reasons, which I desire to state.
>
> First. It contains an affirmation contrary to the fact when it affirms that the Republic of Cuba is now free and independent …, in the face of the declaration, as I understand it, of the person high in command in the troops of the insurgents, who has declared he could prolong the struggle to obtain that independence for twelve years.
>
> Second. It undertakes to take from the Executive his constitutional power, a power affirmed by every Executive from the beginning, a power affirmed by our great authorities on constitutional law from Alexander Hamilton down to the senior Senator from Alabama [Mr. Morgan],. …
>
> Mr. President, I can not vote for the joint resolution because it introduces, and I believe was meant to introduce, discord and divided counsels in what ought to be the act of a united country.
>
> I can not vote for it because it undertakes to direct, contrary to all our legislative precedents, a coordinate branch of the Government, the Executive, ordering him to proceed at once when his constitutional and legal duties are defined by the Constitution, and not by the law-making power.
>
> I can not vote for it because it is contrary to the courtesies which prevail between the legislative and Executive and undertakes to take from the discretion of the Executive what ought to belong to him under the Constitution itself.
>
> I will not vote for it because if it pass and the government of Cuba be now free and independent, the forces of the Army of the United States on Cuban land and the Navy of the United States in Cuban waters must be under the command of the insurgent leader or their presence there is a war against him. (*Cong. Rec.*: 1898, 3992; 3993)

As Senator Hoar noted, the Fifty-fifth Congress was about to sanction a lapse of logic, decorum, and fact. Such a bald-faced lapse would have been incomprehensible to the delegates to the Second Continental Congress. The irrepressible primitive urge to embarrass the president was pushing the Fifty-fifth Congress to assert that the Republic of Cuba was free and independent when the highest authority in the rebellion insisted that independence was in fact at least twelve years away. Further, the Fifty-fifth Congress was infringing on the president's long-acknowledged power to command the armed forces. And, finally, the Fifty-fifth Congress was about to violate all the laws of logic. It was about to assert, on the one hand, that the Republic of Cuba was actually free and independent as a matter of fact, while ordering the armed forces of the United States, on the other hand, to intervene to force Spain to give Cuba the freedom and independence that the resolution claimed it already had. Further, legally and logically, if the assertion of a de facto Cuban independence were true, then either the armed forces must be placed under the command of General Máximo Gómez as the leader of "free and independent Republic of Cuba" or the army and the navy must war against General Máximo Gómez, the leader of the selfsame "free and independent Republic of Cuba." But, to repeat, Senator Hoar's appeal to reason was entirely irrelevant to the primary objective of the Democratic members, which was to impose maximum political costs on President McKinley and the Republicans so as to achieve maximum political benefit in the midterm elections.

When Senator Hoar had completed his last-minute appeal to reason, the yeas and nays were called, and Senate Joint Resolution 149, now substituted for House Joint Resolution 233, passed, sixty-seven to twenty-one. Once Senator Hoar's point of order had been disposed of, Senator Davis again moved to substitute the Senate preamble for the House preamble, which was accomplished without calling the yeas and the nays. With the preamble and the resolutions successfully substituted, it was only logical for Senator Davis to move for the substitution of the title also. But, just to rub salt into the wound, he desired that "and Republic of Cuba" be inserted so that the title ran "for the recognition of the independence of the people and Republic of Cuba" (*Cong. Rec.*: 1898, 3993). These two amendments also passed without the calling of the yeas and nays. Then, in a display of arrogance that went rather too far, Senator Davis moved:

that the Senate insist upon its amendments and ask for a conference. ["No!" "No!"]

Mr. STEWART. I object

Mr. JONES of Arkansas (to Mr. Davis). Do not do that.

Mr. DAVIS. I insist on the motion.

The VICE PRESIDENT. The Senator from Minnesota moves that the Senate insist on its amendments made to the joint resolution.

Mr. FAULKNER. I do not think it is according to parliamentary usage for the Senate at this time to do that. The House has a right to concur in the amendments if it chooses to do so.

Mr. DAVIS. That is true; but nothing is more unusual than for a motion of this kind to be made.

Mr. ALLEN. I shall insist upon following the rule of the Senate, and that is that the joint resolution as amended shall go to the House.

Mr. DAVIS. I withdraw the motion.

The VICE PRESIDENT. The motion is withdrawn.

Mr. DAVIS. I move that the Senate adjourn.

The motion was agreed to; and (at 9 o'clock and 15 minutes p.m.) the Senate adjourned until Monday, April 18, 1898, at 12 o'clock meridian. (*Cong. Rec.*: 1898, 3993)

So ended the fourth day of the congressional games. As the *New York Times* observed:

> The leaders of the movement for the recognition of the Cuban Republic are congratulating themselves on the majority that proposition received, which exceeded their expectations. The resolutions with the recognition paragraph included now go to the House. (17 April 1898, 1:7)

But, not immediately: the next day was Sunday, a day of rest. The outcome of the drama would have to await Monday's session. Would the "recognitionists" be able to roll the House? Would President McKinley and Speaker Reed be able to hold the Republican majority in the House? The suspense was thrilling.

THE "GAMES" RETURN TO THE HOUSE

On Monday, 18 April 1898, the House met at ten o'clock in the morning but immediately adjourned until noon in order to allow the Republican leadership to put some fiber into their more pliant members. As the *New York Times* observed:

> There were signs of open revolt in the Republican ranks. … Cuba, the reconcentrados, and the Maine were forgotten in the fierce struggle to hold the Republican majority in line with the President's policy. (19 April 1898, 1:7)

In the most natural of ways, debate over the actual causes of the war was entirely "forgotten" in the heat of congressional politicking, especially when advantage in the midterm elections was in jeopardy. After all, this was not 1776.

At noon, after the prayer, the secretary of the Senate delivered House Resolution 233 as amended by the Senate to the House, which the clerk of the House read. Representative Nelson Dingley, Republican from Maine, immediately moved

> to concur in the Senate amendments to House joint resolution No. 233 with an amendment striking out in the first paragraph the words "are, and," and also the words "and the Government of the United States hereby recognizes the Republic of Cuba as the true and lawful government of that island;" so that the first paragraph of said Senate amendment will read as follows:

"First. That the people of the Island of Cuba of right ought to be free and independent."

[Applause.]

Also amend the title of said joint resolution by striking out the words "and Republic." (*Cong. Rec.*: 1989, 4041)

After a few sharp exchanges, during which the Minority Leader, Representative Bailey, lost his temper and accused Speaker Reed of falsehoods, the roll was called, revealing that the Republicans had held the line. The Dingley motion had passed one hundred and seventy-nine to one hundred and fifty-six, a margin of twenty-three, with only fourteen Republican "insurgents" breaking ranks and voting with the Democrats. A game of shuttlecock now began:

> The scene of the conflict shifted from one chamber to the other – Senators, specta-
> tors, and newspaper men assembling in the House to watch the proceedings there,
> then moving in bodies over to the Senate; then back to the House, and again back
> to the Senate, following the resolutions in their progress toward an agreement.
> (*New York Times* 19 April 1898, 1:6)

In the Senate, the members roused themselves from consideration of the Sundry Civil Bill at 2:40 pm to hear the message from the House. Senator Davis appealed to his colleagues to settle the matter and accept the House's decision. He was, however, voted down – thirty-two to forty-six. Then, in another show of senatorial arrogance, which Senator Davis did not support this time around, the "recognitionists" voted down a motion to appoint conferees, thirty-four to forty-three, thereby insisting upon the Senate resolutions. The shuttlecock flew back into the House. Would the Republican majority hold on a second vote?

After the resolution had returned to the House, Representative Jacob H. Bromwell, Republican from Ohio, moved that the House recede from the Dingley amendments. To the surprise of many, his motion was defeated: the vote on recession was one hundred and forty-eight for and one hundred and seventy-two against. The Republican majority had grown by one to twenty-four; victory for McKinley and Reed was almost in sight. The House, next, named conferees and adjourned until eight o'clock. Everyone now shuttled back to the Senate, where, at 5:10 pm, the names of the House conference were announced. Unable to cower the House, the Senate accepted the conference but soon fell into a dispute over who should be appointed to the conference committee. By custom the vice president named the chair and the ranking majority and minority members of the relevant committee to the conference. In this case, the custom would exclude all of the "recognitionists" from the conference, leaving the Senate with no one representing its majority on this issue. After some bickering, Senator Frye, an opponent of

recognition who would customarily have been the ranking minority member, withdrew in favor of Senator Joseph B. Foracker from Ohio, the leading Republican "recognitionist." When this squabble had been settled, the Senate adjourned until eight o'clock, as the House had, in order to allow the conferees to meet.

At eight o'clock, the Senate conferees reported that the conference majority had agreed to the deletion of the Turpie amendment on recognition. However, the conference had not been able to agree on the deletion of "... are, and ..." from the first clause of the first resolved. While the House waited, the Senate debated the issue. On a vote of thirty-nine to forty, the Senate decided neither to delete "... are, and ..." nor to seek another conference, hoping that the House would back down. When the Senate message reached the House at 9:50 pm, it was, in turn, rejected. Once again, the House called for a conference and adjourned until eleven o'clock. At 11:30 pm, the House was notified that the Senate had agreed to a second conference, and the six conferees met once again.

During this second conference, the *New York Times* reported that

> the Capitol swarmed like a beehive with visitors. The public galleries overflowed with their throng. Senators and Representatives mingled in the two halls of Congress, lounging idly while the conferees deliberated. The determination was evident everywhere to finish the Cuban matter before adjournment. The talk arose of an all-night session. The basement restaurants did a thriving trade. Jokes were cracked, Congressmen guyed each other. The scene suggested little of the awful possibilities of war. (19 April 1898, 2:1)

At 1:10 am, the conferees reached agreement. The two House Republicans, Acting Chairman Adams and Joel P. Heatwole (Minnesota), relented and admitted the words "... are, and ..." to the first resolved. This ended the impasse, although it did reintroduce the factual and logical inconsistency noted by Senator Hoar. The agreement was reported in both houses at 1:15 am, at which time the Senate voted to adopt the conference report, forty-two to thirty-five. In the House, there was additional tumult; nonetheless, the resolution was, first, adopted one hundred and seventy-one to one hundred and twenty-one. Then, the conference report was accepted three hundred and ten to six.

THE END OF THE "GAMES"

And, so ended the fifth day of the congressional games. President McKinley and Speaker Reed had held the Republican majority in the House and beaten back the "recognitionists" in the Senate. As Senator William E. Chandler, Republican from New Hampshire, explained:

Having accomplished our object [intervention], we did not think it was wise to go
further and delay proceedings and thus play into the hands of the peace men by
continuing to insist upon specific recognition. (Trask 1981, 55)

Senator Chandler is, of course, correct. The "peace men," McKinley and his
colleagues, had not been able either to delay or to avert war.

The next day, Wednesday, 20 April 1898, McKinley signed the joint resolution, thereby making it official, despite the logical and factual flaws found
in its first resolve:

Joint Resolution for the independence of the people of Cuba, demanding that
the Government of Spain relinquish its authority and government in the Island of
Cuba, and withdraw its land and naval forces from Cuba and Cuban waters, and
directing the President of the United States to use the land and naval forces of the
United States to carry these resolutions into effect.

Whereas the abhorrent conditions which have existed for more than three years in
the Island of Cuba, so near our own borders, have shocked the moral sense of the
people of the United States, have been a disgrace to Christian civilization, culminating, as they have, in the destruction of a United States battleship, with two hundred
and sixty of its officers and crew, while on a friendly visit in the Harbor of Havana,
and cannot longer be endured, as has been set forth by the President of the United
States in his message to Congress of April eleventh, eighteen hundred and ninety-
eight, upon which the action of Congress was invited: Therefore,

Resolved by the Senate and the House of Representatives of the United States of
America, in Congress assembled, First. That the people of the Island of Cuba are,
and of right ought to be free and independent.

Second. That it is the duty of the United States to demand, and the Government
of the United States does hereby demand, that the Government of Spain at once
relinquish its authority and government in the Island of Cuba, and withdraw its
land and naval forces from Cuba and Cuban waters.

Third. That the President of the United States be, and he hereby is, directed and
empowered to use the entire land and naval forces of the United States, and to call
into the actual service of the United States the militia of the several States to such
extent as may be necessary to carry these resolutions into effect.

Fourth. That the United States hereby disclaims any disposition or intention to
exercise sovereignty, jurisdiction, or control over said island except for the pacification thereof, and asserts its determination, when that is accomplished, to leave
the government and control of the island to its people. (Pub. Res. No. 55–24, 30
Stat. 738)

President McKinley, then, set about informing the Spanish government of
the resolution. In particular, he decided to recast it in the form of an ultimatum with a forty-eight-hour deadline (*For. Rel.*: 1898, 762–3). The ultimatum was then sent to the American minister in Madrid, General Stewart L.
Woodward, who was to present it to the Spanish authorities on Thursday, 21
April 1898. However, the Spanish minister in Washington, Señor Luis Polo

y Bernabé, forwarded his copy of the ultimatum directly to his government. Upon receiving it, the Sagata government immediately severed relations with Washington, ordering Señor Polo to quit Washington for Canada. He crossed the bridge over the Niagara River at 1:30 pm on Thursday, 21 April 1898, and spent the rest of the afternoon cabling New York, Washington, and Havana, running up a $300 bill for cables to the Foreign Office in Madrid (*New York Times* 22 April 1898, 1:3). In Madrid, the Sagata government refused to allow Minister Woodward to present his ultimatum and instead handed him his passports and ordered him to leave Spain at once. A semiofficial notice explained the Spanish position:

> The Spanish Government, having received the ultimatum of the President of the United States, considers that the document constitutes a declaration of war against Spain and that the proper form to be adopted is not to make any further reply but to await the expiration of the time mentioned in the ultimatum before opening hostilities. In the meantime the Spanish authorities have placed their possessions in a state of defense, and their fleet is already on its way to meet that of the United States. (*New York Times* 22 April 1898, 1:2)

A state of war had been recognized by Spain; McKinley proclaimed a naval blockade of Cuba the next day, Friday, 22 April 1898 *(New York Times* 23 April 1898, 1:6. *For. Rel.*: 1898, 769–70).

> The formal proclamation came none too soon, as American ships had already started capturing Spanish prizes sailing in Cuban waters, the first prize being the *Buena Ventura* taken on the morning of 21 April 1898 by the gunboat *Nashville* and carrying eight hundred and seventy-three thousand feet of pine lumber worth approximately $20,000. (*New York Times* 23 April 1898, 2:2)

Once the ultimatum had been rejected and prizes had been taken, some members of the Fifty-fifth Congress felt that an absolute declaration of war was now called for:

> There is a difference of opinion about the importance or necessity of making a formal [absolute] declaration of war, the President being quoted as opposing such a declaration. ... Some of the Republican members of the Foreign Relations Committee argue that if it is not necessary, it should be omitted, as war may be made without it. Other members insist that all legal disputes about the conditions at a given date would be set at rest by the passage of a resolution recognizing the existence of a state of war. That is the only form of declaration that has ever been used by the United States. (*New York Times* 23 April 1898, 1:5)

But of course the decision to make an absolute declaration did not rest in the hands of the Fifty-fifth Congress anymore. On that, everyone agreed. Custom and precedent dictated that such an important congressional act could only be contemplated with the express approval of the president. Consequently, discussions continued during Saturday and into Sunday:

The Administration and the Congress are not yet quite certain that there is war. Practically it is admitted that a state of war exists, and it is believed that the ships captured from Spain will be declared "good prize" in the courts.

The opinion prevailing in Congress, and which the Administration had not fully admitted up to this afternoon, that war should be declared formally, is now accepted, and is to be declared early next week after the form of the declaration has been subjected to further consideration by the President and Congress. (*New York Times* 24 April 1898, 1:5)

Finally, at a White House conference on Sunday, the text of the absolute declaration was approved by McKinley, and he further agreed to forward a message requesting it. There would be no more presidential "waiting" for congressional "action," as precedent demanded that once again the Fifty-fifth Congress would dutifully concur with a resolution previously approved by the president:

An Act Declaring that war exists between the United States of America and the Kingdom of Spain.

Be it enacted by the Senate and House of Representatives of the United States of America in Congress assembled, First. That war be, and the same is hereby, declared to exist, and that war has existed since the twenty-first day of April, anno Domini eighteen hundred and ninety-eight, including said day, between the United States of America and the Kingdom of Spain.

Second. That the President of the United States be, and he hereby is, directed and empowered to use the entire land and naval forces of the United States, and to call into the actual service of the United States the militia of the several States, to such extent as may be necessary to carry this Act into effect.

Approved, April 25, 1898. (Pub. L. No. 55–189, 30 Stat. 364)

As agreed, McKinley sent his message requesting an absolute declaration of war the next day, Monday, 25 April 1898 (*For. Rel.*: 1898, 771–1; *New York Times* 26 April 1898, 3:1). The House, as usual, acted with dispatch, passing the agreed upon text by acclamation an hour and a half after McKinley's message was read at shortly after noon. The Senate, upon being informed of the House vote at 2:55 pm, immediately went into secret session. It reappeared an hour and a half later, also having passed the agreed text. The only contretemps during the secret session was a motion by Senator Turpie to amend the text to include the recognition of the Cuban Republic. Because that game had already been played out the week before, his attempt was quickly defeated. Like clockwork, Speaker Reed and Vice President Hobart affixed their signatures and the clerk of the Enrolling Division carried the document to the nearly deserted White House, where, after assuring himself that nothing had been altered, McKinley affixed his signature at 6:18 pm (*New York Times* 26 April 1898, 3:2).

And so ended the congressional games. In the course of ten days, President McKinley had not averted war, as he desired. His motivation for relenting may be viewed patriotically, as Margaret Leech does:

> A more aggressive President might have broken with Congress outright, condemned the rabid warmakers, and declined to advise intervention. It would have been a lofty and courageous gesture, applauded by the pacifist minority. It would not have prevented war. The President rightly refused to abdicate his function as Commander in Chief, and leave nation, as well as party, divided and rudderless in a time of crisis. (1959, 185)

Or it can be viewed cynically as petty partisan politics to ensure that the Republicans, and not the Democrats, would reap the electoral benefits of the war against Spain in the upcoming midterm congressional elections. On this cynical view, McKinley was greatly successful. In November, the Republicans gained nine seats in the troublesome Senate and lost only twenty-one seats in the House. Either way, the games of April 1898 represent the only time in more than two hundred years that a president has stepped aside and "awaited" congressional action. With this unheard-of decision, President McKinley opened up the space for the Fifty-fifth Congress to display all the game-playing defects of a bicameral legislature for the declaring of war.

ANALYSIS

Of the lessons to be learned from the "great game of politics" played during April 1898, the least important is that the Fifty-fifth Congress did not play the role of President McKinley's town crier. President McKinley did "convene and give information" to the Fifty-fifth Congress, but not as a dictatorial president to impose his decision upon the country. Hence, the 1898 declarations are the only declarations since 1776 to fall somewhat outside the rule of men or somewhat inside the rule of law. But, again, if these "games" are the best that the Congress can do and if the Congress can do its best only once every two or three hundred years, then its best is not good enough.

Moral Incapacity

More to the point, the "great game of politics" of 1898 demonstrates why the Founders erred in assigning the power "to declare war" to the Congress and why the bicameral Congress ought never again declare war. The ethical arguments are two. The first is empirical; the second is more directly moral. Empirically, "ought not" derives directly from "cannot." Since the Congress cannot declare war in any meaningful sense, it, therefore, should not declare war. Since I cannot figure my income taxes in any meaningful sense, I, therefore, should not figure my income taxes. Let a competent accountant do it. The principal reasons for this "cannot" are the organizational paralysis of the Congress as a large majority-ruled, bicameral body burdened with 1) extremely high transaction costs, 2) enormous difficulties in coordinating its members' shared interests, and 3) huge collective action problems.

Fortunately, this paralysis is easily cured by forceful presidential leadership for the peacetime responsibilities of the Congress. Unfortunately, the peacetime cure makes it impossible for the Congress to exercise its principal wartime responsibility. The paradox turns on the fact that presidential initiative, leadership, and agenda setting are entirely normal and natural in any chief executive–policy board relationship, such as that found between any organization's president and its board of directors. Moreover, this leadership and agenda setting relationship is mandated in times of peace under article II, section 3, clause 1, "He shall from time to time give to the Congress Information of the State of the Union, and recommend to their Consideration such Measures as he shall judge necessary and expedient." In time of war, however, this same presidential initiative, leadership, and agenda setting lead only to dictatorship. The relationship destroys any hope of the Congress's exercising its principal wartime responsibility "to declare war." It transforms the Congress into the president's town crier.

Under normal circumstances, then, the Congress "cannot" declare war because it is paralyzed without presidential initiative, leadership, and agenda setting. What makes 1898 so different, then, is not so much President McKinley's opposition to war, but the absence of congressional paralysis, once McKinley stepped aside. But overcoming one organizational problem only uncovers a more fundamental constitutional flaw: the bicameral structure of the Congress. Splitting the power "to declare war" between two inevitably competitive chambers makes the "great game of politics" seen in 1898 an all but foregone conclusion. Serious debate over true reasons for and against war is abandoned. Instead of engaging in the most difficult task of "let[ting] Facts be submitted to a candid world," the bicameral "game" encourages the electoral ambitions of politicians to motivate the drafting of the declaration. Beyond a shadow of a doubt, the vast majority of the members in 1898, as in 1812, 1917, and 1941, voted their electoral self-interests, not their consciences. Enhancing a member's electoral chances, however, is certainly among the most immoral reasons to support a war.

In this regard, the "games" of 1898 can too easily be looked upon as a precursor for the cold war (1946–89). During the cold war, wars were not declared by the Congress, but they were fought in Korea, Vietnam, and elsewhere motivated largely out of political fear of being called "soft on Communism." Or, more pointedly, Senator Robert A. Taft's meaningless charge, "Who lost China?" (Mann 2001). During the cold war, no attempt was made, certainly not by the Congress, to do the hard work of "let[ting] Facts be submitted to a candid world" for any of the wars fought between 1946 and 1990. Instead, innuendo, falling dominoes, and claims as illogical as the "... are, and ..." in the 1898 declaration were the order of the day. The cold war "games" reached ridiculous heights with Senator Joseph R. McCarthy's search for nonexistent Communists in the State Department and the army.

In fine, the small, unicameral Supreme Court or the small, unicameral Second Continental Congress is the model. For, not only is the U.S. Congress empirically incapacitated, very much more important, its bicameral structure means that it is morally incapacitated.

Decorum and Organization

A number of other less dramatic lessons can also be learned from the 1898 "games." The first useful lesson is how the procedures for declaring war need to reestablish greater decorum, as was seen in 1776. Never should the newspapers be able to report that

> the scene on the floor resembled a political convention more than the House of Representatives. Members were scurrying about, caucusing in groups and discussing the situation. (*New York Times* 19 April 1898, 2:2)

Conflict Resolution Potential The games also provide an initial illustration of one of the primary functions of procedurally perfect declarations of war – their conflict resolution function. Although unrealized in 1898, the sequencing of a conditional before an absolute declaration has great potential. As relations between the conflict partners deteriorate from amity to enmity, the declarer should draft, debate, and vote down a series of conditional declarations of war. These debates should lead to negative votes because the declarer of war has decided that, although worrying and serious, amity still outweighs enmity. Needless to say, both the debates and the failure to declare war conditionally would not be unnoticed by the public, the president, or the conflict partner. Yet, the debates should nudge the situation toward a restoration of amity by clarifying both the casus belli and the possible remedies. Should the nudge prove insufficient and should the situation deteriorate further, the declarer would, then, be duty bound to "let Facts be submitted to a candid world" in the form of a positive vote on a conditional declaration of war. Again, ideally, this would be enough to nudge all toward a restoration of amity. To help this nudge along, the president might decide to attach an ultimatum to the conditional declaration, as President McKinley did in 1898. Or he might decide that forcing the question would not be helpful. In this case, he might use the conditional declaration to impose diplomatic sanctions along with stronger economic sanctions. If, however, amity were not restored in a reasonable period, the declarer of war would meet again, this time to draft, debate, and vote on an absolute declaration of war, and the full tragedy of war would now engulf the conflict partners. Ideally, this vote would also be negative. However, if, after several negative votes, when the point of last resort had been reached, the declarer of war would be obliged to vote for war and against peace. Again, the model to be emulated is the many petitions and remonstrance made by the First and Second Continental Congresses between 1775 and July 1776.

A further lesson is to recognize that this multistage conflict resolution process is, of course, the ideal. In an ideal world, the tautological rule that decision must occur before the declaration would always hold. Yet, in a less than ideal world, events often overwhelm the most ideal of processes. As James Madison and Elbridge Gerry observed on Friday, 17 August 1787, when they proposed substituting "declare" war for "make" war at the Federal Convention, their proposal still required of "the Executive the power to repel sudden attacks" without the benefit of a procedurally perfect declaration of war (Madison 1966, 476). Clearly, a procedurally perfect declaration of war by the authorized declarer of war is not always possible before armed hostilities begin. In this case, the procedurally perfect declaration may occur at any time, even after armed hostilities are over.

A salient example is President Ronald Reagan's decision on Monday, 25 October 1983, to invade Grenada. The turmoil on Grenada happened suddenly. The murder of Prime Minister Maurice Bishop on Thursday, 13 October 1983, called for such immediate action that a full debate, much less a conditional declaration of war, was impossible. More relevant to the present discussion, the fighting, such as it was, was over in days, and American troops had left the island by early December. Yet, the war, as opposed to the combat, was not over. A number of important policy questions still had to be answered to secure the peace. Notably, would the United States complete the work begun by the Cubans on a modern international airport for Grenada? Seeing how vital the airport was to the economic development of Grenada, would the United States cancel or complete the airport? Such questions should be answered by the authorized declarer in an absolute declaration of war, even when the declaration occurred after the combat was over. Such vital policy questions should not be answered by either the chief executive officer or the commander in chief.

Drafting a High-Quality Text: Two Rhetorics A comment on the varying quality of the texts written in 1898 is called for. During the games of 1898, seven different texts floated around the Capitol: the two messages of 11 and 25 April from President McKinley, the two standing committee drafts, the amended Senate draft, and the final conditional and absolute declarations. Neither of McKinley's messages can be faulted in terms of the "information given." In his first message of 11 April 1898, he summarized the history of the conflict, laid out four options, eliminated two, but pointedly did not request a declaration of war, as have all other presidents in similar situations. In his second message of 25 April 1898, he did call for an absolute declaration, but Spain had declared war on the United States at that point using unofficial, imperfect procedures. Consequently, his messages might very well serve as models for the type of "giving information" message that a nondictatorial president should send to the declarer of war.

Of the five remaining texts, the final unreasoned absolute declaration of 25 April 1898 may be passed over, except to note that the backdating of the war to 21 April 1898 is unusual. To the best of my knowledge, it is the first and only time that this has been done, in America or anywhere else. At the time two reasons for doing so were proffered: One was that 21 April 1898 was the date on which the Spanish government had broken off relations. Hence, this backdating assured that both sides began the war on the same date. The other was to ensure that the *Buena Ventura*, which had been captured on the twenty-first, would be declared a "good prize." Whatever the case may be, it seems unlikely that there would ever be a need to repeat this strange precedent again.

That leaves House Resolution 233 and Senate Resolution 149 and their amended versions. Since the Turpie amendment was eventually dropped and the Teller amendment was considered uncontroversial at the time, we need comment only on the two original committee drafts. Not surprisingly, the two drafts are good examples of the two justificatory rhetorics identified by Hatzenbuehler and Ivie in the previous chapter. The rhetoric of the House draft is not diabolic; the Senate draft is. The House draft is not diabolic because it is relatively objective and focused upon negotiable demands that could settle the conflict. The Senate draft is diabolic both in its emotional appeal "to Christian civilization" and in the deaths of the crew of the USS *Maine* in Havana harbor as justifying war, but more so in its vague and ambiguous wording. It lacks both purpose and specificity. The Senate draft says that the conditions in Cuba are "abhorrent." But which conditions? The House draft says explicitly and objectively, "the death by starvation of more than 200,000 innocent non-combatants." The Senate draft calls upon the president to use "the entire land and naval forces of the United States ... to carry these resolutions into effect." But which resolutions? The first of the Senate resolutions states, "That the people of the island of Cuba are, and of right ought to be free and independent." As Senator Hoar pointed out, this is either a factual or a moral assertion. If it be factual, then there is no need for the United States to intervene, since the fact has already been established. If it be moral, then the intervention or nonintervention of the American armed forces will not affect the proposition one way or another. In fine, the first clause makes no sense. While the second resolution does make some sense, it is incomplete, calling only for the armed forces of the United States to force Spain to "relinquish its authority" in Cuba. Unfortunately, though, the relinquishing of authority does not settle the matter. What will happen to Cuba after Spain has relinquished its authority? In a word, what is the purpose of the intervention? The House draft answers clearly:

> That the President is hereby authorized and directed to intervene at once to stop the war in Cuba to the end and with the purpose of securing permanent peace and order there and establishing by the free action of the people thereof a stable and independent government of their own in the Island of Cuba. ...

In fine, Senate Resolution 149 is the better public relations document; House Resolution 233 is the better declaration of war. It is not on a par with the Declaration of 1776, but it is the best effort ever made by the U.S. Congress.

Political Politicians But, again, to say that the members of the Fifty-fifth Congress rejected House Resolution 233, which was a document of some substance, for Senate Resolution 149, which was the better public relations document, is only to say that the members of the Fifty-fifth Congress were politicians first and declarers of war second. Indeed, of all the reasons one might adduce for intervening in Cuba in 1898, embarrassing President McKinley and winning the next election are beyond the very last. Some might even argue that they are entirely immoral. Yet, these are reasons that elected politicians understand instinctively; they are the types of reasons by which elected politicians live and die. Naturally and uncontroversially, they animated all of the parliamentary maneuvering during April 1898.

Yet, to accuse elected politicians of being elected politicians is like accusing sugar of being sweet: true, but not of much use. If one desires politicians who are declarers of war first and elected politicians second, then one must assign the declaring of war to others. The model for these types of politicians, to repeat, is not an elected legislature, especially a bicameral legislature, but an appointed judiciary or the appointed delegates of the First and Second Continental Congresses. Consequently, to repeat one final time, if the games played in April 1898 are the best that the Congress can do and if the Congress can do its best only once every two or three hundred years, then its best is not good enough.

Fortunately, though, no one should fear that the Congress will ever again declare war, since the War Powers Resolution of 1973 has authorized the president lawfully to preempt the congressional power "to declare war."

4   A Plan for Acquiescence

The War Powers Resolution of 1973

The Congress shall have power ... to declare war, grant letters of marque and reprisal, and make rules concerning captures on land and water.

(article I, section 8, clause 11)

Altho' the power of declaring War belongs to Congress, I do not see that it less falls within the scope of the President's constitutional duty to recommend such measures as he shall judge necessary and expedient than any other which, being suggested by him, they alone can adopt.

Speaker Henry Clay to Secretary of State James Monroe

Sunday, 15 March 1812

The declarations of 1812 and 1898 are beyond question the two most important declarations in the history of the U.S. Congress. The former established the controlling precedents; the latter navigated to the furthest reaches of congressional autonomy, only to discover that congressional autonomy consisted mainly in playing political games. Unfortunately, concluding that the Congress is exceptionally adept at deferring to the president and seeking partisan electoral advantage does not take one very far. Neither is an insight of any great value. This is true especially in the current dysfunctional state of affairs because presidents enjoy playing games even more than the Congress. When a disinclined Congress and a reluctant public stand between a president and his war, his natural reaction is to ignore the real substance of the conflict, switch to a more public relations friendly rhetoric of diabolism, and seize every opportunistic event that passes his way. Soon, the formula takes effect; opposition and resistance are overcome, and the war begins.

President Madison, of course, pioneered this game plan, as was seen in Chapter 2. In 1846, however, President James Polk took the game to new heights of cynicism for war with Mexico. Shouting "Manifest Destiny," he deployed forces under General Zachary Taylor onto soil claimed by Mexico along the Rio Grande. He was then somewhat less than candid in what he told the Twenty-ninth Congress. He said that the Mexicans had attacked General Taylor, when General Taylor had in fact attacked the Mexicans. This less than candid information naturally stampeded the Twenty-ninth Congress into, not declaring war, but authorizing fifty thousand volunteers and appropriating monies, as can be read in Appendix I. With money and fifty thousand volunteers in hand, no declaration was needed. In 1964, President Lyndon Johnson read from the same playbook with the same results. He parleyed anticommunist rhetoric and indistinct blips on the radars of two American destroyers operating just off the coast of North Vietnam into the Gulf of Tonkin Resolution (Pub. L. 88–408, 78 Stat. 384). The resolution then formed the less than legal basis for his continued escalation of the war in Vietnam. Soon, billions of dollars and five hundred thousand troops flooded into South Vietnam.

In the case of World War II, President Franklin Roosevelt played a different game. As war raged across Europe and Asia, "America First" rhetoric filled the country and the halls of the Congress. Discretion's being the better part of valor, Roosevelt played a waiting game. His reward occurred on 7 December 1941. With the assistance of the Imperial Japanese Navy, on 8 December 1941, the Seventy-seventh Congress turned volte-face and declared war without the slightest opposition, quibble, or murmur. Since World War II, the diabolic rhetoric of "communist aggression," "falling dominoes," "weapons of mass destruction" (WMD), and such, has combined with manipulatable events to serve a long line of presidents as well as or better than Madison's diabolic rhetoric of "dishonor," "humiliation," and "recolonization" or Polk's "Manifest Destiny."

But President Woodrow Wilson is the president who has played the game with the greatest finesse. His use of Orwellian rhetoric ("armed neutrality") and ambiguous events (the Zimmermann Note) represents the subtlest "gamesmanship" so far in American history. He is conventionally remembered for running for reelection in 1916 on the slogan "He kept us out of war." The use of the past tense, "kept," did much to induce hope for continued peace during the campaign, while masterfully concealing his future policies. By the summer of 1916, after an interview, Walter Lippmann readily concluded that the president had all but decided for war and against continued neutrality. All Wilson was waiting for were reelection and a propitious turn of events (Manicas 1989, 351–5). As is recounted in Chapter 6, Wilson was reelected in November 1916; was sworn in for his second term on Saturday, 3 March 1917; and took the decision for war seventeen days later. Wilson's greater subtly, however, does not change the end result: games were still being played. Men rule, and not law.

AN IMPERIAL PRESIDENCY?

Yet, the opportunist manipulation of events combined with an emotionally appealing rhetoric of diabolism is an epiphenomenon. It is not the heart of the matter. The core reason dictatorial presidents still rule is the congressional failure to declare war. Stunningly, though, this failure has never been identified as the principal cause. Rather, the principal cause has long been misdiagnosed as the rise of what Arthur M. Schlesinger, Jr. called *The Imperial Presidency*:

> In the last years presidential primacy, so indispensable to the political order, has turned into presidential supremacy. ... The constitutional presidency ... has become the imperial Presidency [as shown by the Indochina War and the Watergate affair] and threatens to be the revolutionary Presidency. ... [T]he imperial Presidency received its decisive impetus, I believe, from foreign policy; above all, from the capture by the Presidency of the most vital of national decisions, the decision to go to war. ... It [the growth of the imperial Presidency] was as much a matter of congressional abdication as of presidential usurpation. As it took place, there dwindled away checks, both written and unwritten, that had long held the Presidency under control. The written checks were in the Constitution. The unwritten checks were in the forces and institutions a President once had to take into practical account before he made decisions of war and peace. ... By the early 1970s the American President had become on the issue of war and peace the most absolute monarch (with the possible exception of Mao-Tse-tung of China) among the great powers of the world. (1973, viii-ix; see also Fisher 1995, 57–61, 185–91)

Schlesinger's framing of the issue as a "dwindling away" of written and unwritten checks and balances would be more convincing had he spent more time in a detailed study of actual declarations of war, such as those of 1812 or 1898. Further, and equally important, his hypothesis would be more convincing were it not so hackneyed and obvious. More than a hundred years earlier, during the controversies surrounding President James Polk's initiation of the Mexican-American War (1846–8), Congressman Abraham Lincoln had already observed this same "dwindling away" of the Constitution's "checks." Employing a royal instead of an imperial metaphor, as the "dwindling" had not yet reached imperial dimensions, Lincoln wrote to his law partner, William H. Herndon, on 15 February 1848 that

> the provision of the Constitution giving the war-making power to Congress was dictated, as I understand it, by the following reasons: Kings had always been involving and impoverishing their people in wars, pretending generally, if not always, that the good of the people was the object. This our convention understood to

be the most oppressive of all kingly oppressions, and they resolved to so frame the Constitution that no one man should hold the power of bringing this oppression upon us. But your view [i.e., ... that ... President [Polk] may, without violation of the Constitution, cross the line and invade the territory of another country [Mexico], and that whether such necessity exists in any given case the President is the sole judge.] destroys the whole matter, and places our President where kings have always stood. (Lincoln 1907, 1:111–12)

Yet, Lincoln was still not the first to make the diagnosis. Two score and ten years earlier, in the first month of John Adams's administration, long before the "dwindling away" had begun, James Madison was already making an anticipatory diagnosis. Writing with eighteenth-century optimism to Thomas Jefferson on 2 April 1798, he explained that "the constitution supposes, what the History of all Govts demonstrates, that the Ex. is the branch of power most interested in war, & most prone to it. It has accordingly with studied care vested the question of war in the Legisl." (cited in Schlesinger 1973, 5).

If 1798 were not a sufficiently ancient lineage, just before the lunch break on Friday, 17 August 1787, during the debate in the Federal Convention on what was to become the Declare War Clause, Pierce Butler of South Carolina rose to object to vesting the power "to make war" in the legislature. Instead, speaking prophetically, "He was for vesting the power in the President, who will have all the requisite qualities, and will not make war but when the Nation will support it." Truer words have seldom been spoken. All presidents have indeed demonstrated that they "have all the requisite qualities," and no president has ever made "war but when the Nation will support it." True, some of the wars so made with the initial support of the nation have soured after a time. Still, the nation has always supported the initial making, which is all a president requires, as George W. Bush demonstrated once again.

Upon hearing Butler's objection, however, James Madison of Virginia and Elbridge Gerry of Massachusetts seized the opportunity to introduce their amendment, "to insert '*declare*,' striking out '*make*' war; leaving to the Executive the power to repel sudden attacks." Gerry then commented in Schlesingeresque tones, "[I] never expected to hear in a republic a motion to empower the Executive alone to declare war" (Madison 1966, 476). After a few more minutes of discussion, the Madison-Gerry amendment passed, ayes 7, nos 2, abs. 1.

In fine, the relationship between the Declare War Clause and the Commander in Chief Clause has always been misdiagnosed as a minor glitch in the constitutional system of checks and balances. As a result, instead of revealing the structural defect in the Constitution, the misdiagnosis has always reduced the issue to one of "political will." If only the president had a little less will and the Congress had a little more, the golden age of "balance" would be restored.

And, indeed, it is both natural and convenient to misdiagnose the failure of the Federal Convention in these mechanical, clockwork terms. It is natural because the Constitution is an eighteenth-century document built upon a system of "divided, but shared" powers. It is convenient because it absolves the Congress of all blame for its failure to discharge its constitutional duty to declare war. One observes what looks like the development of an imperial or kingly presidency – but is really congressional silence – and, then, one diagnoses the congressional inaction as a "dwindling away" of a hoped for legislative "check" to "balance" the executive's "proneness" to war. Still, ancient lineage is not always a good thing. Well-worn paths are often little more than mental ruts. A diagnosis that does not cure the disease after more than two hundred years is more than a little suspect. After more than two hundred years, it is not entirely out of place to suggest that the diagnosis might possibly be false, or, at a minimum, that it is clearly inadequate.

EXORBITANT TRANSACTION COSTS, DIFFICULTY COORDINATING SHARED INTERESTS, AND AN EXTENSIVE COLLECTIVE ACTION PROBLEM

In addition to recognizing the fatally impractical division of the sovereign's war powers, the correct diagnosis identifies the rapid and unexpected increase in the size and workload of the Congress since roughly 1812 as that which has made it impossible for the Congress to declare war in any meaningful sense. These unanticipated increases forced the Congress to abandon its original, and extremely inefficient, committee-of-the-whole system for its modern, vastly more efficient standing-committee system. The most complete empirical account of the deleterious effects of the standing-committee system on the declaring of war is found in William G. Howell and Jon C. Pevehouse's groundbreaking study *While Danger Gathers: Congressional Checks on Presidential War Powers* (2007). As their subtitle proclaims, the authors did not study the congressional power to declare war. An analysis of $n = 4$ declarations is clearly insufficient for a statistical study. However, a study of $n = 15,000$ "opportunities" to deploy military forces, 1945–2000, is sufficient (*ibid.*, xxii). Proponents of the New Institutionalism, Howell and Pevehouse employed a rigidly positivist, value-neutral, contranormative statistical methodology:

> Throughout, this book takes a decidedly positive – contra-normative – perspective. We do not consider who ought to declare war. We do not ruminate on the constitutionality of recent presidential uses of force. Nor do we consider whether careful deliberations (which, presumably, Congress can best deliver) or energy and dispatch (mainsprings of executive leadership) contribute more to a

successful foreign policy. Instead, we set our sights on how the federal government works in practice, how powers are asserted, how institutional advantages are advanced, how perceived weaknesses are exploited, and ultimately which decisions [for war or peace] are rendered. We scrutinize how and under what conditions, one branch of government goes about checking the war powers of another. And we leave it to others to decide whether the finding uncovered would please the nation's Founders, or anyone else. (*ibid.*, xiii)

The disadvantage of their positivist methodology is that the questions of how and why an institution other than the Congress might or should or could actually declare war cannot be answered using their contranormative methods, as Howell and Pevehouse acknowledge. The advantage of their methodology, however, is that the data sets provide a detailed, systematic, and very technical explanation of what actually happens in the current dysfunctional system, despite any norms that a republican Constitution might imply. For example, should anyone feel relieved to read that the "one central objective" of Howell and Pevehouse's research is "to investigate the checks Congress intermittently places on presidents who are contemplating the use of the single most potent of government powers – namely, sending young men and women abroad to fight, kill, and die" (*ibid.*, xxiv). "Intermittently?" "Checks?" The Constitution says with exceptional clarity, "to declare war" and implies "always." Or, to take another example, Howell and Pevehouse report that congressional checks arise out of partisan calculations and the potential for controversy, as was the case in 1898. Congressional checks never arise out of any recognized duty "to declare war":

> To the great consternation of constitutional scholars, members of Congress do not feel much duty to thwart any and all challenges to the foreign policy powers and responsibilities laid out in Article I. Rather, congressional checks on presidential war powers materialize under well-specified conditions, having to do with the institution's partisan composition, the size of a potential deployment, and the strength of international obligations. (*ibid.*, 223)

Little surprise here, but Howell and Pevehouse have the numbers and the percentages.

More enlightening, however, a positivist methodology is able to explain why the Congress is inherently dysfunctional without presidential leadership. The basic, unavoidable reason is that "disabling problems are rampant, and they are built into the collective nature of the institution" (Moe and Howell 1999, 862). This is the case because

> in any majority rule institution with diverse members, so many different majority coalitions are possible that, with the right manipulation of the agenda, outcomes can be engineered to allow virtually any alternative to win against any other. Put more simply, agenda setters can take advantage of the collective action problems inherent in majority-rule institutions to get their own way. (*ibid.*)

Without being so clinical as to speak of "manipulation" and "agenda setters" taking "advantage," presidential leadership is absolutely essential in order to stave off the chaos of too many, too busy members, each with his own agenda.

Understanding the disabling problems inherent in any large majority-rule bicameral institution is also valuable when contemplating solutions to the congressional inability "to declare war." If transaction costs, coordination of shared interests, and collective action problems increase with each increase in the size of any majority-rule institution, a large part of any solution must be to decrease the number of people involved in declaring war. For example, under the Articles of Confederation, 1781–8, the Committee of the States, a collective executive of thirteen members, soon proved unworkable. In response, the Federal Convention solved this collective action problem by reducing the executive branch to a single chief executive officer, the president. With this reduction, the transaction costs diminished to near zero, and the impediments to coordinating "shared" interests in the new executive all evaporated as soon as President George Washington took over. Hence, if the U.S. Congress cannot declare war because "disabling problems are rampant, and they are built into the collective nature of the institution," as both history and the New Institutionalism demonstrate in great detail, then obviously a smaller, less disabled unicameral institution needs to be created. The fact that the Second Continental Congress was composed of fifty-six delegates, and not five hundred and thirty-five members, is significant, as is suggested in Part III, later.

Despite the great value of a positivist methodology and its conclusions, even greater insight can be had by performing a necropsy of the War Powers Resolution of 1973. Such an autopsy illustrates in concrete terms the disabling problems that are "built into the collective nature of the institution."

A CONGRESSIONAL DESIRE TO COOPERATE

On Wednesday, 7 November 1973, the Ninety-third Congress passed the War Powers Resolution of 1973 over President Richard Nixon's veto. In doing so, it raised the false hope that a much needed special wartime procedure was now in place to "check and balance" future presidents "prone" to war. Because President Nixon's veto did not quash the resolution, every president since has taken every opportunity to assert that the resolution is unconstitutional, an unjustified infringement on his own powers as commander in chief. These protestations are most ironic since the principal effect of the resolution has been to put the presidential power to deploy the armed forces at will on a much firmer legal foundation than ever before.

For example, consider the next presidential protest after Nixon's – President Ronald Reagan's signing statement of Wednesday, 12 October 1983, protesting the Multinational Force in Lebanon Resolution (Pub. L. 98–119, 97 Stat. 805). In his statement, President Reagan not only welcomed this expression of congressional support for his policies in Lebanon, but also argued:

> I do not and cannot cede any of the authority vested in me under the Constitution as President and as Commander in Chief of the United States Armed Forces. Nor should my signing be viewed as any acknowledgement that the President's constitutional authority can be impermissibly infringed by statute, that congressional authorization would be required if and when the period specified in section 5(b) of the War Powers Resolution might be deemed to have been triggered and the period expired. (Reagan 1983a)

As President Reagan's confrontational tone indicates, the expected response to any discussion of the relationship between the Congress and the president is to slip immediately into the language of checks and balances. The doctrine of "divided, but shared powers" is both infinitely complex and subtle. It is infinitely complex because the actual powers of the two branches are not fixed. Instead, they "must, of necessity, be determined in the ongoing practice of politics" (Moe and Howell 1999, 853). What is a "check" today may well be a "balance" tomorrow. More important than the doctrine's radically contingent complexity is its subtlety. It hovers somewhere between cooperation and conflict, with the balance tipped toward conflict. This "tip" is especially pronounced for journalists, who are always counting up the president's wins and losses. However, as is well known, conflict is fundamentally a form of cooperation. And, of course, the government would cease to operate altogether if the president and the Congress were ever to enter into a sustained conflict. Consequently, despite appearances, the relationships between the two branches are basically those of cooperation and complementarity. Go along to get along better describes the reality of their relationship.

And, indeed, this is the story told by the text of the War Powers Resolution. The provisions of the text enter in as the lion of a confrontational "check" to "balance" the president, but leave as the lamb of congressional cooperation with whatever the president initiates. Cooperation is also the story of the struggle of both the president and the Congress to deal with the untenable aftermath of the resolution. After all, only confusion and inconvenience can be built on the sands of a false hope. The text of the War Powers Resolution of 1973 (Pub. L. 93–148; 87 Stat. 555) begins on a conventional note of conflict:

PURPOSE AND POLICY
Sec. 2. (a) It is the purpose of this joint resolution to fulfill the intent of the framers of the Constitution of the United States and insure that the collective judgment of both the Congress and the President will apply to the introduction of United States

Armed Forces into hostilities, or into situations where imminent involvement in hostilities is clearly indicated by the circumstances, and to the continued use of such forces in hostilities or in such situations.

(b) Under article I, section 8, of the Constitution, it is specifically provided that the Congress shall have the power to make all laws necessary and proper for carrying into execution, not only its own powers but also all other powers vested by the Constitution in the Government of the United States, or in any department or officer thereof.

(c) The constitutional powers of the President as Commander-in-Chief to introduce United States Armed Forces into hostilities, or into situations where imminent involvement in hostilities is clearly indicated by the circumstances, are exercised only pursuant to (1) a declaration of war, (2) specific statutory authorization, or (3) a national emergency created by attack upon the United States, its territories or possessions, or its armed forces.

As befits the antagonisms at the end of the war in Vietnam, the tone of section 2 implies that the president should take heed. All is not right with the world, the Ninety-third Congress lectures, and a new dispensation is needed. New checks to balance *The Imperial Presidency* are needed. However, if one approaches section 2 from a constitutional perspective, one sees immediately the fundamental flaw in the resolution. The resolution's purposes and policies do not elaborate procedures "to declare war." From this fundamental flaw, all the resolution's false hopes follow.

In the first place, section (a) is little more than a paraphrase of Speaker Henry Clay's constitutional dictum of Sunday, 15 March 1812:

Altho' the power of declaring War belongs to Congress, I do not see that it less falls within the scope of the President's constitutional duty to recommend such measures as he shall judge necessary and expedient than any other which, being suggested by him, they alone can adopt. (Clay 1959–84; 1:637; see also Monroe 1960)

The essential purpose of the War Powers Resolution is clearly not to promote the capacity of the Congress "to declare war." Instead, without realizing it, the essential purpose is to codify Speaker Clay's dictum. As is expressed even more clearly in section 3, cited in the following, the Ninety-third Congress cannot imagine that any Congress would, first, take the decision for war or peace on its own constitutional authority and, then, declare its decision. All it can imagine is waiting upon the president's decision. Only then should the president involve the Congress, making his "recommendation" to or "consulting" the Congress to "insure that the collective judgment of both the Congress and the President will apply," whatsoever that means.

In the second place, upon what constitutional authority is the resolution based? Should a resolution "Concerning the War Powers of Congress and the President" not be based upon "the war powers of Congress and the President"? What, then, are these powers? Are they not the congressional power "to declare war" and the presidential powers as commander in chief? Why, therefore, does subsection (b) cite instead the catch-all clause of article I, section 8, clause 18 investing the Congress with a general legislative power, "to make all laws necessary and proper for carrying into execution, not only its own powers but also all other powers vested by the Constitution in the Government of the United States, or in any department or officer thereof." Does this not strike one as a little off the mark? Could the Ninety-third Congress be preparing to micromanage the commander in chief, to legislate a check to balance?

Returning to subsection (a), the Ninety-third Congress further claims to know "the intent of the framers," who desired to "insure that the collective judgment of both the Congress and the President will apply." Yet, does the Congress not possess sufficient "collective judgment" within its own chambers to exercise its own congressional power "to declare war"? Why embroil the president in the exercise of a congressional power? Why not follow Hamilton's suggestion toward the end of his first *Pacificus* paper that "the Legislature is free to perform its own duties according to its own sense of them" (1961–87, XV: 42)? But, then, both Hamilton's suggestion and the question are misdirected and impertinent. The "collective judgment" is not to be applied to the declaring of war at all. Rather, according to the resolution, "collective judgment" is to be applied to "introductions": that is, "to the introduction of United States Armed Forces into hostilities, or into situations where imminent involvement in hostilities is clearly indicated by the circumstances, and to the continued use of such forces in hostilities or in such situations." This legalistic mouthful is repeated in subsection (c).

In subsection (a), the mouthful raises perplexing questions of definition. How does one define "hostilities" or, better yet, "imminent involvement in hostilities"? At which point during the forty-five years between 1945 and 1990 did the United States become "involved in *imminent* hostilities" with the Soviet Union? Can "imminence" be sustained for forty-five years? Or, consider the marines deployed to Beirut by President Reagan for service with the Multinational Force Lebanon (August 1982–March 1984). They were "peacekeepers." By definition, then, they had not been introduced into "hostilities." They had been introduced into "peace," which they strove to "keep." Not even the Sunday, 23 October 1983, truck bombing of the marines' barrack at the Beirut airport, which killed two hundred and forty-one, created a "situation where imminent involvement in hostilities is clearly indicated by the circumstances." At least, President Reagan said so, and the Ninety-eighth Congress agreed, as will be seen. In fine, as a practical matter, the convoluted legalese of section 2 cannot be defined. Yet, more to the point, the Constitution says most clearly, "to declare war." Euphemisms such as the artless term "introductions" are not to be found there.

In subsection (c), the question of micromanagement is added to the mysteries of definition. Presumably, the president still possesses full powers to command the armed forces. The only restriction to be imposed by the resolution will be on his ability to "introduce" the armed forces. In the future, these "introductions" will be "checked and balanced" because they will be "exercised only pursuant" either to a constitutionally sanctioned "declaration of war" or to an extraconstitutional "statutory authorization," or because of "a direct attack." The intention of the Ninety-eighth Congress to micromanage presidential "introductions" is clear. Or, as the politically correct might say, the intention to "check and balance" an "imperial presidency" is clear. However, intentions and ability are two different things. If future introductions of the armed forces are to be checked and balanced "pursuant" to congressional desires, the Congress must have a means, a procedure by which it can impose its desires. Ignoring the "direct attack" option (3), both the constitutionally sanctioned "declaration of war" and the extraconstitutional "statutory authorization" require a "trigger" to get them started. If neither procedure is initiated, micromanagement will not happen. What then might these micromanaging procedures be? Section 3 suggests gently an antiprocedure:

CONSULTATION

Sec. 3. The President in every possible instance shall consult with Congress before introducing United States Armed Forces into hostilities or into situations where imminent involvement in hostilities is clearly indicated by the circumstances, and after every such introduction shall consult regularly with the Congress until United States Armed Forces are no longer engaged in hostilities or have been removed from such situations.

Before considering the practical fallout of this "consultation," consider its political strengths. Politically, such presidential "consultation" is where the common ground is to be found. To be sure, the constitutional responsibility of the Congress "to declare war" cannot be found here, but a solid, mutually agreeable, politically sustainable common ground can. For, cooperative "consultation" also marks the limits of presidential indulgence. As President George H. W. Bush noted most succinctly during his dedication of the new Social Science Building at Princeton University on Friday, 10 May 1991, at 11:45 am:

This does not mean that the executive may conduct foreign business in a vacuum. I have the greatest respect for Congress and I prefer to work cooperatively with it wherever possible. Though I felt after studying the question that I had the inherent power to commit our armed forces to battle [in Kuwait] after the U.N. resolution, I solicited congressional support before committing our forces to the Gulf war. So while a President bears special foreign policy obligations, those obligations do not imply any liberty to keep Congress unnecessarily in the dark. (Bush 1992, 497; see also *ibid.* 19–20)

In fine, section 3 is politically viable because it requires presidents to do that which they are most happy to do, not "to keep Congress unnecessarily in the dark." As long as the initiative and the decision remain with the president, as long as the Congress does not exercise its constitutional mandate "to declare war" on its own authority, presidents are more than willing to "consult" as often and as long as the Congress may please. Or, as James Madison expressed the same thought more positively, "The executive [after having decided the question of war or peace] has no other discretion than to convene and give information to the legislature" (1900–10, 6:160).

The practical "trigger" for these section 3 "consultations" is found in sections 4 and 5. This is where the unsustainable political confusion and drafting errors slip in (Glennon 1995; Fisher and Adler 1998; The National War Powers Commission Report 2008). In sections 4 and 5, the Ninety-third Congress pushed the envelope and overstepped the bounds of cooperative "consultations." It had the temerity to suggest that the president might not just "consult" *before* he "introduced" the armed forces, but that he might also "report" any "introductions" *after* they occurred, so that his "report" could "trigger" congressional action:

Sec. 4. (a) In the absence of a declaration of war, in any case in which United States Armed Forces are introduced –

(1) into hostilities or into situations where imminent involvement in hostilities is clearly indicated by the circumstances;...

(3) ... the President shall submit within 48 hours to the Speaker of the House of Representatives and to the President pro tempore of the Senate a report, in writing,. ...

(c) Whenever United States Armed Forces are introduced into hostilities or into any situation described in subsection (a) of this section, the President shall, so long as such armed forces continue to be engaged in such hostilities or situation, report to the Congress periodically on the status of such hostilities or situation as well as on the scope and duration of such hostilities or situation, but in no event shall he report to the Congress less often than once every six months.

Sec. 5. (b) Within sixty calendar days after a report is submitted or is required to be submitted pursuant to section 4(a) (1), ... the President shall terminate any use of United States Armed Forces with respect to which such report was submitted (or required to be submitted), unless the Congress (1) has declared war or has enacted a specific authorization for such use of United States Armed Forces, (2) has extended by law such sixty-day period, or (3) is physically unable to meet as a result of an armed attack upon the United States.

On the one hand, the requirement to make two different types of reports creates a hole that can be looped. On the other hand, an inability to define prospectively when the armed forces have been "introduced – (1) into hostilities or into situations where imminent involvement in hostilities is clearly indicated by the circumstances" makes it impossible to determine when the initial "triggering" report has been or is required to be submitted. Unless one can define this starting point with precision, the sixty-day clock cannot begin ticking. How much simpler it would be if the Congress were simply "to declare war" on its own authority.

The loophole in this tangle was quickly revealed when the resolution was put to its first test. As already mentioned, in 1982, President Reagan ordered the marines afloat with the Sixth Fleet ashore to serve with the Multinational Force Lebanon. The marines landed in Beirut on Wednesday, 25 August 1982. Concurrent with his order, the president sent a *Letter to the Speaker of the House and the President Pro Tempore of the Senate on the Deployment of United States Forces in Beirut, Lebanon,* dated 24 August 1982. In his *Letter,* President Reagan said, "In accordance with my desire that the Congress be fully informed on this matter, and consistent with the War Powers Resolution, I am hereby providing a report on the deployment and mission of these members of the United States Armed Forces." So far, so good.

Yet, the key words in the president's sentence are "I am hereby providing a report." Which report? About what? A triggering report under section 4(a)? or a periodic report of section 4(c)? or, perhaps, just a report? After all, like all presidents, President Reagan did not want "to keep the Congress unnecessarily in the dark." Whichever type of "report" it was, President Reagan was at pains to assure the Ninety-eighth Congress that the War Powers Resolution did not apply to this peacekeeping mission. In the first place, the marines would leave Beirut long before the lapse of the sixty days that could trigger any congressional action under section 5(b), "According to our agreement with the Government of Lebanon, the United States military personnel will be withdrawn from Lebanon within thirty days." In the second place, he was certainly not introducing the marines "into hostilities or into situations where imminent involvement in hostilities is clearly indicated by the circumstances." "I want to emphasize that there is no intention or expectation that U.S. Armed Forces will become involved in hostilities." And, finally, if any doubt remained, "This deployment of the United States Armed Forces to Lebanon is being undertaken pursuant to the President's constitutional authority with respect to the conduct of foreign relations and as Commander in Chief of the United States Armed Forces." Beyond question, the War Powers Resolution did not apply. However, President Reagan did want to keep the Ninety-eighth Congress informed. So far, so good.

More to the point, events unfolded just as the president said they would. As promised, the marines withdrew from Beirut in less than thirty days, in sixteen days to be exact, on Friday, 10 September 1982. The 24 August 1982 letter, therefore, was just "a report." The War Powers Resolution clearly did not apply to a sixteen-day deployment during which no shots were fired. Retrospectively, one could say that "hostilities" had absolutely not been "imminent." But the world is not static; circumstances change, sometimes unexpectedly. The next week, between 16 and 18 September 1982, one of the Christian militias in Lebanon massacred more than eight hundred Palestinians in the Sabra and Shatila refugee camps, under the watchful eye of the Israeli Defense Force. Horrified, President Reagan ordered the marines to return to Beirut, as they did on Monday, 20 September 1982. This redeployment prompted a second "report" to the Speaker and the President Pro Tempore, dated Wednesday, 29 September 1982 (Reagan 1982a). The second letter was virtually a carbon copy of the first. "Hostilities" were not "imminent"; the deployment was short-term; he had ordered it under his authority as commander in chief. Two "reports" had now been submitted that were "consistent" with the resolution, but concerning situations to which the resolution did not apply. President Reagan was consistently fulfilling his gentlemanly duty not "to keep the Congress unnecessarily in the dark." So far, so good.

Duty in Beirut passed uneventfully enough during the remaining winter months and into the spring and summer of 1983. However, the marines began taking fire from various factions in the Beirut area in late August 1983. Two marines were killed on Monday, 29 August 1983. This prompted a third "report" to the Speaker and the President Pro Tempore of 30 August 1983 (Reagan 1983). The third "report" was again a virtual carbon copy of the first two. Individual acts of violence were occurring, but neither "hostilities" nor "imminent hostilities" could be observed. A year into the deployment, three "reports" had been made "consistent" with the resolution about a situation to which the resolution did not apply. However, if one wished to argue that the resolution did apply, the best one could do would be to argue that the three "reports" were "periodic" reports made under section 4(c). Attempting to argue that any of the three constituted an initial forty-eight-hour triggering "report" under section 4(a) (3) would be exceptionally arbitrary. More to the point, a congressional debate to determine which "report" was the "triggering" report would be an utter disaster, a partisan train wreck. A finer loophole is difficult to imagine.

Be the illogic of the resolution as it may, continued fighting and casualties into the fall fueled congressional and public concern to the point where President Reagan felt he had to do something. Naturally, he turned to the usual peacetime procedures of the Congress and negotiated passage of the Multinational Force in Lebanon Resolution of 12 October 1983 (Pub. L. 98–119, 97 Stat. 805). This resolution provided an extraconstitutional "statutory authorization" for the Multinational Force in Lebanon going forward from that date out another eighteen months. To mollify the Ninety-eighth Congress, several sections of the authorization were prefaced with the phrase "authorized for purposes of the War Powers Resolution." To mollify himself, President Reagan issued the signing statement cited previously, welcoming congressional support for his policies in Lebanon but denying vigorously the constitutionally of the War Powers Resolution (Reagan 1983a).

Nine days later, on Sunday, 23 October 1983, a truck bomb struck the marine barrack at the Beirut airport, killing two hundred and forty-one. From this point, events moved rapidly. Four months later, on Thursday, 7 February 1984, President Reagan announced the final withdrawal of the marines. By Sunday, 26 February 1984, the marines had redeployed afloat. President Reagan sent his final "report" to the Speaker and the President Pro Tempore on 30 March 1984 (Reagan 1984). Because the marines had left Beirut, this "report" must be seen as an after-action report, as part of the president's efforts to keep the Congress informed, and not as part of the War Powers Resolution.

ANALYSIS

The first lesson to be learned here is that the primary effect of the resolution is to facilitate a president's use of the armed forces. Under the resolution, a president can deploy the armed forces for sixty days secure in the knowledge that the Congress cannot legally object. Then, should the operation extend beyond sixty days, either he can use the "reporting" loophole, or he can rely upon congressional fears of being charged with "not supporting our troops" to forestall any congressional action occurring without presidential approval.

The second and very much more important lesson is that the members cannot imagine the U.S. Congress's declaring war. They can imagine the Congress's "consulting" the president. This involves negotiating with the president and employing its normal peacetime standing-committee structure to pass extraconstitutional "authorization of force" resolutions. But the members cannot even begin to imagine the procedures by which the Congress might possibly declare war on its own authority. Hamilton said, "The Legislature is free to perform its own duties according to its own sense of them." But no member of the Congress has ever believed these words. Since Sunday, 15 March 1812, no member of the Congress has ever imagined breaking free from presidential leadership. The exorbitant transaction costs, the extreme difficulty in coordinating shared interests, and the very large collective action problem make such a thought suicidal.

The third and final lesson that emerges is the tautological principle that war is not peace, and peace is not war. And, what is true of the phenomenon itself is also true of its structures and procedures. Hence, the ways of peace are not the ways of war, any more than the ways of war are the ways of peace.

Structures and procedures that are most excellent for enacting peacetime legislation fail entirely during times of war, and vice versa. Special circumstances require special structures and procedures.

For example, unlike the members of the U.S. Congress, the delegates to the Second Continental Congress could imagine themselves declaring war. They could imagine this because the Second Continental Congress possessed a suitable unicameral organization and procedures to declare and wage war. As a revolutionary assembly, it was purpose built for times of war. However, when peace followed, it tied itself into knots. When the basic committee-of-the-whole organization and procedures of the Second Continental Congress were rewritten as the Articles of Confederation, the resulting gridlock, it was argued by Madison, Washington, and others, was unsupportable (Jillson and Wilson 1994). This perception prompted the convening of the Federal Convention in Philadelphia in 1787. The Constitution that emerged from that convention was purpose built for times of peace. It reorganized the government of the United States from wartime exigencies to peacetime governance. The words of the preamble are unusually clear on this point: The Federal Constitution was built "to form a more perfect Union, establish Justice, insure domestic Tranquility, provide for the common defence, promote the general Welfare, and secure the Blessings of Liberty to ourselves and our Posterity." In particular, the new peacetime government was to "provide [*by peacetime appropriations*] for the common defence." As more than two hundred and twenty years of American history demonstrate, the U.S. Congress has so provided in an exemplary manner. Since World War II, it has even built and nourished a military-industrial complex. However, more than two hundred and twenty years of American history also demonstrate that the Congress cannot possibly imagine itself "declaring war." Consequently, unlike the Second Continental Congress, the U.S. Congress has always organized itself to legislate for peace, allying itself with the president as the natural leader of a peacetime government and attending to his agenda.

As the sad tale of the War Powers Resolution shows, the job of work begun in Philadelphia is yet to be completed. If one desires to create a constitution that is fully republican in time of war as well as time of peace, then one must begin to imagine how the wartime organization and procedures of the Second Continental Congress can be adapted to the peacetime Constitution of 1789. No less is required.

PART II

WHAT IS A DECLARATION OF WAR?

5   Declaring and Commanding

Forms, Functions, and Relationships

The Congress shall have power ... to declare war, grant letters of marque and reprisal, and make rules concerning captures on land and water.

(article I, section 8, clause 11)

The contracting powers recognize that hostilities between themselves must not commence without previous and explicit warning, in the form either of a reasoned declaration of war or of an ultimatum with conditional declaration of war.

Hague Convention III, 1907
Relative to the Opening of Hostilities

The President shall be commander in chief of the army and navy of the United States, and of the militia of the several states, when called into the actual service of the United States.

(article II, section 2, clause 1)

After more than two hundred and twenty years, the consequences of the Founders' fatally impractical division of the sovereign's war powers are plain for all to see. The inescapable conclusion is that the Congress simply cannot, should not, and will not in the future exercise its power to declare war. The otherwise simple act of recognizing rising tensions and seizing the initiative to draft, debate, and vote up or down a declaration of war is entirely beyond the organizational capacity, the moral vision, or the political ambition of the U.S. Congress. Indeed, despite its dictatorial consequences, energetic and persistent presidential leadership is required simply to maneuver an indifferent and reluctant Congress into fulfilling its constitutional mandate in the most minimal manner possible on the fewest number of possible occasions.

Before one can propose a remedy for the Founders' impractical division of the sovereign's war powers, one clearly needs a better explanation and understanding of the power to declare war. No need exists for a better explanation and understanding of the *congressional* power to declare war. Returning to the unproductive congressional scholarship of the past two hundred and more years is not a viable option. To do so is only to spin the wheel one more time in order to go nowhere, like a squirrel in a cage. In order to prevent this fate, as a first step, one requires a clear and accurate vocabulary, a set of terms that enable one to say what one means when speaking of the power to declare war, and not just to mean what one says. This, needless to say, is the main task for this chapter: first, to reject the commonly used, but misleading and obfuscating, modern terms and, then, to rediscover the classical vocabulary of Roman law. Once that is accomplished, one can then move on to appreciate the functions of a declaration of war and the relationship between the declarer and the commander.

In order to say what one means, one must use terms that capture the fact that war is not a natural phenomenon, like an earthquake, but, instead, a socially constructed phenomenon, like money. The social construction of war is dealt with more fully in Chapter 11. For present purposes, however, one must capture the fact that war is socially constructed of two primary elements: the sufficient material acts and the necessary speech acts. The sufficient material acts are the kinetic part of war – the various diplomatic, economic, or military sanctions that can be imposed when the amity of peace turns to the enmity of war. The necessary speech acts are the aesthetic, moral, and legal part of war – the policy for the sake of which the diplomatic, economic, or military sanctions have been imposed. The speech acts are of two kinds: the "commands" or "orders" given by commanders and the "declarations" or "public announcements" given by declarers of war. Without a commander's necessary "commands" or "orders," the sufficient material or kinetic part of war simply will not occur. The soldiers will not march, and the ships will not sail. Without the declarer's necessary "declaration" of war, the reasons, justifications, or policy for which the war is being fought will not be known and the commander's "orders" will produce only an ugly, immoral, and illegal effusion of blood – ugly, immoral, and illegal because without purpose, reason, or justification.

If this were the end of the matter, terminology would not be a problem. Unfortunately, a further division of "declarations" of war must be taken into account. For, declarations of war either may be spoken in accordance with long recognized procedures by competent declarers or may be spoken tyrannically in violation of long recognized procedures by incompetent declarers. When an authorized declarer of war "declares" war according to long recognized procedures, the initial presumption is that the war so declared is justified and legal because the declarer is speaking within his area of competence. He who should declare war has done so. When an unauthorized declarer of war "announces" war tyrannically in defiance of long recognized procedures, the initial presumption is that the war is unjustified and illegal because the declarer is speaking outside his area of competence. He who should not declare war has done so. Needless to say, the legal competence of the declarer and the legal quality of the procedures used to declare any war are two vital pieces of information. They cannot be overlooked in any useful and accurate terminology.

Two strategies exist in order to express accurately all this complexity. During the early Middle Ages, the Franks used the first strategy. They employed two different nouns. The Latin term *bellum* was used to describe a calling of the host for a public "war." This had to be done by a competent public authority, normally the king, by means of a long recognized, solemn ceremony, including a mass presided over by a bishop. In contrast, the Germanic *warra* (or *guerra*) was used to describe a private "war" that had been announced by a competent private authority, usually a baron, by means of an unsolemn ceremony employing no particular procedures (Duby 1990, 110–11).

The alternative is to modify the noun "war" with a suitable adjective. That is, to employ a noun, "war," to capture the sufficient material condition and to employ a descriptive adjective to express the necessary speech act condition, the aesthetic, moral, and legal value to be placed upon the kinetic part of war. This alternative approach was, of course, the one taken most successfully by Roman law, as will be seen in a moment.

Modern legal scholars have struggled with a mixed approach. Commonly, they employ the adjective-noun approach, relying on the misleading terms "declared-undeclared" and "formal-informal" to express the aesthetic, moral, and legal status of a "war." Frequently, however, they employ the two-noun approach, relying on the reductionist term "armed conflict" and contrasting it with "war."

"ARMED CONFLICT" VERSUS WAR

The term "armed conflict" is, of course, not a noun, but a noun phrase. Yet, it is used in the same spirit as the Frankish *bellum-warra*, as can be seen by recalling common articles 2 and 3 of the 1949 Geneva Conventions.

> Art. 2. In addition to the provisions which shall be implemented in peacetime, the present Convention shall apply to all cases of *declared war* [i.e., *bellum*] or of any other *armed conflict* [i.e., *warra*] which may arise between two or more of the High Contracting Parties, even if the state of war is not recognized by one of them.

> Art. 3. In the case of *armed conflict* [i.e., *warra*] not of an international character occurring in the territory of one of the High Contracting Parties, each Party to the conflict shall be bound to apply, as a minimum, the following provisions:

(1) Persons taking no active part in the hostilities, including members of armed forces who have laid down their arms and those placed hors de combat by sickness, wounds, detention, or any other cause, shall in all circumstances be treated humanely, without any adverse distinction founded on race, colour, religion or faith, sex, birth or wealth, or any other similar criteria. (Italic added)

Yet, as a matter of fact, no material difference exists between a "declared war" and an "armed conflict." "Declared wars" are no less "armed conflicts" than are "armed conflicts." What sense does it make to call the Spanish-American War a "declared war" and the Vietnam War an "armed conflict"? Is the changed terminology supposed to indicate that "arms" were not used during the Spanish-American War? In fine, both wars meet the sufficient material conditions for war equally well; they differ only in the constitutive aesthetic, moral, and legal quality of their necessary speech act conditions. The Spanish-American War was declared in accordance with the Constitution, whereas the Vietnam War was declared in defiance of the Constitution. Both were wars, however. In sum, the term "armed conflict" provides the reader with no new information; it creates a redundancy in the text, a distinction where no material difference exists. It is a euphemism like "toilet," "water closet," or "comfort station" for something that is more accurately described with a two-syllable Anglo-Saxon term. The term implies that a "declared war" is different from an "armed conflict" without explaining what that difference is. This can only be confusing and misleading.

To be sure, no lawyer worth his salt would write an international convention that used language highlighting the fact that the high contracting parties were often in violation of their own constitutions and laws. To preserve decorum, lawyers must use terms that obscure the lawlessness of their clients, the high contracting parties. Still, the term "armed conflict" fosters an impoverished reductionist conception of "war" that reduces war to "conflict" and encourages the declaring of war to escape from the rule of law. Such a term is inappropriate.

And, finally, the only benefit to adopting the term "armed conflict" is that it creates the cynical observation that World War II was the last "war" in human history because it was the last "declared war" anywhere in the world since 1945. However, the end of legally "declared wars" has not stopped the substance of war in the material sense. It has only fostered the initiation of war outside the rule of law. It has only encouraged the more than two hundred and forty-four "armed conflicts" that have occurred between 1946 and 2009 (Harbom and Wallensteen 2010, 501). Somehow this statistic does not feel like progress.

THE IMPOSSIBILITY OF AN "UNDECLARED" WAR

Precisely because war is a socially constructed combination of material and speech acts, no war can be "undeclared." All wars are inescapably and necessarily "declared." The point of confusion, of course, is that, while the negative prefix "un-" says that no "declaration" was made, for the war in Vietnam, for example, what the speaker really means is that no *legal* "declaration" was made. Thus, both the Spanish-American War and the war in Vietnam are equally "declared" wars. The only difference is that the former was "declared" legally in accordance with the Constitution, whereas the latter was "declared" tyrannically in defiance of the Constitution. Again, this not-saying-what-one-means can only be confusing and misleading.

In this regard, war is different from marriage. Because of the way in which the number of participants can be restricted, the necessary speech act component of marriage, if not the sufficient material component, can be hidden and denied. For example, Louis XIV could marry his second wife, Madam de Maintenon, in a severely restricted private ceremony without informing his ministers or publishing the usual public proclamation. The restriction on the number of participants and the subsequent destruction of the official records permitted the king and Françoise to appear in public as if they were not married, as if she were simply his latest official mistress. Yet, the king could not similarly declare war in private and, then, neglect to inform his ministers, his generals, and the public. Even if Louis XIV did not issue a public declaration, his ministers and generals had to be told of his decision and "orders" had to be given to mobilize tens of thousands of troops, set them en route, and initiate battle. All this activity would soon becomes public knowledge, if not before the first shot was fired, then after. Likewise, the "undeclared" so-called secret wars in Laos, Nicaragua, or elsewhere hardly deserve the title when they are reported on regularly in the *New York Times* soon after the president issues his "findings," official hypocrisy and subterfuge notwithstanding. Furthermore, even a private war must be declared publicly so as to distinguish it from a vendetta or predatory brigandage. As Jean-Jacques Rousseau observed, "The foreigner, whether king, individual, or people, who robs, kills or detains the subjects, without declaring war on the prince, is not an enemy, but a brigand" (Rousseau 1950, p. 10).

"FORMAL" VERSUS "INFORMAL" DECLARATIONS OF WAR?

The contrasting terms "formal-informal" represent a problem of an entirely different order. The objection is not that the terms are misleading or false, as is the case with "declared-undeclared." To describe the 1898 declaration against Spain in the traditional manner as a "formal" declaration accurately tells the hearer that the authorized declarer used constitutionally mandated procedures. To describe the war in Vietnam as "informally" declared accurately tells the hearer that an unauthorized declarer used unconstitutional procedures. Rather, the issue is that the terms "formal-informal" can be used in several incompatible ways, each of which hits a different mark. In particular, the terms are used sometimes in the sense of "official-unofficial," at other times in the sense of "perfect-imperfect" procedures, and at still other times in the sense of "correct-incorrect" literary forms.

To sort out these three senses, consider briefly President George H. W. Bush's 7:20 am televised address from the Oval Office of Wednesday, 20 December 1989, announcing his invasion of Panama, "My fellow citizens, last night I ordered U.S. military forces to Panama. No President takes such action lightly. This morning I want to tell you what I did and why I did it" (1990, 1722–3). Notice that the president did not "declare" war. Only the Congress can do that. Instead, he "ordered" a war. He issued a military "order" and, then, made a "public announcement" of the military "order" he had given the night before. At one level, then, President Bush was merely exercising his constitutional responsibilities as commander in chief. At another level, needless to say, he was simultaneously usurping the congressional power to declare war.

This Janus-faced usurpation occurs because President Bush's necessary speech act produces a double effect. Viewed as a "formal" "order," his words produce the intended military effect. Yet, his "formal" "order" also produces the unintended effect of an "informal" declaration of war against Panama. This Janus-faced effect is analyzed in greater detail in Chapter 11. In the meantime, consider three different senses of the "informally" functionally equivalent, secondary effects of President Bush's "formal" "order."

In the literary sense of distinguishing a text's substantive content from its literary form, President Bush's "order" was certainly a "formal" order. His speech act possessed the necessary literary form and content that marked it as an easily recognized "order": ". . . last night I ordered U.S. military forces to Panama." Yet, his "order," combined with his public "announcement" of it, was simultaneously an "informal," functionally equivalent declaration of war. Unequivocally, his speech act did not possess the necessary literary form and content of an easily recognized "declaration" of war, such as the Declaration of Independence.

In the sense of distinguishing "official" acts that the president is duty bound to perform from acts he is not duty bound to perform, President Bush's "order" was certainly a "formal" duty he was constitutionally bound to perform as commander in chief. It was an act well within his competence to do. Yet, his "order," combined with his public "announcement" of it, was simultaneously an "unofficial" or "informal," functionally equivalent declaration of war. It was, therefore, well outside his "official" or "formal" competence to do.

In the sense of distinguishing constitutional from unconstitutional procedures, President Bush's "order" was certainly a "formal" order. It was issued in a procedurally "perfect" manner by the competent "order" giver. The rule of law was not skirted when he issued his "order." Yet, his "order" was simultaneously an "informal," functionally equivalent declaration of war. It was a procedurally "imperfect," public "announcement" by an incompetent "declarer" of the end of the state and condition of amity and the beginning of the state and condition of enmity. The rule of law was clearly skirted when he allowed his "formal" "order," combined with his public "announcement" of it, to produce an "informal" or procedurally "imperfect" declaration of war. In all three senses, President Bush's speech act was simultaneously Janus-faced, simultaneously "formal" and "informal."

As can be seen, the terms "formal-informal" are overburdened with diverse meanings and fine distinctions, each of which talks about a different area of concern. How is the author, much less the reader, to keep all of these senses straight? This is especially the case since Roman law provides untroubled alternative adjectives, such as "perfect-imperfect" or "solemn-unsolemn." With that last comment, perhaps it is time to turn from terminological problems to solutions. As an initial step, the connection between the national and the international law must be made.

THE IMPACT OF UNCONSTITUTIONAL DECLARATIONS ON INTERNATIONAL LAW

Seeking a fuller appreciation of the *power* to declare war, one must begin by searching out the forms, functions, and relationships that constitute a declaration of war. In truth, to research these topics, one must return to and reconstruct the *jus fetiale* of the early Roman republic from its remaining fragments. This will be done more fully in Chapter 10. As a quick introduction to these issues, however, consider for a moment how abandoning the rule of law at the national level makes nonsense of the rule of law at the international level. As just noted, no nation has declared war in a procedurally perfect, constitutional manner since World War II. This means that all of the two hundred and forty-four so-called armed conflicts between 1946 and 2009 were necessarily declared in a procedurally imperfect, unconstitutional manner (Harbom and Wallensteen 2010, 501).

As a consequence of this lack of constitutional rule at the national level, Hague Convention III, *Relative to the Opening of Hostilities* of 1907, has been desuetude since 1946, and the declaring of war is no longer a topic of interest to international law scholars. However, the situation before World War II was different. Hague Convention III was considered fully in force – belligerents made procedurally perfect declarations for both world wars – and international law scholars were still interested in the topic. Unfortunately, though, the positivist legal scholarship of the time was not up to the challenge. Basing itself solely on the empirical data of state practice, this pre–World

War II scholarship could see that some wars were declared in a procedurally perfect, constitutional manner and others not, but this critical difference was not appreciated. Instead, it was evaluated as merely a variation in state practice and, hence, as a legal distinction without any important nonlegal consequences.

As a first example, consider Clyde Eagleton's 1938 *American Journal of International Law* article, "The Form and Function of the Declaration of War." In what one might kindly call a conclusion, Eagleton opines, "We may say, then, with confidence, only one thing: that a declaration establishes the legal status of war. It is not always clear what is to be regarded as a declaration, nor what authority can issue it, nor when it is to be regarded as in effect" (29). From a positivist perspective, Eagleton's conclusion is solid and uncontroversial. As his many examples document, this is precisely the value-neutral, contranormative conclusion one must draw from state practice. Yet, his conclusion is not untroubling, especially in light of his title, "The Form and Function of the Declaration of War."

In the first place, his conclusion means that declarations of war have no form. Or, rather, they may take an indefinite number of varied forms such that "it is not always clear what is to be regarded as a declaration." This complete informality, in the second place, frustrates the performance of any useful functions that declaration might have had in the past. According to Eagleton:

> The situation has been so greatly changed [in recent years] that the declaration of war has become inadequate. It does not, today, perform satisfactorily the tasks for which it was intended, that is, to determine the existence of a legal status of war, and to differentiate it, on the one hand, from the status of peace, and on the other hand, from lesser hostilities. It seems to be accepted, among international lawyers, that the legal status of war may exist in the case of hostilities without a declaration. … (*ibid.*, 34–5)

And, of course, in the third place, Eagleton's conclusion largely frustrates any hope for the rule of law, and not men, at the international level: "If one says that a use of force is not war unless so declared by a state employing it, then it becomes possible for a war-making state, simply by failing to issue a declaration, to avoid the opprobrium of waging war, … and … [this possibility] makes it probable that undeclared wars, rather than declared wars, will be the rule [in the future]" (*ibid.*, 35).

Eagleton's final point is, of course, prophetic. The "probability" that procedurally imperfect "undeclared" wars will become the rule quickly reached 100 percent in the aftermath of World War II. Is it any wonder, though? In addition to avoiding "the opprobrium of waging war," why would states bother to make formless, apparently functionless declarations of war? To point to the obvious, however, the natural solution to all the lawless, nonfunctional unconstitutionality documented by Eagleton at the international level is for states to abide by their constitutionally mandated procedures at the national level. As soon as states did so, it would always be clear what was to be regarded as a declaration, what authority issued it, and when it was to be regarded as in effect. Form and function would be restored by the dictates of municipal law, by the constitutional mandates of each nation.

Therefore, might it be possible that the primary "intended" function of declarations of war is not "to determine the existence of a legal status of war, and to differentiate it, on the one hand, from the status of peace, and on the other hand, from lesser hostilities." Instead, might it just be possible that the legal status of war at the international level falls out naturally as a secondary effect from the legal status of the declarer at the national level and the legitimacy of the procedures he uses? Whensoever the constitutionally recognized declarer of war declares war in accordance with the constitutionally recognized procedures of the nation, the legal status of the war is not in question. Questions arise only when war is declared by a constitutionally unrecognized declarer in defiance of the constitutionally recognized procedures of the nation. If this possibility be true, then the primary functions of declarations of war would be other than legal. Perhaps, they might even be integral to conduct of war, and not just legalistic flourishes.

A second and equally interesting example is found in Quincy Wright's *When Does War Exist?* In this 1932 comment, Wright opines that war possesses a terribly fragile and contingent existence because one needs to distinguish "between war in the legal sense and war in the material sense" (362). While certainly true and valid in a positivist sense, the distinction is less than limpid:

> War in the legal sense means a period of time during which the extraordinary laws of war and neutrality have suspended the laws of peace in the relations of states. A state of war may exist without active hostilities, and active hostilities may exist without a state of war. ... It is clear, however, that an act of war starts a state of war only if there is a real intention to create a state of war. ... Suppose, however, that a state commits acts of war on a large scale [as with the Japanese invasion of Manchuria in 1931], but with repeated assertions that it is not intending to make war, is it possible for its acts to speak louder than its words? It is believed that such a situation may become a state of war, but only if recognized as such by the victim or by third states. ... It is submitted that in case a state using military force disclaims an intention to make war, and the victim cannot or does not recognize war [as China did not in 1931], a state of war does not exist until such time as third states recognize that it does. (*ibid.*, 363, 365, 366)

As the square brackets indicate, Wright was trying to parse the strange circumstances of the 1931 Japanese invasion and occupation of Manchuria. Just as Eagleton had prophesied, Imperial Japan was trying "to avoid the opprobrium of waging war" by denying that it was waging war. Most conveniently, the Chinese government of the day agreed, as a certain amount of gold had changed hands, or so it was rumored at the time. Because the fact of "war in the material sense" was incontestable, according to Wright, the joint Japanese-Chinese denial forced the responsibility to declare the existence of "war in the legal sense" on to a third party. For example, Secretary of State Henry Stimson played this role when he declared, "it is clear beyond peradventure that a situation has developed [in Manchuria] which cannot under any circumstances be reconciled with [Japan's obligation to resolve her dispute with China pacifically]" (*ibid.* 368).

Superficially, Wright's distinction looks like so much splitting of "material" and "legal" hairs. More fundamentally, though, Wright's positivist distinction between "war in the legal and material senses" is only the positivist symptom for the speech act disease. The speech act disease is caused by an improper ordering of names, which must be rectified: "When names are not properly ordered, what is said is not attuned; when what is said is not attuned, things will not be done successfully" (*Analects* 13/3, cited in Hall and Ames 1987, 269–70). For, as Confucius would no doubt confirm, if "war" were always declared in a procedurally perfect manner in tune with the mandate of the declarer's constitution, then no gap or ambiguity could exist "between war in the legal sense and war in the material sense." But, of course, as Eagleton demonstrated, state practice, including American practice, makes this solution impractical. What international body or convention would dare to demand that the United States, much less any other state, follow its own Constitution?

Eagleton and Wright's positivistic way of looking at the declaring of war is clearly a most unhelpful perspective. It reduces war to an insensate natural occurrence devoid of human agency. Like the tree that falls in George Berkeley's forest, if no one is around to hear the roar of the cannon, war does not exist "in the legal sense." What is needed is a rectification of names that abandons a state-practice perspective and restores a rule-of-law perspective. And, indeed, two thousand five hundred years ago, just such a nonpositive, normative, rule-of-law perspective existed. In early republican Rome, the *collegium fetialis* possessed a body of law, the *jus fetiale,* that reversed the order of "material act" and "legal state." This reversal was possible because the *jus fetiale* was based upon a commensurate normative distinction between legitimately and illegitimately declared wars, and not on an incommensurate distinction between "material" and "legal" wars. Under the *jus fetiale,* the "state and condition" of "war in the legal sense" were constituted by a procedurally perfect declaration of war from the Senate before the "act" of "war in the material sense" could occur. In consequence, the existence of "war in the material sense" depended upon the existence of an objective moral and legal act – a procedurally perfect declaring of war by the constitutionally recognized declarer of war – the Roman Senate. Indeed, it was this object-ive, visible legal act that constituted each war as this specific, "material" war. Depending upon how the declarer wrote each declaration, the subsequent war might be a war for independence, a war to liberate Cuba, or some other specific type of war. This constitutive or definitional power of the performa-tive speech act, needless to say, is the first and most fundamental function of a declaration of war.

Unfortunately, this first and foremost function depends upon declarers of war to follow their constitutional mandates, which, of course, is a very simple, but revolutionary idea. Therefore, the double challenge for the rest of this chapter is, first, to rediscover what the Romans of the republic once knew and, then, to turn to Carl von Clausewitz's *On War* (1976) to deter-mine the appropriate relationship between the declarer of war and the com-mander of the diplomatic, economic, or military means. With regard to the first task, some wars are declared in accordance with the nation's constitu-tionally mandated procedures; others are not, but all wars are declared. Why is this so?

WAR AS A SPEECH ACT: ALTERNATIVE TYPES

In order to speak clearly and accurately about declarations of war, one must be able to identify and describe their alternative types and functions. Ultimately, these forms and functions derive from the nature of human language and have been recognized in customary law for more than five thousand years. Indeed, they can be traced back at least to the Sumerian epic *Agga and Gilgamesh* (Pritchard 1955, 44–7). More immediately, the terms used are taken from the Latin as found ultimately in the *jus fetiale*. In point of fact, two different, but complementary, sets of terms exist. The one set of terms derives from the unique compositional elements that distinguish declarations of war from other performative speech acts, from disaster declarations, for example. The point of entry into this compositional vocabulary is, of course, the text of the Declaration of Independence, as will be discussed in a moment.

The other set derives more directly from the conflict resolution function of declarations of war. This set of terms was in common usage until roughly the end of the nineteenth century. For example, during the litigation over good prizes following the Quasi-War with France (1798–1800), the Supreme Court justice Bushrod Washington employed the technical terms "perfect-imperfect" and "solemn-unsolemn" to distinguish a war declared "in form" from a quasi-war declared "out-of-form":

> If it [war] be declared in form, it is called solemn, and is of the perfect kind; because one whole nation is at war with another whole nation. ... But hostilities may sub-sist between two nations more confined in its nature and extent; being limited as

to places, persons, and things; and this is more properly termed imperfect war; because not solemn,... (*Bas v. Tingy*. 4 U.S. (4 Dall. 37) 40 (1800))

One not particularly good point of entry into this second set of terms is article I of Hague Convention III, *Relative to the Opening of Hostilities* of 18 October 1907: "The contracting powers recognize that hostilities between themselves must not commence without previous and explicit warning, in the form either of a reasoned declaration of war or of an ultimatum with conditional declaration of war."

Although not particularly important, it is interesting to note that Convention III was ratified by the Senate on 10 March 1908, was approved by President William Taft on 23 February 1909, and is found in the 37th volume of the Statutes at Large, page 2259. Consequently, in the United States, the declarer of war is legally bound by its procedures. Because this is the case, the Declare War Clause is not the only legal pillar upon which the power to declare war rests. Hague Convention III adds further support and shape to the illusion of a congressional obligation to declare war. Needless to say, of course, since 1909, no Congress has abided by Convention III. Neither the Sixty-fifth Congress for World War I nor the Seventy-seventh Congress for World War II met its responsibilities under Hague III, since neither made a reasoned declaration. This, however, is not surprising given that they are the only two Congresses since 1909 to have abided by the Declare War Clause even minimally.

As just mentioned, Hague III is a less than perfect entry point into the conflict resolution functions of declarations of war. This is the case because the "declaring of war" is not the same as the "opening of hostilities," any more than the signing of the contract for the Bears to play the Lions next season is the same as the referee's blowing the starting whistle at game time. The principal reason for this confusion in the convention is that the authors of Hague III were nineteenth-century romantics who did not fully understand the conflict resolution purposes of declarations of war. Instead, they thought of "declarations of war" as primarily minatory, as the giving of "previous and explicit warning" before the "opening of hostilities." This, of course, is the traditional reason for or explanation of the function and purpose of declarations of "war." Contestants in "war" should be chivalrous, gentlemanly, sportsmanlike, and it is decidedly unsportsmanlike to "commence hostilities" before the referee blows his whistle. Beyond question, all must agree that this fine romantic idea is romantic.

What the authors of Hague III did not understand was how declarations of war are concerned more with establishing a process or a procedure to make a conflict public and manifest as the first step toward resolving it (Kriesberg 1998). To take a sequential view of the process, as illustrated in Figure 2, the declaring of "war" is first and foremost about constituting a conflict as a war.

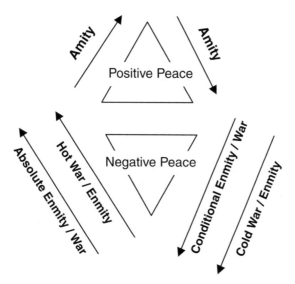

Figure 2. Declarations of War as a Conflict Resolution Process.

This speech act requires the declarer to define the fissure between the amity of a positive and the enmity of a negative peace characterized by diplomatic and economic sanctions, whereas the "opening of armed hostilities" is about defining the fissure between the enmity of a negative peace and the beginning of military sanctions upon the failure of less forceful diplomatic and economic conflict resolution means.

Ignoring the romance of the minatory "previous and explicit," the viable heart of Hague III is the presentation of alternative types of declarations of war and the technical terms needed to describe each alternative. The structure of human speech is such that wars are declared either with "a reasoned declaration," such as the Declaration of Independence, or with "an ultimatum and a conditional declaration," such as the conditional declaration of 19 April 1898 to which President William McKinley appended an ultimatum.

But, in order to understand and speak about these two options more fully, one must also know the technical terms that are not used in Hague III. For, a reasoned declaration must be contrasted with an unreasoned declaration, and a conditional declaration must be contrasted with an absolute declaration, not forgetting the contrasting paired synonyms: "solemn-unsolemn" and "perfect-imperfect."[1] The purpose of these four contrasting pairs is to enable one to identify and speak about the four different qualities that define and describe the performative speech act by which a declarer of war makes a

[1] Traditionally, the contrasting pair, formal-informal, is included in this list. It has been dropped as misleading for the reasons given.

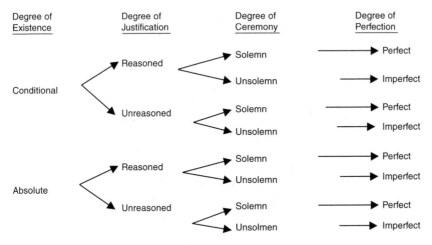

Figure 3. Alternative Types of Declarations of War.

conflict public and manifest. In this way, the declarer constitutes or defines a given conflict as a "war" and takes the first steps to resolving it. Furthermore, the four contrasting pairs are related one to the other by the way in which they define and describe differences in the degree of existence, justification, ceremony, and procedural perfection of war, as is illustrated in Figure 3.

Degrees of Existence

With respect to a war's *degree of existence*, both a war and a declaration of war may be either conditional or absolute. Such is the nature of human language that a conditional war or cold war is constituted by a conditional declaration as the war's necessary, but not sufficient, speech act condition. Pending the results of further negotiations, a conditional declaration of war documents the slippage from amity to enmity and establishes a state and condition of negative peace between the conflict partners, thereby constituting the state and condition of war conditionally. The conditional declaration of war argues that gravamina x, y, and z have caused concern and may well lead to deeper enmity if the stated remedies or peace terms/war aims a, b, and c are not accepted. When accepted, the amity of the state and condition of positive peace are restored. When a deadline is attached to a conditional declaration of war, it becomes an ultimatum, as was the case in 1898.

An absolute war or hot war is constituted by an absolute declaration as the war's necessary, but not sufficient, speech act condition. An absolute declaration declares that, with the failure of the negotiations provoked by the conditional declaration to reestablish the amity of positive peace, a deepened enmity now exists such that the state and condition of war between the conflict partners are no longer conditional, but absolute, as, for example, was the case in 1776.

Although the vital importance of conditional declarations of war for conflict resolution is explored more fully at the end of this section, one must note in passing that, from a political perspective, the writing of conditional declarations is the main work of a fully empowered declarer of war because most conflicts can be resolved through negotiations if the gravamina and remedies are clearly articulated early on in a conditional manner. Once they are resolved, no need exists to go to the next step and declare war absolutely.

To anticipate a troublesome issue, the role of authorizing clauses in declarations becomes clearer as soon as one realizes that they may appear promiscuously in both conditional and absolute declarations. Their promiscuity arises because they are truly an unimportant optional feature, like power windows on a new car. Power windows are nice, but the car runs just as well, if not better, without them. The two 1898 declarations were purchased with authorizing clauses, but the Second Continental Congress, being more frugal, passed on this luxury and declared independence without authorizing the use of the armed forces. Instead, it authorized the use of the Continental Army in the old-fashioned roll-up way, by appropriating money. That which makes a declaration of war absolute is a sentence declaring war, "That war be, and the same is hereby, declared to exist. ... between the United States of America and the Kingdom of Spain." That which makes a declaration of war conditional is the absence of an absolute declaration of war. An authorizing clause is entirely superfluous and optional.

Two examples of conditional declarations without "authorizing" clauses may help clarify the point. The more restrained is found in Livy:

> Whereas Perseus, son of Philip, King of Macedonia, contrary to the treaty made with his father Philip and renewed with himself after the death of his father, had invaded allies of the Roman people, had devastated their land and seized their cities, and whereas he had entered on plans for preparing war against the Roman people, and had assembled arms, soldiers and fleet for the said purpose, resolved that, unless he offered satisfaction in these matters, war against him be undertaken. (XLII, xxx, 10–11)

Frequently, however, the declaration's conditional quality sounds very much more like an ultimatum or an overwrought challenge, as, for example, the letter delivered by the sultan's ambassador, Kubat, on Tuesday, 28 March 1570, to the signory of Venice:

> Selim, Ottoman Sultan, Emperor of the Turks, Lord of Lords, King of Kings, Shadow of God, Lord of the Earthly Paradise and of Jerusalem, to the Signory of Venice: We demand of you Cyprus, which you shall give us willingly or perforce; and do you not irritate our horrible sword, for we shall wage most cruel war against

you everywhere; nor let you trust in your treasure, for we shall cause it suddenly to run away from you like torrent; beware to irritate us. (Hill 1940–8, 3:888)

Despite Selim's less than conciliatory language, war has not been declared absolutely. Relations between the Ottoman sultan and the signory of Venice are no longer those of the amity of a positive peace, but, rather, of the enmity of a decidedly negative peace; yet, negotiations and a resolution of the conflict over Cyprus short of the sultan's "horrible sword" are possible, if not very probable. In fine, the frequent making of conditional declarations of war, using less wrought language, is the key to unlocking the conflict resolution potential of the Declare War Clause.

Degree of Justification

With respect to a war's *degree of justification*, both a war and a declaration of war may be either reasoned or unreasoned. A fully reasoned declaration justifies the resort to war in terms of the just-war criteria (Hallett 2008; 2008a). The only fully reasoned declaration in American history is the Declaration of Independence (Hallett 1998, 53–6); the House draft of the conditional declaration of 19 April 1898 is another, lesser example. An unreasoned declaration of war does not justify the resort to war. It gives no reasons; it states neither the casus belli nor the preferred remedies, or does so only minimally, as for example, the final Senate draft of the conditional declaration of 19 April 1898. Instead, it simply declares an end to the amity of peace and the beginning of the enmity of war. All four of the absolute declarations made by the Congress, those of 1812, 25 April 1898, 1917, and 1941, are unreasoned absolute declarations of war. To repeat, the 19 April 1898 conditional declaration for the Spanish-American War is, exceptionally, the only reasoned declaration made by the U.S. Congress in its history. With the exception of this single attempt, the Congress has never attempted to explain itself by modeling itself on the Second Continental Congress. Not emulating the Second Continental Congress is undoubtedly a mistake.

Degree of Ceremony

With respect to a war's *degree of ceremony*, because of the nature of human language, both a war and a declaration of war may be either solemn or unsolemn. A solemn war is declared by the constitutionally recognized declarer of war with respectful ceremony according to the customs and laws of the land. An unsolemn declaration of war is declared without respectful ceremony. But note the problem: Because the declaration is not made according to the customs and laws of the land, no laws or rules exist to identify the declarer or to specify the necessary procedures and ceremonies. This lack of laws or rules, needless to say, leads directly to the rule of men, and not law.

As already noted in this chapter's Introduction, failure to recognize the critically important difference between procedurally solemn and unsolemn speech acts has plagued modern legal scholars, confusing and befuddling them. This befuddlement, of course, arises only because they are caught in the trap "state practice," in the trap of their contranormative, positive methodology. Consequently they are unable to deploy a normative methodology such as speech act theory. Like Eagleton and Wright, they are left to report the material or positive fact that unsolemn declarations are totally ambiguous. This ambiguity is caused by irregularities on the part of the declarer or by the declarer's use of irregular ceremonies or procedures.

With regard to the declarer, an unsolemn declaration may be made by the constitutionally recognized declarer of war speaking in an unsolemn manner, as the Congress frequently does; or it may be made by a constitutionally unrecognized declarer, as the president frequently does; or it may be made by any common warlord. An example of this latter might be Osama bin Laden's 23 February 1998 declaration (World Islamic Front Statement 1998). With regard to the form, an unsolemn declaration may be made by means of any sort of public announcement, such as a televised presidential address, or by no public announcement at all, such as when Philip II of Spain sent the Armada against Elizabethan England in 1588. So-called secret or covert wars are also unsolemn private wars. Such wars, like the Armada, announce themselves publicly only when the first shot is fired, as with the April 1961 Bay of Pigs invasion of Cuba.

Not unexpectedly, the use of unsolemn, functionally equivalent speech acts creates a slipshod world. As Charles Molloy observed, with a solemn denunciation, one does not "slip into war" unnoticed:

> A general war is either solemnly denounced or not solemnly denounced; the former is when war is solemnly declared or proclaimed by our [English] king against another state. Such as the Dutch war, 1671. An unsolemn war is when two nations slip into a war without any solemnity; and ordinarily happeneth among us. Again, if a foreign prince invades our coasts, or sets upon the king's navy at sea, hereupon a real, though not solemn war may, and hath formerly, arisen. Such was the Spanish invasion in 1588. So that a state of war may be between two kingdoms without any proclamation or indication thereof, or other matter of record to prove it. (*De Jure Maritimo* 1672, I, c, l)

Degree of Perfection

With respect to a war's *degree of perfection*, both a war and a declaration of war may be either procedurally perfect or imperfect. A procedurally perfect war is one that is declared by the constitutionally recognized declarer with due solemnity and ceremony according to the customs and laws of the land. A procedurally imperfect war is one that is declared either by a constitutionally unrecognized declarer or by the constitutionally recognized declarer, without due solemnity and ceremony, presumptively, in violation of the laws and customs of the nation.

The point of the contrasting terms "perfect-imperfect" is not to facilitate ironic or cynical humor. Sophisticated comments such as how World War II was not only "a good war," but a "perfect" war as well, because the Seventy-seventh Congress failed to shirk its responsibility to declare war in accordance with the Constitution, are not the point at all. Nor is the point ironic commentary to the effect that the Korean, Vietnam, and Iraqi wars were not only "bad wars," but "imperfect" as well, because the respective Congresses succeeded brilliantly in shirking their constitutional responsibilities. Such cynical observations are not the point at all.

Rather, the point of the terms is to identify or summarize the quality of the necessary, but not sufficient, speech acts by which a war is constituted and, hence, the degree of ambiguity that shrouds the war. Did the nation "slip into a war" because the war was initiated in some unsolemn unconstitutional manner? Or did the nation initiate the state and condition of war clearly and unambiguously by declaring it in a solemn and constitutional manner? Needless to say, the difference between a procedurally "perfect" and a procedurally "imperfect" war is the tragic dilemma that hovers over every page of this book.

WAR AS A SPEECH ACT: THE COMPOSITIONAL ELEMENTS

But declarations of war possess not just a constitutive grammar, but an interior structure as well. Their interior structure is critical because the presence or absence of one or more of the elements of composition establishes whether a declaration is conditional or absolute, reasoned or unreasoned, solemn or unsolemn: in other words, whether a given declaration is procedurally perfect or imperfect.

Again, the terms derive from the Latin as developed in the *jus fetiale* of the early Roman Republic. However, no single source can be consulted to learn this technical vocabulary. One begins by wondering what one calls the list of gravamina in the Declaration of Independence, or why the word "denounce" is used: "We must therefore, acquiesce in the necessity, which denounces our Separation." Then, one comes across "denunciation," along with "indictment," in Renaissance texts, and, finally, one sees a reference in Cicero's *De Officiis*, for example, and the connections between the technical vocabulary and their meaning is made:

Ac bell quidem acquitas sanctissime fetiali populi Romani iure perscripta est. Ex quo intellegi potest nullum bellum esse iustum, nisi quod aut rebus repetitis geratur aut denuntiatum ante sit et indictum.

As for war, humane laws [i.e., most holy or solemn laws] touching it [war] are drawn up in the fetial code of the Roman People under all the guarantees of religion; and from this it may be gathered that no war is just, unless it is entered upon after an official demand for satisfaction [i.e., a conditional declaration of war] has been submitted [to the conflict partner] or a denunciation was before [made] and indicted. (1928, I. xi. 31; translation modified; see also *De Re Publica* 1928, II, xvii 31)

Once these ancient terms are rediscovered, the interior form of a well-drafted declaration of war is easily seen and the compositional logic of the Declaration of Independence is revealed. After a preamble:

I. For a Conditional Declaration of War:

   A. *The Indictment*: The grievous conduct of the conflict partner must be indicted. That is, the grievances, causes, reasons, or justification for the war must be analyzed and listed ("To prove this [King George's tyranny], let Facts be submitted to a candid world."),

   B. *The Declaration of Peace Terms*: The preferred peace terms/war aims must be declared. That is, as a consequence of the indictment, the preferred remedy for the enmity so indicted must be articulated and published as the basis for continuing negotiations to restore the amity of peace. ("We, therefore, the Representatives of the united States of America, in General Congress, Assembled, appealing to the Supreme Judge of the world for the rectitude of our intentions, do, in the Name, and by authority of the good People of these Colonies, solemnly publish and declare, That these United Colonies are, and of Right ought to be Free and Independent States, ...").

II. For an Absolute Declaration of War: In addition to a restatement of the indictment and declaration of peace terms,

   A. *The Denunciation of War*: The unwanted change in the relationship from amity to enmity must be denounced. That is, the failure of the negotiations over the gravamina indicted and the peace terms proposed in the conditional war must be condemned. ("We must therefore, acquiesce in the necessity, which denounces our Separation,...").

   B. *The Declaration of War*: The existence of an absolute state and condition of enmity must be declared. That is, the conditional declaration of war having led to negotiations that failed to restore amity; the absolute character of the enmity so indicted and denounced conditionally must be declared. ("... and [we] hold them, as we hold all the rest of mankind, Enemies in War, in Peace Friends." or "*Be it enacted by the Senate and House of Representatives of the United States of America in Congress Assembled*, First. That war be, and the same is hereby, declared to exist. (25 April 1898))

As already noted, optionally, a fifth clause authorizing hostile activities may be included in either a conditional or an absolute declaration. Notably, no such clause was included in the Declaration of Independence.

> *The Authorization*: Optionally, the condition and state of enmity having been declared absolutely, permission from the declarer of war to the executive authority to commence coercive diplomatic, economic, or military operations may be included. ("Hereby Willing and Requiring Our General of Our Forces, Our Commissioners for Executing the Office of High Admiral, Our Lieutenants of Our several Counties, Governours of Our Forts and Garisons, and all other Officers and Soldiers under them, by Sea and Land, to do, and execute all acts of Hostility in the Prosecution of this War against the French King, his Vassals and Subjects, and to oppose their Attempts." At Hampton-Court, William and Mary, 7 May 1689. (Brigham 1968 (1911), 147–50)

Considering the troublesome authorization clause further, three points need to be made: First, as will be further illustrated in the next chapter, "authorization of force resolutions" are merely precatory and hortatory because an "authorizing" clause is not what makes a declaration of war a declaration of war. Delete either the indictment or the declaration of peace from a conditional declaration, and the utterance is no longer a conditional declaration. Delete either the denunciation or the declaration of war from an absolute declaration of war, and the utterance is no longer an absolute declaration. Delete an "authorizing" clause, and nothing happens; nothing is missing. The car runs just as well without power windows.

Second, just to confound and confuse, an "authorizing" clause can just as easily be turned on its head to become a "prohibiting" clause. In Chapter 6, the *Joint Resolution Justifying the Employment by the President of the Armed Forces of the United States* of 22 April 1914 will be analyzed. For the moment, consider the 1998 *Supplemental Appropriations and Rescissions Act of 1 May 1998*:

> SEC. 17. It is the sense of the Congress that none of the funds appropriated or otherwise made available by this Act [for use by the Iraqi opposition] may be made available for the conduct of offensive operations by United States Armed Forces against Iraq for the purpose of obtaining compliance by Iraq with United Nations Security Council Resolutions relating to inspection and destruction of weapons of mass destruction in Iraq unless such operations are specifically authorized by a law enacted after the date of the enactment of this Act. (Pub. L. 105–174; 112 Stat. 66)

And, third, no reason exists to limit the authorizing clause to authorizing the "use of the Armed Forces" only. I know of no examples of this in procedurally perfect declarations of war; I do, however, know of several examples in procedurally imperfect declarations of war, such as the Iraq Liberation Act of 1998. After the recital in section 2 of twelve findings, which begin

> (1) On September 22, 1980, Iraq invaded Iran, starting an 8 year war in which Iraq employed chemical weapons against Iranian troops and ballistic missiles against Iranian cities.

and conclude with

> (12) On May 1, 1998, President Clinton signed Public Law 105–174 (the *Supplemental Appropriations and Rescissions Act of 1 May 1998* cited previously), which made $5,000,000 available for assistance to the Iraqi democratic opposition for such activities as organization, training, communication and dissemination of information, developing and implementing agreements among opposition groups, compiling information to support the indictment of Iraqi officials for war crimes, and for related purposes.

Section 3 all but declares war, whereas section 4 authorizes President William Clinton to do everything but use the armed forces of the United States.

SEC. 3. SENSE OF THE CONGRESS REGARDING UNITED STATES POLICY TOWARD IRAQ.

It should be the policy of the United States to support efforts to remove the regime headed by Saddam Hussein from power in Iraq and to promote the emergence of a democratic government to replace that regime.

SEC. 4. ASSISTANCE TO SUPPORT A TRANSITION TO DEMOCRACY IN IRAQ.

(a) Authority to Provide Assistance. – The President may provide to the Iraqi democratic opposition organizations designated in accordance with section 5 the following assistance:
   (1) Broadcasting assistance. – (A) Grant assistance to such organizations for radio and television broadcasting by such organizations to Iraq.
(B) There is authorized to be appropriated to the United States Information Agency $2,000,000 for fiscal year 1999 to carry out this paragraph.
   (2) Military assistance. – (A) The President is authorized to direct the draw down of defense articles from the stocks of the Department of Defense, defense services of the Department of Defense, and military education and training for such organizations.
(B) The aggregate value (as defined in section 644(m) of the Foreign Assistance Act of 1961) of assistance provided under this paragraph may not exceed $97,000,000.
(b) Humanitarian Assistance. – The Congress urges the President to use existing authorities under the Foreign Assistance Act of 1961 to provide

humanitarian assistance to individuals living in areas of Iraq controlled by organizations designated in accordance with section 5, with emphasis on addressing the needs of individuals who have fled to such areas from areas under the control of the Saddam Hussein regime.

(c) Restriction on Assistance. – No assistance under this section shall be provided to any group within an organization designated in accordance with section 5 which group is, at the time the assistance is to be provided, engaged in military cooperation with the Saddam Hussein regime. (Pub. L. No: 105–338; 112 Stat. 3179–80)

In his signing statement of 31 October 1998, still trying to undo the mischief of section 17 of the 1 May 1998 act, President William Clinton made note of the incongruity of the "additional, discretional authorities" provided to him by the 105th Congress. The incongruity arose because several Security Council resolutions had already authorized President George H. W. Bush and him to use the armed forces of the United States to enforce the no-fly zones and to impose economic sanctions against Iraq. Consequently, the value and purpose of these new nonmilitary "authorities" were difficult to fathom. Nonetheless, President Clinton welcomed them and said he would make use of them, "to further the objectives" of his own Security Council–based policies (Clinton 2000, 1938–9). Exactly how and why the Security Council possesses the authority to authorize the use of the armed forces of the United States in Iraq is a rock best left unturned.

Ignoring the politics of the president's signing statement then, with the recital of findings in section 2, the unsolemn declaration of war in section 3, and the authorization of Broadcasting, Military, and Humanitarian Assistance in section 4, the Iraq Liberation Act of 1998 may be described as a procedurally imperfect, reasoned, absolute declaration of war. The act is procedurally imperfect, despite the fact that the constitutionally recognized declarer of war made it. The reason is that war was declared unsolemnly in an appropriations act, just as in 1846 when the Twenty-ninth Congress "declared war" against Mexico with an appropriations act. That it is not considered illegal, illegitimate, and unconstitutional is neither surprising nor encouraging.

To conclude, a second primary purpose and function of a well-drafted declaration of war, most notably a conditional declaration of war, is to establish the preconditions for successful conflict resolution by making the conflict publicly and officially manifest. This basic function was well recognized by the Roman *jus fetiale*. Unfortunately, the drafters of Hague III did not understand the conflict resolution purposes of declarations of war and, sadly, focused instead on the romantic need for "a previous and explicit" warning before "opening hostilities." Yet, with a stronger understanding of the *jus fetiale*, one can begin to see how Hague III could be interpreted so as to emphasize the conflict resolution potential of well-drafted declarations of war, such as the Declaration of Independence.

The disappointment that follows from what was just said is that two hundred years of data demonstrate that the Congress sees declarations of war as neither minatory nor preconditional for successful conflict resolution. The two declarations of 1898 are close, but, even if counted as near-misses, they represent a one-off, unique, never to-be-repeated exception. Basically, the record demonstrates that the Congress sees the declaring of war as a congressional prerogative, but a presidential function. The historical reality of this conclusion notwithstanding, such cannot possibly represent either the proper or the appropriate relationship between the declarer of war and the commander of the diplomatic, economic, or military means.

ENDS AND MEANS, DECLARER AND COMMANDER

In order to consider the relationship between declarer and commander, one must put aside the two functions just discussed and engaged with two additional very closely related functions. Unlike the constitutive and conflict resolution functions, which derive from the compositional elements of the written text, the relationship between declarer and commander derives from the complex interrelationship of closely related performative speech acts. For, both declaring and commanding are performative speech acts. A commander gives "orders"; a declarer makes "public announcements." Consider this relationship, first, in a contranormative, positive manner. Superficially, the difference between the two is that a command leads obviously and directly to "war in the material sense," to the movement of men and machines, whereas a declaration leads to no obvious or direct action. A declaration appears to lead nowhere, to be just talk, some mumbo jumbo to allow for the "recognition" of "war in the legal sense," as positivist legal scholarship has long held. If true, if declarations lead only to the "recognition" of the obvious, then they are truly useless.

Consider next the relationship between the declarer and the commander in normative speech act terms: If one assumes that the declarer of war is not just a town crier, that it, and not the commander, should actually decide the question of war or peace, then the declarer must speak before the commander. Tautologically, the decision for war or peace must be made and "announced" before "orders" can be given. This means that the relationship between the declarer of war and the commander is not one of either subordination or the one "checking and balancing" the other. Instead, the relationship is a temporal and coordinate one. By announcing its answer to the question of war and peace in a fully reasoned, solemn declaration, as did the Second Continental

Congress, the declarer of war, first, constitutes and justifies the existence of the war as either conditional or absolute. But, crucially, in so doing, the declarer also articulates both the causes of the war and the political ends for which it is now necessary to employ some combination of diplomatic, economic, or military means. In other words, diplomatic, economic, or military "orders" must now be given because of the solemnly indicted and denounced gravamina so as to accomplish the peace terms/war aims declared.

Fully reasoned declarations, then, serve the additional functions of articulating the political ends for which warlike means are to be employed. This, in turn, establishes the terms of the relationship between the declarer and his commander. But where might one look to expand upon and develop further this tautological, temporal understanding of the relationship between the political ends and the operational means, and, hence, between the declarer of war and his commander? What body of knowledge might illuminate this relationship?

The Difference between War in Theory and in Practice?

Carl von Clausewitz (1780–1831) was a veteran of the entire sweep of the French wars of revolution and empire (1792–1815); a Prussian general, he began his service as a thirteen-year-old infantry ensign in 1793 and was chief of staff to General Johann Adolf von Thielmann's III Army Corps at Ligney and Wavre in 1815. Ligney was the prelude to the Battle of Waterloo. It was fought on Friday, 16 June 1815, two days before Napoleon met Field Marshal Arthur Wellesley, duke of Wellington, at Waterloo. At Ligney, the French Armée du Nord under Napoleon's personal command defeated, but did not scatter General Gebhard Leberecht von Blücher's Prussians. Thielmann's III Army Corps held Blücher's right wing at Ligney, and formed his rear guard during the retreat northwest toward Waterloo. Teilmann withstood Marshal Emmanuel de Grouchy's attack upon his position at Wavre on 18 June 1815, thereby securing Blücher's rear as he moved to support Wellington at Waterloo. Without the timely arrival of the Prussians at the end of the day, Napoleon might possibly have prevailed at Waterloo.

As a writer and philosopher of war, Clausewitz created a dialectical argument that opposed a theoretical conception of "war" to the actual practice of war. Theoretically, he suggested, "*War is thus an act of force to compel our enemy to do our will*" (1976, 75). In theory, he continued, "there is no logical limit to the application of that force. Each side, therefore, compels its opponents to follow suit; a reciprocal action is started which leads, in theory, to extremes" (*ibid.*, 77). In other words, in theory, "war" is characterized as a radical form of noncooperation, a reciprocal acting together without a conscious sense of partnership. Morally, each agent views the other as an enemy who is thwarting his will. The material or physical means to remedy the subjective situation, is, in theory, the direct application of force upon the enemy's physical substance, to attack his soldiers, his cities, and his civilian population, so as to force his will into line with our will. Once the enemy's will is realigned with our will through these forceful material means, cooperation and the amity of peace will be restored, in theory.

In fine, Clausewitz suggests that, in theory, "war" possesses the self-contained, self-directed, "us-them" structure of a reciprocal Manichaean struggle between good and evil that escalates ever upward to extreme applications of force without end. The inevitable result of this escalation toward the absolute was well described by the British rebel chieftain Calgacus before leading his men into battle against the Romans, "East nor West has glutted them. ... They make a desolation [*solitudinem*] and call it peace" (Tacitus, *Agricola Germanica* 1970, 30.5).

Clausewitz, however, was not interested in making a Manichaean desolation. After twenty-two years of participation in nearly continuous warfare, he understood that theory was theory, but actual practice was actual practice. And, actual practice teaches those who reflect upon it that, in his words, "war is the continuation of policy by other means" (*ibid*. 87). He continued:

> We maintain, on the contrary, that war is simply a continuation of political intercourse, with the addition of other means. We deliberately use the phrase "with the addition of other means" because we also want to make it clear that war in itself does not suspend political intercourse or change it into something entirely different. In essentials that intercourse continues [as in any good conflict resolution strategy], irrespective of the means it employs. The main lines along which [diplomatic, economic, or] military events progress, and to which they are restricted, are political lines that continue throughout the war into the subsequent peace. How could it be otherwise? ... But it is yet more vital to bear all this in mind when studying actual practice. We will then find that war does not advance relentlessly toward the absolute [application of force], as theory would demand. Being incomplete and self-contradictory, it cannot follow its own [theoretical] laws, but has to be treated as a part of some other whole; the name of which is policy. (*ibid*., 605–6)

In fine, Clausewitz argues that, in reality, war is not a Manichaean "us-them" battle of opposed wills, escalating ever upward to an application of absolute force. "War" may very well appear as such, especially in Hollywood films, but, in actual practice, it is a cooperative enterprise, a certain style of political intercourse between conflict partners. "War is," in practice, "the continuation of policy by other means." The immediate consequence of this insight is that declarations of war are decidedly neither minatory nor intended for the purpose of marking the "recognition" of "war in the material sense" so as to baptize "war in the legal sense." Instead, declarations are absolutely necessary, nonoptional public announcements that embody, define, or constitute the political ends for which "other means" are deemed necessary. In a word, if war be policy, then an absolute need exists to articulate that policy publicly. The declaration of policy may be either procedurally perfect or imperfect, but it cannot be omitted under any circumstances. As a practical matter, an "undeclared war" cannot possibly exist.

More fully, on each side of the partnership, war possesses an ends-means/whole-part structure, according to Clausewitz. In actual practice, the political ends declared by each conflict partner govern and restrain the material diplomatic, economic, or military means so that the unrestrained material means do not destroy the declared ends. The point is common sense. In theory, the more one jogs the better one's health. In actual practice, though, well-defined limits exist between jogging that enhances one's health and jogging that endangers one's health. To jog a few miles two or three times a week enhances one's health. The material means is fully coherent with the aesthetic, moral, and legal ends desired. To jog twenty miles every day compromises one's health. The material means are now incoherent with the moral end desired and soon destroy that end. The jogger's knees soon buckle under the strain.

Consequently, despite the theory, extremely forceful military means are not the actual practice of war. At least, they are not the whole of war. At most, they are only a small part. Therefore, to conceive of war, even theoretically, as "*an act of force to compel our enemy to do our will*" is to misconceive of war in actual practice. Such a misconception ignores the instrumental ends-means structure of all action, in general, and the whole-part structure of war, in particular. It also turns the whole-part structure of war on its head. Instead of viewing the military means as a small part of the whole, it views the military means as the whole of "war." Yet, and this is Clausewitz's critical insight, only when the declared ends cohere with the material means employed, so as to restrain and constrain the material means employed, can the whole achieve integrity and, thereby, the ends sought. Or, as Martin Luther King, Jr., expressed the same thought from the prospective of process rather than logic:

> This [civil rights] movement is based on the philosophy that ends and means must cohere. ... This is where the student [civil rights] movement ... would break with communism and any other system that would argue that the end justifies the means. For in the long run, we must see that the end represents the means in process and the ideal in the making. In other words, we cannot believe, or we cannot go along with the idea that the ends justify the means because the end is preexistent in the means. (1986, 45; see also 1986, 255; 1972, 945)

While King's words are certainly true, one might still ask what they mean. What does it mean to say that the ends declared in speech do not justify the material process employed unless "the end already preexists in the means," unless "the end represents the means in process," unless "the end and means cohere"? King, in his own reflection on the problem, has clearly pushed beyond Clausewitz's commonsense, consequentialist analysis of the relationship between declared aesthetic, moral, and legal ends and the chosen material means. When the end declared merely justifies the means employed, as Machiavelli suggested, all integrity between speech act and material act is lost. For integrity, something more is needed. One way to approach this question is to ask, "What are the ends or purposes of war?"

What Are the Ends of War?

Each war has, of course, its own unique purposes, which are constituted or defined in the text of that war's declaration. Some wars are fought for the purpose of independence, others for the purpose of discovering weapons of mass destruction and ending support for terrorism, and still others for the purpose of annihilating a hated enemy or conquering a vulnerable people. If the particulars are infinitely varied, ranging from the sublime to the ridiculous to the perverse, still, in general, war has always been recognized to possess a single, overarching purpose, a purpose that, not incidentally, excludes the perversions of war. Classically, this general desire or purpose has been expressed as "therefore the only justification for war is that peace and justice should afterwards prevail," as Cicero wrote to his son, at the time studying in Athens (*De officiis* 1967, I, xi, 35). A more modern, and hence, a more pragmatic translation of this general ideal might read, "Therefore, the only justification for war is to resolve the conflict in hand." For, is it not the case that all conflict resolution is also an ends-means/ideal-in-process problem? The desire sought is resolution of the grating grievances; the obstacles to be overcome are the irreconcilable remedies put forth by each of the conflict partners.

The initial consequence of this overarching desire for resolution is that, in actual practice, if not in theory, the ends desired cannot be "*to compel the enemy to do our will.*" The point, of course, is that reducing war to a test of willpower leaves no room for either resolution or "political intercourse." True, Manichaean struggles between good and evil with their noncooperative, "us-them" structure do eventually terminate, but not through either resolution or "political intercourse"; rather, they end through exhaustion, as was the case with the dissolution of the Soviet Union at the end of the cold war. Another example is the collapse of American public opinion at the end of the war in Vietnam. In order to begin to resolve a conflict, "intercourse," if not "political intercourse," is necessary. At a minimum, three steps are needed. First, at least one conflict partner must recognize that the conflict is neither an eternal test of willpower nor an eternal Manichaean struggle: that amity characterized the conflict partners' relationship before the conflict and will again characterize their relationship after the conflict. Or, as the Declaration of Independence put it, we "hold them, as we hold all the rest of mankind, Enemies in War, in Peace Friends." This temporary period of enmity should not, therefore, be allowed to becloud the fundamental cooperation and respect between humans that undergird the amity of a positive peace. Second, from this first realization it follows that one must accord one's conflict partner his full rights under the laws and customs of war. This places the material means employed under the rule of law, limiting those means and fostering not only resolution, but reconciliation as well.

And, third, at least one conflict partner must recognize that conflict resolution, as opposed to termination or "victory," needs to occur despite personalities. Structure, not will, is the issue. For, true conflict resolution is never personal – what one desires – but always impersonal – what needs to be done by both conflict partners to resolve the situation, what needs to be done so "that peace and justice should afterward prevail." In actual practice, if not in theory, then, the challenge is not to articulate our "will" so as to compel our enemy to do it, but to articulate the ideal for which the conflict or war is the process. To recall King's words, resolution, with or without reconciliation, occurs when "the end [that] is preexistent in the means" comes into existence after the conflict process has transformed the declared ideal into an existential or material fact. Or, as Samuel Coleridge captured the thought, "And in today already waits tomorrow."

"The End Is Preexistent in the Means"

For example, consider two contrasting events: first, the coherent process by which the American colonists transformed the ideal of independence into its reality between 1776 and 1783; second, the incoherent material means by which successive American administrations failed between 1949 and 1972 to impose their will in Vietnam.

In theory, one can allege that the American colonists "compelled" the British government to do their "will" during the seven years between the Declaration of Independence in 1776 and the signing of the Treaty of Paris in 1783. And, to all appearance, it may well appear as such. Yet, in actual practice, if one looks closely at what the colonists did on the ground, what one observes is an ideal in process, a declared end preexistent in the material means employed to create the new social reality. For, if the declared aesthetic, moral, and legal ideal was "independence," the actual process was a systematic plan "to assume among the Powers of the Earth, the separate and equal Station to which the Laws of Nature and of Nature's God entitle them."

The first step toward realizing this ideal was to break British control over local colonial government. The necessary, but not sufficient, speech act condition for this step was taken on Friday, 19 May 1776, when the Second Continental Congress:

> resolved, That it be recommended to the respective assemblies and conventions of the United Colonies, where no government sufficient to the exigencies of their affairs have been hitherto established, to adopt such government as shall, in the opinion of the representatives of the people, best conduce to the happiness and safety of their constituents in particular, and America in general. (*Journals of the Continental Congress* 1904–37, IV: 342)

With the colonial governments no longer under British control, the second, third, and fourth steps toward the realization of independence were taken two weeks later, on Friday, 7 June 1776. On that day, Richard Henry Lee took the floor of the Second Continental Congress to introduced three Virginia resolutions, which were seconded by John Adams of Massachusetts:

> That these United Colonies are, and of Right ought to be, Free and Independent States, that they are absolved from all allegiance to the British Crown, and that all Political connection between them and the State of Great Britain is, and ought to be, totally dissolved.

> That it is expedient forthwith to take the most effectual measures for forming foreign Alliances.

> That a plan of confederation be prepared and transmitted to the respective Colonies for their consideration and approbation. (*ibid*. V: 425)

The passage of these four resolutions, however, was the necessary speech act that constituted and articulated the end or ideal desired. In 1776, the coherence and integrity of the material means employed to achieve the aesthetic, moral, and legal ends declared still needed to happen. And happen they did. By 1781, the former colonies had won the military battles; formed foreign alliances with France, Spain, and the Netherlands; and formed a confederation. As a result, the former British colonies had in fact assumed "among the Powers of the Earth, the separate and equal Station to which the Laws of Nature and of Nature's God entitle them." The British had not been "compelled to do our will." What changed during those seven years were the material facts on the ground. The new political structures, which were preexistent as ideals in the four resolutions, made it impossible to turn the clock back. Not incidentally, the conflict was resolved in a manner that ensured "that peace and justice would thereafter prevail."

Turning from a good example to a bad example, in his 1975 article Official Justifications for America's Role in Indochina, 1949–67, Hugh M. Arnold found twenty-three official rationales for American intervention in Vietnam, including the catchall category "Others." Analyzing 2,002 statements found in the *Pentagon Papers* (Gold et al., eds. 1971), the number one rationale given for the war was countering the "Communist threat" at 57 percent, while "other" ranked seventeenth at 11.5 percent, just above stopping the "dominoes" from falling at 8.9 percent (Arnold, 1975, 35–6). Sorting the rationales by administration to show a certain indecisiveness of will, anticommunism constituted 19.4 percent of the citations for the Truman administration, 26.6 percent for the Eisenhower administration, and 20 percent for the Kennedy administration (*ibid.* 37–42). Anticommunism dropped to the number four position at 6.8 percent for the Johnson administration, replaced by "a simple response to aggression against an ally; self defense" at 23.1 percent (*ibid.* 42–4). Given the indecision about the end desired, one is perhaps not surprised to learn that "almost 70 percent of the Army generals who managed the war [in Vietnam] were uncertain of its objectives," according to a 1974 survey carried out by Douglas Kinnard (1977, 25). Uncertain material means used to attain unclear moral ends lead naturally to "*an act of force to compel our enemy to do our will.*" Expedient principles of this sort lead to a "theoretical" war of unbounded devastation, but not to a "practical" war of declared ends, as Clausewitz argued. And, the reason for this, as King argued, is that, in actual practice, the moral ends and the material means must cohere, as in 1776. The moral end must represent the material means in process and the ideal in the making, because the moral end is preexistent in the material means.

In fine, the two examples illustrate how the relationship between the declarer of war and the commander of the diplomatic, economic, or military means follows naturally from the structure of war, from its ends-means/ideal-in-process structure. The declarer of war speaks in order to articulate the aesthetic, moral, and legal ends desired, the ideal to be created. The commander speaks in order to manage the process, employing the material means at hand. When the ends and ideals declared are coherent with the means employed by the commander, success is likely, as in 1776. When not, success is unlikely, as is the case most of the time. For example, not one of the twenty-three official ends desired in Vietnam ever preexisted in the military means employed. No shot fired or bomb dropped ever stopped a single domino from falling.

The only loose end left to tie up is whether the two functions of declaring and commanding are best exercised by a single individual – a king, emperor, or dictatorial president – or whether they are best exercised by two different bodies. On the one hand, no doubt exists that single individuals can exercise both functions. To repeat, this is the verdict of more than five thousand years of world history. Kings, emperors, and dictatorial presidents have always both commanded and declared. In addition, a number of individuals have been unusually successful in exercising both functions. Clausewitz's Prussian hero,

Frederick the Great, immediately comes to mind. Abraham Lincoln, Franklin D. Roosevelt, and Martin Luther King, Jr., are certainly other, more recent, examples. On the other hand, while exceptions may well prove the rule, they do not make the rule, especially the rule of law. And, indeed, the functions of declarer and commander are best kept separate. The history of republican Rome provides particularly salient evidence to this effect, as is discussed in Chapter 10. More to the point, James Madison claimed without explanation that "those who are to *conduct a war* cannot in the nature of things, be proper or sage judges, whether *a war ought* to be *commenced, continued,* or *concluded*" (1906, VI, 148). What reasons might Clausewitz adduce to support Madison's claim?

Is Declaring Separable from Commanding?

One must begin by recognizing the intimate connection between Clausewitz's "remarkable trinity" passage and his ends-means/ideal-in-process analysis of the actual structure and practice of war:

> The passions that are to be kindled in war must already be inherent in the people; the scope which the play of courage and talent will enjoy in the realm of probability and chance [i.e., in the contingent world of military operations] depends on the particular character of the commander and the army; but the political aims [of the war] are the business of the government. (1976, 89)

According to Clausewitz, the three principal agents of war are 1) the "people," whose spirit or genius determines which types of war – dynastic wars, *levée en masse*, guerrilla war, or other – the nation will or will not support; 2) the "commander and his army," whose spirit and genius determine strategy – how the war will be waged in the material realm of contingency and chance; and 3) the "government," whose spirit and genius determine the moral, legal, and political ideals of the war. Ultimately, neither the commander nor the government can succeed without the support of the people, as the tragedy of both the French and American wars in Vietnam demonstrates. Yet, the people neither declare nor command a nation's wars. Hence, the ultimate importance of the people notwithstanding, the relationship between the commander and the government is the determining factor when it comes time for a society to answer the question of war or peace, as is illustrated in Figure 4.

Focusing on the commander and the government, Clausewitz further suggests that, if war is to escape the extremes of hatred and destruction implied by its theory, "its element of subordination as an instrument of policy [must come to the fore], which makes it subject to reason alone" in actual practice (*ibid.*). It follows, therefore, that, because the instrument of policy must be

	According to Tradition	According to Clausewitz
Articulation of the Ends/Ideal	King or Dictatorial President	The "Government"
Articulation of the Means/Process	King or Dictatorial President	The "Commander"

Figure 4. Declarations of War as an Ends-Means/Ideal-in-Process Problem.

coordinate with the aesthetic, moral, and legal dictates of policy, so also the commander of that instrument must be coordinate with the declarer of the moral and legal policy, the government. The desired political ends declared must cohere with the instrumental means commanded.

Consequently, Clausewitz, the Prussian royalist, appears to agree fully with Madison, the Jeffersonian republican that "those [commanders] who are to *conduct a war* cannot in the nature of things, be proper or sage judges [of the moral and political aims desired]." Letting a single individual, even a dictatorial president, exercise these two functions simultaneously destroys "the remarkable trinity" by mixing two "realms" that should remain separate. The destruction occurs because, according to Clausewitz, the commander of the material means operates "in the [operational] realm of probability and chance" – the hard world of time and space, fog and friction, men and machines – whereas the government operates in a soft world of morality and legality, of international diplomacy, domestic political opinion, and economic sanctions. The skills, experience, and knowledge required to be successful in one realm are significantly different from the skills, experience, and knowledge needed to be successful in the other realm. Hence, to repeat, according to the Romans, Clausewitz, and Madison, the roles and functions of the declarer of the war's moral, legal, and political ends are best separated from the roles and functions of the giver of operational orders because of the ends-means/ideal-in-process "nature" of both conflict and war. Were war not an ends-means problem, the division of these two powers would be impossible.

For Clausewitz, if not Madison, the image provoked by this separation of "government" and "commander" is of a king who reigns but does not rule. As an example, one might look to the history of the unification of Germany. Chancellor Otto von Bismarck as the government made all the political decisions; Field Marshal Helmuth von Moltke as chief of the General Staff "commanded" the military means. Neither interfered in the realm of the other. Be that as it may, of greater interest is that the division of roles as between declarer and commander follows, not from the Constitution, but from "the nature of things," according to both Madison and Clausewitz.

The Constitution's separation of the power to declare war from the power to command the armed forces is but a carbon copy of "nature." And, this is the case even if the Congress is incapable of declaring war. The constitutional principle is sound; only the locus of execution is in error.

In addition, one cannot help noticing the way in which well-drafted declarations map smoothly onto Clausewitz's "remarkable trinity." At the level of morality and emotion, the Declaration of Independence established a three-way bond connecting both the people and Commander in Chief Washington to the Second Continental Congress. The Second Continental Congress did this by distilling the grievances, hopes, and desires expressed in the long line of procedurally imperfect conditional declarations of war. These included a long line of petitions and pamphlets from before the Stamp Act Congress of 1765, including notably Thomas Paine's *Common Sense* (1989). As a result of this distillation, the Second Continental Congress and its declaration "kindled" the passions of the people, drew them (or at least a sufficient number of them) into the Second Continental Congress's cause, and fortified them against the trials and deprivations of the revolution. At the same time, the declaration also bound Commander in Chief Washington and his army to both the people and the Second Continental Congress. The Declaration of Independence explained to the people, to Commander in Chief Washington, and to his army why the "government" had decided to pursue independence from Great Britain by "other means." The morality and legality of the declarer's ideals were clearly articulated for all to see and hear.

At the level of grand strategy, the Declaration of Independence defined and constituted the war as a "revolutionary" war for independence, informing it with an ends-means/ideal-in-process structure. So constituted and structured, the declaration set moral and legal limits on and gave essential direction to the "play of courage and talent" in the "realm of probability and chance" displayed by Commander in Chief Washington, his commanders, and the army. By indicting the gravamina that had caused the enmity, by denouncing George III as the cause of those grievances, and by declaring the remedies that would restore peace and justice, the Second Continental Congress did its share of the work. Now, it was up to Commander in Chief Washington to employ the military means as the executive agent of the Second Continental Congress to achieve the aesthetic, moral, and legal ends desired. In the absence of the government's shouldering its share of the work, exceptional commanders can, of course, wear both hats. Abraham Lincoln was able to do such; George Washington, however, did not have to. Unlike the U.S. Congress, the Second Continental Congress shouldered its "governmental" responsibilities; it transformed a scattered rebellion into a Revolutionary War. It reconstituted thirteen colonies into an independent nation-state.

A. **Primary Functions**
  1. Toward recognition and resolution of the conflict through negotiation:
      a. To manifest a conflict publicly and initiate resolution of it,
      b. To define a conflict as a war.

  2. Toward decision and deployment of the operational means:
      a. To establish a coherent relationship between political ends and the diplomatic, economic, or military means to be employed.

      b. To establish a coherent end-means/ideal-in-proces relationship between declarer and commander.

B. **Moral & Legal Functions**
  1. To give the government authority to war,
      a. To legitimize the war in the eyes of domestic and foreign publics
      b. To legitimize the actions of the government during the war,
      c. To legitimize the actions of the commander during the war.

C. **Public Relations Functions**
  1. To inform the public of their changed legal and material situation,
  2. To provide the decision with appropriate solemnity and sobriety,
  3. To motivate the public to support the war.

D. **Functions in a Republic**
  1. To ensure the rule of law in times of war as well as peace,
  2. To ensure the consent of the representatives of the governed,
  3. To uphold the republican principles of the Constitution,
  4. To reduce the frequency of war, because few declarations can survive rigorous scrutiny of a solemn, procedurally perfect process.

Figure 5. Functions of Fully Reasoned, Solemn, Procedurally Perfect Declarations.

And, finally, at the level of government-commander relations, the Declaration of Independence provided the "element of subordination as an instrument of policy, which made it [war] subject to reason alone" (Clausewitz 1976, 89). That is, to repeat one more time, the declaration tied Commander in Chief Washington and his army to the Second Continental Congress as its executive agent by indicting British tyranny, denouncing the resulting enmity, declaring its preferred peace terms, and thereby establishing the organic, ends-means/ideal-in-process relationship with Commander in Chief Washington so necessary for the successful prosecution of military operations.

THE PRIMARY FUNCTIONS OF DECLARATIONS OF WAR

As summarized in Figure 5, the primary functions of a well-drafted declaration of war consist of two pairs of two functions each. The first pair aims toward resolution of the conflict through negotiations. Since resolution is unlikely as long as the conflict is not taken seriously, the declarer of war speaks publicly to redefine and reconstitute a growing conflict as a war. Redefinition and reconstitution, however, require the declarer to articulate the issues that constitute the casus belli. That is, by indicting the gravamina, denouncing both them and those responsible for them, and declaring its preferred peace terms, preferably conditionally, but absolutely if need be, the declarer articulates the conditions for a negotiated resolution from his perspective. The second pair of primary functions aims toward the operational resolution of the conflict. Operationally, it is absolutely necessary to establish a coherent relationship between the ends sought and the means employed. This should already have been accomplished with the text of the fully reasoned declaration. Once the relationship between the political ends and operational means has been established, the relationship between the political authority that declared war and its commander in chief follows naturally and conveniently.

The primary functions of the Declare War Clause, therefore, are not minatory, as Hague Convention III suggests. Nor are they intended to express congressional pique and outrage that Britain, Mexico, Imperial Germany, or Imperial Japan should have the temerity to attack the United States; even less is the primary function of a declaration of war to "authorize" the use of the armed forces. None of those functions or purposes contributes an iota either 1) toward constituting the war, 2) toward resolving the conflict, 3) toward relating political purposes to operational means, or 4) toward defining a coherent relationship between the declarer and its commander.

6   Lawful and Unlawful Declarations of War

Quantity over Quality

> The Congress shall have power ... to declare war, grant letters of marque and reprisal, and make rules concerning captures on land and water.
>
> (article I, section 8, clause 11)

> The domestic political world changes, as it were, the instant that presidents formally decide to engage the enemy.
>
> William G. Howell and Jon C. Pevehouse (2007, xix)

By now, it should be clear that the history of declaring of war in the United States is a story of extreme ambiguity and confusion. In terms of the competence of who makes the declaration, of the quality of the texts written, and of the procedures by which the texts are produced, no consistency can be found. For example, even when the Congress meets the minimal constitutional procedures for declaring war, as in 1812, 1917, and 1941, the process is still entirely insufficient because the text lacks all substance. The 1812, 1917, and 1941 declarations are like passing a law saying, "that taxes be increased, and the same is hereby increased, and that the president be, and he is hereby, directed and empowered to use the entire Internal Revenue Service to increase taxes." Such a law would meet the minimal constitutional criteria for law-making, but most people, not including the president of course, would observe that the text is not really adequate to its purposes. Something important is missing; a necessary specificity is missing. Ideally then, the rule of law requires not only a performative speech act by a competent speaker, attention to proper procedures, but a substantive text as well. Sadly, this chapter catalogues the results of more than two hundred years of inattention to these three elements of the rule of law.

The only ray of hope in all this bleak landscape is that the Declare War Clause has so far been interpreted to mean that the Congress, and only the

Congress, can declare war in a procedurally perfect manner, and this interpretation has not yet been challenged. Most certainly it has yet to be challenged by any president, as will be noted in a moment. But to say that presidential tyranny has yet to manifest itself explicitly and nakedly is cold comfort, since it leaves entirely unspecified the role and status of procedurally imperfect declarations of war. Which branch can legitimately declare war in a procedurally imperfect manner? Both? Only one? Neither? Logically, the rule should be neither, as in the *jus fetiale* of the Roman Republic. However, by a well-accepted two-hundred-year-old custom and tradition, both the Congress and the president are free to declare war in a procedurally imperfect manner as promiscuously as they please.

In addition, and perhaps more important, the simple existence of procedurally imperfect declarations of war has been completely ignored in the scholarly literature. Instead of recognizing that declarations of war may be spoken in either a procedurally perfect or imperfect manner, the debate and scholarship for the past two hundred years and more have been monopolized by relational politics, by ideological polemics over the relationship between the executive and the legislative. For more than two hundred years, readers have been assaulted by the endless ebb and flow of contradictory opinions: Alexander Hamilton said that the Constitution mandated a "strong executive"; James Madison argued for a "weak executive"; John Hart Ely (1993) believed that the Congress needed to "check and balance" an executive "prone" to war; and John Yoo (2005) said something else altogether, arguing that the congressional "power of the purse" was the real "check" to "balance" the president's "inherent" power to make war, not the Declare War Clause. The only innovation since 1793, when Hamilton and Madison first wrote, is the heartfelt search for the "original intent," or, lately, the "original understanding" of the Founding Fathers. And, indeed, the unknowable psychological state and motivation of men two hundred years dead are endless fascinating topics.

The inherent pleasures of ideological polemics notwithstanding, as soon as one turns one's attention to the importance of the rule of law when declaring war and, hence, to the speech act heart of the power to declare war, one soon discovers a debilitating matrix of four cells: the president and the Congress, both enabled by the fatally impractical division of the sovereign's war powers in the Constitution to declare war, sometimes with a procedurally perfect speech act, sometimes with a procedurally imperfect speech act. Figure 6 presents the matrix.

DEFINING THE PROBLEM

Because of the unrestrained ambiguity of procedurally imperfect speech acts, identifying and counting declarations of war constitute, to say the least, a

	Constitutional	Unconstitutional
President	0	12 to 329
Congress	2 to 11	300+

Figure 6. Presidential and Congressional Declarations of War.

hazardous occupation. The number of procedurally perfect congressional declarations varies from two to eleven as a result of uncertainty as to how to handle double counting – should the six declarations made during World War II count as one or six? – and whether declarations that meet only the absolutely minimal criteria truly count. These questions are dealt with fully in a moment. The number of procedurally imperfect congressional declarations is unknown because no one has ever counted them. A number of reasons exist for this lack of enterprise: First, no one is interested because procedurally imperfect congressional declarations have no legal standing; second, they are difficult to recognize because they possess no set, easily identifiable form, as do procedurally perfect declarations of war; and, third, most of them are buried here and there in acts and resolutions on other topics. Still, since the Congress is reacting to the same events and circumstances as is the president, the general impression is that procedurally imperfect congressional declarations are at least as numerous as are procedurally imperfect presidential declarations, probably more numerous, because the Congress is more garrulous.

On the presidential side, no president has ever asserted the full extent of his royal prerogative to declare war. Kings, emperors, and dictators, by definition, possess the constitutional authority to declare war both in accordance with and contrary to constitutionally recognized procedures, as they best please. American presidents have so far limited themselves to declaring war in a procedurally imperfect manner. No president has so far contested the standard interpretation of the Declare War Clause as conferring the constitutionally proper power to declare war to the Congress alone. Because of this, the question on the presidential side is not what counts as a constitutionally proper presidential declaration of war, since all presidential declarations are constitutionally improper, but what counts as a "war." This is the case because not all military operations are "wars"; hence, when does the size, duration, or some other characteristic push one of the numerous military operations ordered by the president over the line into "war"? At one extreme, the Congressional Research Service counts three hundred and twenty-nine *Instances of Use of United States Armed Forces Abroad, 1798–2008* (Grimmette 2009). But, of course, how many of these "instances of use" actually count as "war"? As Kenneth Moss (2008) has exhaustively described and analyzed, trying to sort out those "instances" that make the cut from those that do not is a diffi-cult and thankless task. At the other extreme, the Office of the Secretary of Defense (N.D.) recognizes ten *Principal Wars In Which The United States Participated* between 1775 and 1991 – the Revolutionary War, the War of 1812, the Mexican-American War, the Civil War, the Spanish-American War, World War I, World War II, the Korean War, the Vietnam War, and the Persian Gulf War – to which one must add the 2001 invasion of Afghanistan and the 2003 invasion of Iraq, to make twelve. But minor wars are no less wars. Until 1920, the *Statistical Abstract of the United States* listed thirty wars between 1775 and 1900 of which twenty-one were Indian wars (Department of Commerce 1921, 757). Fortunately, though, the exact number of "wars" is of no particular interest. Rather, it is the lurid imbalance between pro-cedurally perfect and imperfect declarations that is the critical piece of the puzzle.

The matrix, therefore, identifies one positive, one neutral, and one nega-tive conclusion: The positive conclusion is the existence of complete agree-ment on the question of which branch should declare war in a procedurally perfect, constitutionally legitimate manner. The uncontested answer is the Congress, and only the Congress. This is not unexpected. The neutral con-clusion is that both the president and the Congress are equally able to declare procedurally imperfect wars, as one would expect given the nature of human language unrestrained by the rule of law. The negative conclusion is that the Congress, like the president, is well organized to declare procedurally imper-fect wars, but not procedurally perfect wars: the opposite of the way it should be for anyone concerned with the rule of law. In light of the uncontested agreement that only the Congress can legitimately declare procedurally per-fect wars, should it not be organized to do so? Should it not be organized to fulfill its constitutional mandate for all wars, of which there have been many more than eleven?

The overall conclusion, then, is that the bone of contention has never been an ideological dispute such as a "strong" versus a "weak" executive. Nor has it ever involved "inherent" executive powers versus "inherent" legislative powers or who "checks and balances" whom. Nor has it ever been about the relationship between the "power of the purse" and the "power to declare war," to include John Yoo on this list of false ques-tions. All of these two-hundred-year-old ideological controversies recede into irrelevance, as soon as one recognizes that the very nature of human language is the source of the problem. Had the Framers recognized this fact and responded to it by drafting language that reduced the four cells of the matrix to one, no controversy would ever have arisen, and law would have ruled the declaring of war. For the moment, though, consider each cell of the matrix in turn.

THE CONGRESSIONAL DECLARATIONS OF WAR

No one can complain that the Congress has been inactive in making warlike pronouncements of one sort or another. The fundamental problem, however, is that one sort – nine of the eleven procedurally perfect declarations – meet only minimal meaningless technical requirements, whereas the other – the procedurally imperfect sort – do not meet even the minimal standard. In light of all this misdirected activity, how does one sort out the data, winnowing the useful wheat of the rule of law from the unhelpful chaff of the rule of men?

Second Continental Congress: The Declaration of Independence, 1776

Beginning with the very first "congressional" declaration, the U.S. Congress obviously cannot take credit for the Declaration of Independence, which is reproduced in Appendix I. However, it is the touchstone, one of the two seminal documents in American history, and is not easily disregarded. Very much more important, it also just happens to be the gold standard against which all exercises of the power to declare war – whether presidential or congressional, whether procedurally perfect or imperfect – must be measured. In particular, by comparing it to the texts of the eleven procedurally perfect declarations of the U.S. Congress, one sees clearly why all the congressional declarations, except the two declarations of 1898, meet only the minimal, meaningless technical requirements. To ignore the Declaration of Independence, therefore, is to deprive oneself of the only good model – with respect to both content and process – in American history. It is certainly not chaff. Indeed, it is the single most useful example for anyone trying to understand the power to declare war. It bears repeated study because it is the only declaration to advance the rule of law, and not men.

Procedurally Perfect Congressional Enactments to Suppress Piracy, 1798–1823

    A. Quasi-War with France, 1798
    B. Tripolitan Cruisers (Pirates), 1802
    C. Algerine Cruisers (Pirates), 1815
    D. Suppression of Piracy, 1819–1823 (Elsea and Grimmett 2006)

Between 1798 and 1823, the Congress enacted a number of laws to combat piracy in the Caribbean and Mediterranean Seas. These enactments cannot properly be seen as exercises of the power to declare war. They are more properly seen as an exercise of the congressional power to "grant Letters of

Marque and Reprisal," since this was the practical effect of the legislation. Various presidents from John Adams on relied upon these enactments to issue commissions to public vessels to seize pirate ships, recapture American vessels taken by pirates and privateers, and otherwise suppress piracy and privateering. The presidents also relied on these laws to arm merchant vessels and to commission privateers.

Because these enactments are not declarations of war, they are neither chaff nor wheat. Still, they underscore the foresight of the Framers of the Constitution in providing not only for the declaring of public war but also for the enactment of private war and the suppression of pirates, or "nonstate actors," as they are now called. The early nineteenth-century Congresses carefully and sensibly framed their legislative response to attacks by nonstate actors on the basis of the Letters of Marque and Reprisal Clause. This care stands in sharp contrast to the panicky precipitateness with which the 107th Congress enacted its response to the attacks of 11 September 2001. Again, the procedural perfection of the enactments conformed to and advanced the rule of law, and not men.

Miscategorization: An Act for the Prosecution of the Existing War between the United States and the Republic of Mexico, 1846

The 1846 enactment against Mexico is usually included on lists of official congressional declarations, but this is questionable in the extreme. As can be read in Appendix I, the 1846 act is really an appropriations bill that was already under debate when President James Polk announced that General Zachery Taylor had been attacked by Mexican forces at Matamoros. It later turned out that it was General Taylor who had attacked the Mexicans, instead of the Mexicans' attacking him. But at the time President Polk was less than precise on that point. The 1846 act is the "Gulf of Tonkin Resolution" before its time.

In response to what it was told was a Mexican attack, the Twenty-ninth Congress took up the pending appropriations bill, added a single recital – "Whereas, by the act of the Republic of Mexico, a state of war exists between that Government and the United States" – and inserted a new section stating that the bill was now "for the purpose of enabling the Government of the United States to prosecute said war to a speedy and successful conclusion" and authorizing the president "to employ the militia, naval, and military forces of the United States."

While the intention to declare war against Mexico is certainly present, the 1846 act does not so declare, as can be seen by comparing it with the other declarations found in Appendix I. It recognizes that war exists; it appropriates monies to prosecute the war in great detail ("musician and artificers, shall be allowed 40 cents per day for the use and risk of their horses"); and it authorizes the president to employ the armed forces, but it does not actually declare war. Hence, the 1846 act is the chaff of the rule of men, and not wheat of the rule of law. It is a procedurally imperfect, functionally equivalent legislative enactment, and not a procedurally perfect declaration of war. It is helpful only to the extent that it is an excellent example of how not to declare war, demonstrating how and why an exercise of the congressional "power of the purse" cannot substitute for the congressional power to declare war.

Procedurally Imperfect Congressional Declarations of War

A. Without Authorization to Use the Armed Forces

1. An Act to Declare the Treaties heretofore Concluded with France, no longer obligatory on the United States of 1798
2. Resolution in Relation to the Conduct of F. J. Jackson, Minister Plenipotentiary from Great Britain of 1810
3. A Resolution for the Adjustment of difficulties with the Republic of Paraguay of 1858
4. Joint Resolution Calling on the President to Take Such Measures As He May Deem Necessary to Consummate the Agreement between the Governments of Spain and the United States for the Relief of Antonio Mora, a Naturalized Citizen of the United States of 1895
5. The Comprehensive Anti-apartheid Act of 1986
6. Cuban Democracy Act of 1992
7. Syria Accountability and Lebanese Sovereignty Restoration Act of 2003
8. Public Law 105–235, Joint Resolution: Finding the Government of Iraq in Unacceptable and Material Breach of Its International Obligations, 1998.
9. Iraq Liberation Act of 1998

The resolutions and acts listed represent a random selection of a much larger category, probably numbering several hundred, although no one has ever thought to count them. This category consists of official congressional acts that can also be interpreted as procedurally imperfect, functionally equivalent conditional declarations of war. These imperfect declarations of war are "conditional" because they are not "absolute," because they do not declare "absolutely" the existence of the state and condition of war, as do the perfect declarations of 1812, 25 April 1898, 1917, or 1941 found in Appendix I.

The actual import and status of these resolutions and acts are infinitely ambiguous. On the one hand, none of them was intended by the Congress to function as a procedurally perfect conditional declaration of war – quite the opposite. Nor were they taken as such by the president or anyone else. Rather, they were passed as a sign of congressional indignation with respect to some action or activity by Paraguay or Venezuela or whichever state was the target of congressional fury. On the other hand, howsoever innocuous were the intentions of the Congress, the targets of these resolutions and acts could reasonably view them as tantamount to a declaration of war. To take only the most outrageous example, the government of Iraq and Saddam Hussein could easily be forgiven for interpreting either the *Joint Resolution: Finding the Government of Iraq in Unacceptable and Material Breach of Its International Obligations* or the *Iraq Liberation Act of 1998* as casus belli. If an accusation of a serious violation of international law is not casus belli, then a public call for the overthrow of a government, backed up by an appropriation to train a group of subversives and support propaganda efforts, certainly is. Two key sections of the Iraq Liberation Act were reproduced in Chapter 5.

Still, this body of documents is all chaff of the rule of men, and not the wheat of the rule of law. The documents are fundamentally unhelpful because the resolutions and acts were specifically intended not to be lawful declarations of war; the views of the targets of congressional indignation were irrelevant to the Congresses that passed them. Except to demonstrate the tautology that procedurally imperfect, functionally equivalent declarations may take many and varied forms, nothing useful can be learned from this very large body of documents.

B. With Authorization to Use the Armed Forces

1. Authorization for the President to Employ the Armed Forces of the United States for Protecting the Security of Formosa ... 1955
2. Promotion of Peace and Stability in Middle East, 1957
3. Maintenance of International Peace and Security in Southeast Asia (Gulf of Tonkin Resolution), 1964
4. Multinational Force in Lebanon, 1983
5. Authorization of the Use of U.S. Armed Forces Pursuant to U.N. Security Council Resolution 678 with Respect to Iraq, 1991
6. Authorization of the Use of U.S. Armed Forces against Those Responsible for the Recent Attacks Launched against the United States, 2001
7. Authorization of the Use of Force against Iraq Resolution of 2002 (Elsea and Grimmett 2006)

As can be seen by the dates of these seven resolutions, this group of congressional authorizations to use the armed forces is a post–World War II, cold war innovation. Crucially, these authorizations are not sanctioned by the Declare

War Clause. To be simplistic about the matter, the Declare War Clause mandates that the Congress shall "declare war." Since an authorization to use the armed forces is obviously not a declaration of war, at least in any constitutionally appropriate sense, these authorizations do not fulfill the procedural requirements of the Declare War Clause. As Gregory Sidak has explained the illogic of the situation:

> If hostilities do not amount to "war," the President requires no prior congressional authorization to engage in them; if Congress "authorizes" the President to use offensive military force in such a situation, its action is precatory or hortatory, but legally insignificant. On the other hand, if hostilities do amount to war (as one reasonably would have expected before the war against Iraq to liberate Kuwait, and as Judge Greene so concluded in *Dellums v. Bush*), then a [procedurally perfect] declaration of war by Congress is the constitutionally preferred means to authorize the initiation or continuation of the offensive use of American military forces. (Sidak 1991, 120–1)

In sum, the only excuse for the Congress's passing "authorizations" to use the armed forces lies in the fact that the Congress is free to implore and exhort the president to do that which the president has already decided to do whensoever it wishes. No dictator has ever had a more congenial and sycophantic legislature.

To be sure, these "authorizations" can easily be viewed as procedurally imperfect, functionally equivalent substitutes for a procedurally perfect declaration of war. But, besides the nullity of their legal status, as Sidak has noted, they are always requested by the president and function only as harmless vehicles by which the Congress can be associated with the president's decision to defend Formosa, fight in South Vietnam, deploy the marines to Lebanon, liberate Kuwait, or invade Afghanistan and Iraq. In saying this, however, one observes another of the ways in which, for more than two hundred years, "decision" has been separated from "declaration."

In conclusion, then, this group of congressional acts is pure chaff, exceptionally unhelpful. They can be viewed as procedurally imperfect, functionally equivalent declarations of war, but they are really little more than a town crier's script, scene setters, preparing public opinion and hyping the situation. Moreover, this town crier's script only enhances the rule of men and denigrates further the rule of law.

Procedurally Perfect Congressional Declarations of War

A. War of 1812
B. Spanish-American War, 1898
   1. The conditional declaration of 19 April 1898

2. The absolute declaration of 25 April 1898
C. World War I
  1. Imperial Germany, 1917
  2. Austro-Hungry, 1917
D. World War II
  1. The Empire of Japan, 1941
  2. Germany, 1941
  3. Italy, 1941
  4. Bulgaria, 1942
  5. Hungary, 1942
  6. Rumania, 1942 (Elsea and Grimmett 2006)

Finally, some useful examples, wheat almost without chaff. Beyond question, the eleven declarations listed all meet the minimal, meaningless technical requirements for a procedurally perfect, constitutionally appropriate declaration of war. They are all public announcements that unambiguously "declare" the existence of the state and condition of war, either conditionally or absolutely. Hence, they all meet the minimal, meaningless technical requirements for the rule of law.

For the sake of simplicity, though, the eleven can be reduced to five, because the wording of the two declarations for World War I are virtually identical, as is the wording for the six declarations for World War II; only the names of the countries change. In addition, the United States did not fight two separate wars during World War I and six during World War II, only one war each time. Thus, if this simplification is accepted, then the data demonstrate that the Congress is capable of meeting the minimal, meaningless technical requirements of its constitutional responsibilities under the Declare War Clause at a rate of two and a half procedurally perfect declarations per hundred years. Or, at least it was capable of doing so during the nineteenth and twentieth centuries.

For the sake of even greater simplicity, the five declarations can be further reduced to two cases: the technically minimal, but meaningless, declarations of 1812, 1917, and 1941 and the more meaningful declarations of 1898. The 1812, 1917, and 1941 declarations are all technically minimal, but meaningless, because their texts were all written by the State Department on the order of Presidents James Madison, Woodrow Wilson, and Franklin Roosevelt; the respective Twelfth, Sixty-fifth, and Seventy-seventh Congresses only made the public announcement, as the president's town crier. These three documents are less *congressional* declarations of war than legislative ratifications of presidential decisions. Viewed in terms of procedure, these technically minimal, but meaningless, declarations conceive of the unique congressional power to declare war as a "divided, but shared power" consisting of 1) the president's deciding the question of war or peace, 2) the State Department's drafting the declaration of war, 3) the president's officially requesting passage of the draft declaration, 4) the Congress's complying with his request, and 5) the president's then "ordering" military operations to begin. An account of George W. Bush's innovation on this town crier model is found in Chapter 10.

In contrast to the technically minimal, but meaningless, model, both the Second Continental Congress and the Fifty-fifth Congress composed their own declarations. The importance of who drafts the declaration cannot be overemphasized. For, drafting – as opposed to debating or amending – presupposes decision making. The Second Continental Congress was forced to decide and write its own declaration because it was a revolutionary assembly. Neither an executive nor a judicial branch existed at the time to aid it. "Dividing, but sharing" this unique power was simply not possible in 1776. If the Declaration of Independence was going to be made, the Second Continental Congress would have to decide and declare on its own initiative.

The Fifty-fifth Congress was also forced to write its own declarations. But in its case the reason was that President William McKinley opposed war with Spain over Cuba, as had President Grover Cleveland before him. Consequently, without the president's overt aid and assistance, the Fifty-fifth Congress could not avoid drafting its own declaration. As a result, the first, conditional declaration of 1898 was a *congressional* declaration in a fuller sense of the word than all the other congressional declarations. The Fifty-fifth Congress did not function solely as the president's town crier. The 1898 declaration was, therefore, an exercise of the rule of law, and not men. This cheery factoid means that the Congress is able to meet its responsibility "to declare war" in more than a technically minimal manner once every two hundred years.

THE PRESIDENTIAL DECLARATIONS OF WAR

A. Procedurally Perfect: None
B. Procedurally Imperfect: 12 to 329 statements of various types between 1798 and 2008 informing the public of either
   1. a military order to deploy the armed forces (e.g., 1810: West Florida, Spanish territory. Governor Claiborne of Louisiana, on orders of the president, occupied with troops territory in dispute east of the Mississippi River as far as the Pearl River, later the eastern boundary of Louisiana. He was authorized to seize as far east as the Perdido River).
   2. an acknowledgment that the armed forces had been deployed without out previous orders. These incidents occurred mainly during the

nineteenth century and concerned actions taken by naval commanders on the scene on their own authority to protect American citizens or interests overseas (e.g., 1840: Fiji Islands. July. Naval forces landed to punish natives for attacking American exploring and surveying parties (Grimmette 2009; see also Wormuth and Firmage 1989, 135–51).

What is there of interest to be wrung from this mass of presidential data? What can be wrung about the rule of men depends on the approach one takes, whether one employs a contranormative positive approach or a normative approach. A contranormative, positive approach assumes that the parameters of the power to declare war, like all governmental powers, "must, of necessity, be determined in the ongoing practice of politics. And this ensures that the [three] branches [of government] will do more than struggle over day-to-day policy making. They will also engage in a higher order struggle over the allocation of power and the practical rights to exercise it" (Moe and Howell 1999, 853). In this case, one certainly needs to "scrutinize how, and under what conditions, one branch of government goes about checking the war power of the other" (Howell and Pevehouse 2007, xiii). Yet, such close scrutiny of the "is" neglects the "ought." It leaves "to others to decide whether the findings uncovered would please the nation's Founders, or anyone else" (*ibid.*). This "leaving to others" would not excite concern, if only the contranormative, positive approach itself did not exacerbate such concerns: "The fact that we are able to document [some] congressional checks [and influence] on presidential war powers may not, and we believe do not, allay critics' [or Founders'] concern that Congress is not presently doing as adequate job of restricting presidential power in matters involving war" (*ibid.*, 224).

In the present failed system, therefore, just describing and quantifying the procedurally imperfect presidential declarations in a contranormative, positive manner is inadequate. All that one achieves is a better, more detailed description of the systemic failure. Likewise, one needs to move beyond the "higher order struggle over the allocation of power and the practical rights to exercise it," which leads only to a better and more detailed description of how participants struggle to make a failed system work. What one needs to do, instead, is to reframe three of the four temporal modes of declaring war outlined briefly in Chapter 2. Instead of looking at who decides and when, one now needs to ask whether the president's town crier is 1) speaking in a procedurally perfect manner, 2) not speaking at all, or 3) speaking in a procedurally imperfect manner. That is, viewed from a congressional perspective, the three procedures may be described as follows:

The Town Crier Reads a Procedurally Imperfect Declaration of War

For potentially controversial operations that do not reach the scale of a world war, the president makes his decision but does not issue the public "announcement." Instead, he "convenes and gives information" to the Congress, "requesting" a legally vacuous precatory and hortatory resolution of support or "authorization" from the Congress in lieu of a procedurally perfect declaration of war. Since the procedurally imperfect congressional declaration often occurs in a timely manner, the president usually waits until the Congress has complied with his "request" before "ordering" military operations to commence.

The Town Crier Rests

For small uncontroversial operations, the president makes his decision and, then, both "orders" military operations to commence and issues the public "announcement," which is in effect a procedurally imperfect declaration of war. In this case, the president cooperates with the Congress by not disturbing it with small, unimportant matters.

The Town Crier Reads a Procedurally Perfect Declaration of War

For entry into world wars, the president makes his decision but, again, does not issue the public "announcement." Instead, he "convenes and gives information" to the Congress, this time requesting a procedurally perfect, but meaningless, absolute declaration of war from the Congress. Since the procedurally perfect congressional declaration occurs in a timely manner, the president waits until the Congress has complied with his "request" before "ordering" military operations to commence.

As can be seen, the three structures or procedures are built on the fact that the Congress cannot and will not discharge its constitutional responsibility to exercise its unique "unshared and undivided" power "to declare war," the Spanish-American War excepted. In the first and third, however, the president generously "divides and shares" the congressional power "to declare war" with the Congress. To illustrate these three evasions of the rule of law, consider President Woodrow Wilson's management of the Sixty-third, Sixty-fourth, and Sixty-fifth Congresses in 1914, 1916, and 1917, respectively.

The Town Crier Reads a Procedurally Imperfect Declaration of War

On Monday, 20 April 1914, shortly before three o'clock in the afternoon, President Wilson drove to the Capitol to address a joint session of the Sixty-third Congress and request a *Joint Resolution Justifying the Employment by the President of the Armed Forces of the United States*. The reason for his request was to intercede in the Mexican civil war then being fought (Wilson 1966–93, 29:471–4). The singular theory behind the resolution was as follows:

The president, of course, had no need for a congressional resolution, but an official congressional recognition that he was "justified" in intervening in the internal affairs of Mexico would be both proper and useful.

The stated purpose of Wilson's twelve-minute address was to report on certain "slights and affronts" to the "dignity" of the United States that had recently occurred in Mexico. Since Thursday, 9 April 1914, several American sailors had been arrested for short periods in Tampico and Vera Cruz, and telegraphic services had been temporarily denied to diplomatic personnel by the de facto government of President José Victoriano Huerta. The unstated purpose was to intercept the Hamburg-American Lines' freighter *Ypirange*, which was due to arrive in Vera Cruz shortly with a cargo of fifteen million rounds of ammunition that President Huerta had purchased in Germany. Since President Wilson favored General Venustiano Carranza and his Constitutionalist forces in the civil war, he, obviously, could not allow General Huerta to be resupplied in this manner. Unfortunately, congressional dispatch was of the essence since the *Ypirange* was due very soon.

On returning to the White House after his address, Wilson was informed by a dispatch from the American consul in Vera Cruz that the *Ypirange* was to land on 21 or 22 April 1914, the next day or the day after. Under pressure of this turn of events, Wilson issued the necessary orders and made a public announcement, rendering the "justificatory" resolution superfluous. Sailors and marines occupied Vera Cruz the next morning at a cost of four Americans killed, twenty wounded, and a reported two hundred Mexican lives lost. The occupation of Vera Cruz, along with other developments, led to the resignation of General Huerta on Wednesday, 15 July 1914, whereupon General Carranza assumed presidential powers, as had been the unstated object of Wilson's policy all along. The American troops withdrew from Vera Cruz on 23 November 1914, taking with them the custom duties and other taxes they had collected, which were to be handed over to the de jure government whenever it was recognized, but leaving the fifteen million rounds of ammunition that the *Ypirange* had off-loaded in the possession of General Carranza, who made good use of them in his final conquest of power.

Meanwhile, no real opposition to Wilson's request existed in the Sixty-third Congress. However, the Republicans in the Senate saw an opportunity to embarrass the president by delaying the vote on his "justificatory" resolution. As in 1898, playing "political games" and embarrassing the president was an opportunity few Congresses can resist. Led by Senator Henry Lodge, their vehicle for this delay was to propose several amendments to broaden the resolution to include the atrocities committed by General Carranza's Constitutionalists as well: Why was Wilson proposing such limited operations? Why not a general invasion, such as Winfield Scott led in 1847? Why were the operations directed against General Huerta exclusively? Why not against others? While Senator Lodge's attempt to widen the war failed for lack of support, he was able to delay a vote just long enough. As the *New York Times* of Wednesday, 22 April 1914, summarized Wilson's embarrassment:

> The President and his advisors realized that unless an actual state of war existed the seizure of the German vessel and her supplies would be illegal and might bring about difficulties with Germany, which has shown a decidedly friendly feeling toward the United States throughout the Mexican crisis.

> In determining to act without waiting for the tardy Senate to finish its deliberation, the President exercised the discretion of which he made mention [in his address of 20 April 1914]. (1:5, 2:6)

In the end, as a result of Senator Lodge's delaying tactics, the original House draft was extensively amended in the Senate to the point of meaningless banality, absentmindedly agreed to by the House, and approved by Wilson a day too late, on 22 April 1914:

> Joint Resolution Justifying the employment by the President of the armed forces of the United States.

> In view of the facts presented by the President of the United States in his address delivered to the Congress in joint session on the twentieth day of April, nineteen hundred and fourteen, with regard to certain affronts and indignities committed against the United States in Mexico: Be it

> *Resolved by the Senate and House of Representatives of the United States of America in Congress assembled*, That the President is justified in the employment of the armed forces of the United States to enforce his demand for unequivocal amends for certain affronts and indignities committed against the United States.

> *Be it further resolved*, That the United States disclaims any hostility to the Mexican people or any purpose to make war upon Mexico. (Pub. Res. No. 63–10, 38 Stat. 770)

As the *New York Times* reported, Wilson was motivated to request the resolution because he felt he needed "an actual state of war" to exist before he seized the *Ypiranga*. This need raises an uninteresting question. Which of the two procedurally imperfect declarations is the "real" declaration of war – the day-late congressional "justificatory" resolution or the president's military "order" and his public "announcement" of that order? Consider the congressional resolution first. Its first "justificatory" clause does not declare war, at least, not clearly and unambiguously in the way that a procedurally perfect declaration of war would. Even worse, the second resolving clause states clearly "that the United States disclaims any hostility to the Mexican people or any purpose to make war upon Mexico." How is it possible to institute "an actual state of war" when one "disclaims any hostility or purpose to make war"?

As a passing observation, what was needed in 1914 for this military operation short of war was an exercise of the power to grant letters of marque
and reprisals. Such a grant would have obviated the need for the illogical,
contradictory second resolving clause in the 1914 resolution. Instead of
complete ambiguity about what the Sixty-third Congress meant to do, the
grant would have clearly and unambiguously commissioned the intervention
without declaring, constituting, or creating the state and condition of enmity
toward Mexico on the part of the United States. The Mexican response to
the grant would have been, of course, for the Mexican government to decide
and declare. It could either accept the bona fide of the grant, as the French
government did during the Quasi-War with France, 1798–1800, or, alternatively, it could interpret the intervention as tantamount to an act of war and
so declare.

In effect, what a grant of marque or reprisal does is to separate the sovereign's public enactments from his private activities. As a public matter,
from the perspective of the government of the United States, relations
with the government of the Republic of Mexico would have remained
those of peace and amity. Yet, as a private matter, as was the case during
the Quasi-War with France, 1798–1800, the government of the United
States would have asserted a compelling need to intervene for a determined purpose in a limited geographic area for a limited time. To repeat,
how the government of Mexico would respond to the American assertion
of a "compelling need" was for the government of Mexico to determine
and declare.

Be that as it may, while a tortured case can be made that the resolution is
the procedurally imperfect, functional equivalent of a procedurally perfect
declaration of war – the intent, after all, is present – neither the captain of the
Ypiranga nor the German foreign minister is going to pay the least attention
to such tortured language. Instead, their eyes were firmly fixed on the president's "orders." If Wilson "ordered" forces to land at Vera Cruz, they would
conclude that "an actual state of war" existed. If he did not, they would
conclude that "an actual state of war" did not exist. Thus, because President
Wilson had "divided and shared" the congressional power to declare war, confusion and ambiguity were the natural outcome. Not only was the situation
confused by the existence of two procedurally imperfect declarations of war,
but the congressional resolution was also both self-contradictory and contradictory with regard to the circumstances as well. The Sixty-fifth Congress
appeared to declare a nonwar against Mexico the day after American forces
had landed with the deaths of two hundred Mexicans. In sum, the 1914
resolution is another example of both the rule of men and the congressional
penchant to play "political games."

The Town Crier Rests

Two years later, Wilson wisely decided to ignore the Sixty-fourth Congress in this noncontroversial case. On Thursday, 9 March 1916, "Pancho" Villa's forces raided Columbus, New Mexico. Initial reports listed eight townspeople killed, including one woman, seven soldiers killed and five wounded, and the bodies of twenty-seven of Villa's men buried (Wilson 1966–93, 38:218). Not wishing to deal with Republican partisanship again, President Wilson saw no reason to reject Representative Edward Pou's advice, which the honorable representative offered in a letter of Monday, 13 March 1916:

> This morning I made a point to talk with every member of the House I saw. Without exception they are with you and almost without exception they feel that the matter should be left in the hands of the administration without discussion of any kind on the floor of the House. In my judgment very great harm might result from debate in either the House or the Senate at this time and I am glad to say that, so far as I can judge, there is no disposition to debate the matter in the House. (*ibid.*, 38:300)

Eliminating the town crier greatly increases the dispatch and efficiency with which the president can deal with crises. Crucially, though, once the power to declare war has been "divided and shared," it is the town crier that can be ignored, and not the "order" giver. Supported by Representative Pou's display of initiative in defense of congressional responsibilities, Wilson "ordered" Major General Frederick Funston to order Brigadier General John Pershing to lead a punitive expedition to "disperse or capture" "Pancho" Villa's forces, announcing his decision on Friday, 10 March 1916 (*ibid.*, 38:285–7). A self-contradictory "justificatory" resolution was obviously not needed, as long as no controversy surrounded the president's decision. In sum, the 1916 deployment is another example of the rule of men, and not law.

The Town Crier Reads a Procedurally Perfect Declaration of War

And, finally, American entry into World War I was clearly of an entirely different order of magnitude than occupying Vera Cruz for seven months or chasing Mexican bandits through the mountains of Chihuahua. For the Vera Cruz or Chihuahua operations, the small American standing forces were fully adequate. No extra legislation or appropriations were needed. Fighting a world war, however, would require an enormous expansion of the armed forces, financed by equally enormous congressional appropriations. Ignoring the Congress, as in 1916, was not possible. Managing it with a legally vacuous "justificatory" resolution, as in 1914, would also not suffice. Something legally stronger, but effectively meaningless, was needed.

During 1916, Wilson had run for reelection on a platform that appeared to promise keeping the United States out of the war in Europe. But then, seventeen days after he was sworn in for his second term, after a fateful cabinet meeting on Tuesday, 20 March 1917, Wilson changed his mind. In this, he was supported by his entire cabinet. All agreed that war was now inevitable. The failure of his peace initiative during January; the resumption of unrestricted submarine warfare by the Germans on Thursday, 1 February 1917; the subsequent sinking of the British passenger liner *Laconia*, with the loss of American lives; and, finally, the torpedoing of three American merchant ships – the *Illinois*, the *City of Memphis*, and *Vigilancia* – on the same day, Sunday, 18 March 1917, with the loss of fifteen lives from the *Vigilancia*, forced Wilson's hand. Continued neutrality was no longer tenable (*ibid.*, 41:vii–viii).

When the decision had been made, Wilson issued a proclamation on Wednesday, 21 March 1917, to convene an extra session of the Sixty-fifth Congress on Monday, 2 April 1917, a month before the regular session, so as to "give it information." As in 1812, the "information" to be given was that the president had changed his mind and had, now, decided for war and against peace. Wilson spent most of the day before the special session, Sunday, 1 April 1917, sitting upright before his typewriter composing his request for a declaration against Imperial Germany. When he had finished, at about 10:00 pm, Wilson sent a message to his secretary of state, Robert Lansing, requesting that the secretary draw up a resolution "in the sense of these words":

> I advise that the Congress declare the recent course of the Imperial German Government to be in fact nothing less than war against the government and people of the United States; that it formally accept the status of belligerent which has thus been thrust upon it; and that it take immediate steps not only to put the country in a more thorough state of defense but also to exert all its power and employ all its resources to bring the Government of the German Empire to terms and end the war. (*ibid.*, 41:516)

The State Department's draft was approved by Wilson and submitted to the House leadership the next day shortly before Wilson spoke to the Joint Session at 8:32 pm. After some minor revisions in the Senate, as can be read in Appendix I, the amended declaration passed both chambers on 6 April 1917, Good Friday. At 12:14 pm the same night, President Wilson approved the Sixty-fifth Congress's approval of his decision to enter the war in Europe (*ibid.*, 41:ix). As town crier, the Sixty-fifth Congress acquitted itself with dispatch and decorum, unlike the obstructionism of the Sixty-third Congress in 1914 or the missing Sixty-fourth Congress in 1916. In sum, the magnitude of a world war in relation to the minuscule size of the pre-1945 American military forced President Wilson to create the appearance of the rule of law. Still, the reality was of the rule of men.

ANALYSIS

First and foremost, the root problem with the unique, "undivided and unshared" congressional power to declare war has always been the confusion and ambiguity inherent in human language. The simple truth of the matter is that the Framers failed to pay attention to the fact that procedurally perfect declarations of war are performative speech acts that are shadowed by a plethora of procedurally imperfect, functionally equivalent, declarations of war. Second, because of the first, the irrelevance of the ideological polemics over the relationship between the executive and the legislative of the past two hundred and twenty years should be obvious.

Third, whereas both the president and the Congress are well organized to make procedurally imperfect declarations war, neither is organized to make procedurally perfect declarations of war. The Constitution bars the president from doing so, as kings and emperors have always done, while the internal organization of the Congress clearly does not permit it to do so without strong presidential leadership. This impasse means that the United States seldom enters wars with clarity of purpose, certainly not with the clarity of purpose achieved in 1776. Instead, the norm is for the United States to slip into war in a very ambiguous manner, without much clarity of purpose, as the president and the Congress struggle to make an unworkable system work. Naturally, the president works harder than the Congress, because "disabling problems [in the Congress] are rampant, and they are built into the collective nature of the institution" (Moe and Howell 1999, 862).

Fourth, sad to say, the procedures used in 1898 by the Fifty-fifth Congress do not offer a robust model to be emulated by other Congresses. They only demonstrate the difference between the merely possible and the consistently improbable. Yes, 1898 proves that it is *possible* for the Congress to go beyond both indifference and the minimal technical requirements for a town crier, that it is *possible* for it to draft its own declaration relatively independently of the president. Yet, doing so only once in two hundred and thirty years also proves that a repetition is exceedingly *improbable*, that, on any given occasion, the Congress will most *probably* fail to meet its obligations once again.

Fifth, and finally, the specific mechanism by which the president exercises his power to declare war in an unconstitutional, procedurally imperfect manner results naturally and logically from his "undivided and unshared" power as commander in chief. By "ordering" the commencement of military operations and "announcing" this publicly – as President Wilson did in 1916 – a president, in effect, declares war, albeit without following proper procedures. As a result of the feature of human language that permits this type of functionally equivalent speech act, the president is, thus, empowered either to circumvent the Congress or, alternatively, to acknowledge its existence by requesting that it pass some sort of a legally vacuous resolution of "justification" or "authorization" – as Wilson did in 1914. Exceptionally, for world wars, after the president has decided, but before he "orders" military operations, he can request a technically minimal, meaningless, but procedurally perfect declaration of war from the Congress. Still, in all cases, the president decides the question of war or peace, thereby promoting the rule of men, and not law.

7   Six Possible Structures

The Congress shall have power ... to declare war, grant letters of marque and reprisal, and make rules concerning captures on land and water.

(article I, section 8, clause 11)

It may well be that the problem of "democracy," construed as an ideal, cannot be solved until there is a solution to the problem of war.

(Peter Manicas 1989, 1)

A review of the six possible procedures or structures for declaring war is needed before proposing solutions. The purpose of the review is to capture the full range of possible alternatives. In passing, though, the story of how successive presidents have radically reduced the amount of time that the Congress devotes to the declaring of war may prove of some interest. During the nineteenth century, the stiff resistance of the Jefferson Republicans meant that the Twelfth Congress took essentially its entire seven-month session, from 4 November 1811 until 18 June 1812, to find the votes needed for passage of Secretary Monroe's State Department–drafted declaration. In 1898, efficiency grew exponentially. Under expedited rules, the Fifty-fifth Congress took, not seven months, but seven days, 13–19 April 1898, to pass the conditional declaration against Spain and less than a day to pass the absolute declaration on 25 April 1898, after the commencement of armed hostilities.

During the twentieth century, President Wilson achieved moderate gains in efficiency by calling a special session. During the session, the Sixty-fifth Congress followed the regular peacetime procedures to amend slightly and then pass the State Department's resolution in three days, between 2 and 5 April 1917 (Elsea and Grimmett, 2006, 77–9). However, President Roosevelt achieved the greatest gains in efficiency when the Seventy-seventh

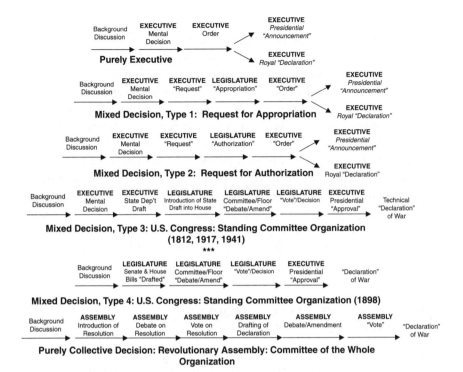

Figure 7. Six Possible Structures.

Congress completed the whole process in three hours and forty minutes on 8 December 1941. The president spoke to a joint session from 12:30 pm until 12:36:06 pm. The Senate returned to its chamber and both houses suspended the rules so as to pass the State Department–drafted resolution in thirty-three minutes, by 1:09 pm. It took until 3:23 pm to prepare the paperwork, and President Roosevelt approved the declaration at 4:10 pm (Kluckhohn 1941, 1).

As can be seen, each time the president's management of the Congress improved. With each congressional declaration, successive presidents were able to produce a much more efficient and expedited procedure. This no doubt represents the principal success of the current procedures. However, efficient management of the Congress by the president is not necessarily a desirable outcome. Perhaps a less efficient, but more thoughtful and lawful management of the process is what is needed. To this alternative end, consider following six structures in Figure 7.

A PURELY ROYAL OR EXECUTIVE DECISION

This executive decide-order-announce structure is unquestionably the most frequently used performative structure for declaring war, not just in the

United States, but around the world and throughout history as well. No
dictatorial president, emperor, king, or warlord worth his salt would permit
any other option. In outline, the procedure begins when 1) a king or dictatorial president decides the question of war or peace, on his own authority,
in his privy council. His decision becomes known and manifest to his privy
council in a personal and private performative speech act. Depending on
the circumstances, this personal and private speech act leads either 2a) to an
official "order" for his forces to deploy against the enemy and then 3a) to a
public "announcement" or 2b) to a public "announcement" and then 3b)
to an official "order" for his forces to deploy against the enemy. The public
"announcement" may be either a royal declaration of war, if the king is the
constitutionally recognized declarer of war, as in Great Britain, or a functionally equivalent unsolemn declaration of war, if the king is not the constitutionally recognized declarer of war, as in the United States. In sum, this
procedure advances the rule of men, and not law.

A MIXED DECISION, TYPE 1, REQUEST
FOR AN APPROPRIATION

In her circa 1434 *The Book of Fayttes of Armes and of Chyualrye* (1937), Christine
de Pisan writes that a purely executive or royal decision is not in the best interest of a prince. Instead, a wise prince should follow the example of the Romans
and "assemble to counseil the four estates of his countree whiche ought to be
called or he emprise so chargeable a thyng [as war]" (*ibid*. I, v). According to
Christine, the principal reason for this is to give a king's subjects the opportunity to express their loyalty and love, for, "O how is that a proffitable thynge
in seygnourye / Royame / or Cyte to haue true subgettis / & of grete loue"
(*ibid*.). As a modern illustration of this principle, she cites the "wel gaaf ensample the good wyse kyng charles the fythe of that name" who, in 1369

> asse*m*bled at parys [Paris] at his parliame*n*t the forsaid foure estates / ... / and
> to theym purposed his reasons ayenst thenglyssh men [against the English men]
> demaundyng theyr aduys / yf he had cause to bygynne warre / for without iuste
> cause / the regarde & deliberac*i*on emonge theym / and the consente & wylle of
> his good subgetts in no wyse he wold doo it at whiche counseyl by long delibera-
> c*i*on was concluded that he had good & iuste cause to begynne agayn the warre &
> thus the good wise kynge entreprysed it /. (*ibid*.)

"Demanding their advice" on the question of war or peace may well have
been Charles V's principal motivation. However, another very much more
pragmatic outcome may not have escaped his attention. For, once he had convinced his four estates "that he had good & iuste cause to begynne agayn the
warre," it then voted new taxes, without which he could not have restarted
armed hostilities, "*nervos belli, pecuniam infinitam*" ("the sinews of war, infi-
nite treasure"), as Cicero has observed (1969, *Philippics* V, ii, 5). His funding

assured, Charles V then issued a royal declaration of war against Edward III, king of England, as was the custom during the Hundred Years War. More recently, of course, approval of new funding would be followed, not by a royal declaration of war, but by a functionally equivalent presidential declaration. At this point, the matter can become rather confusing. On the one hand, the appropriations act can itself be considered as the "real" procedurally imperfect, functionally equivalent declaration of war, as, for example, the one passed by the Twenty-ninth Congress on 13 May 1846 against Mexico (Pub. L. 29–16, 9 Stat. 9). On the other hand, if the president also issues an executive proclamation or manifesto, such as that issued by President James Polk on that same day, most people would accord the president pride of place and consider his manifesto the "real" procedurally imperfect, functionally equivalent declaration (Polk 1846, 6).

Although this performative structure acknowledges the legislature's "power of the purse" and, therefore, seems to involve it in the king's decision making, this is more appearance than reality. It is very much more a "grace and favour" gesture on the part of the king or dictatorial president than any true sharing of power, or even an exercise in "collective judgment." The actual decision, after all, has already been made privately by the king or dictatorial president in his privy council before he "convenes and gives information" to the four estates.

Furthermore, to point to the obvious, the "power of the purse" is not the power to declare war. The two are entirely different. To see this, consider the performative structure in outline: 1) The king decides the question of war or peace in his privy council. His decision becomes known and manifest to his privy council in a personal and private performative speech act. His private decision then leads 2) to a public speech act, a "request" from the executive to the legislature for funding. Since the request for funding is usually granted, this means that 3) the legislature performs another series of public, collective speech acts to appropriate new funding and, usually, to levy new taxes. Subsequently, with new funding in hand, the king returns to his privy council and 4) decides on the precise moment to open armed hostilities. His decision again becomes known and manifest to his privy council in a personal and private performative speech act. Next, 5) the king issues official military "orders" detailing the precise moment to open armed hostilities. His decision, again, becomes known and manifest to his privy council in a personal and private performative speech act. When all is ready, 6) the king makes a public "announcement" of the commencement of armed hostilities.

Again, either the public "announcement" may be a royal declaration of war, if the king is the constitutionally recognized declarer of war, as was Charles V of France, or the appropriations act itself may serve as a functionally equivalent public "announcement," if the commander in chief is not the constitutionally recognized declarer of war, as was the case in 1846. Or, to elaborate the full confusion, the dictatorial president may also issue a manifesto or proclamation as the functional equivalent of a procedurally perfect declaration of war.

Unlike a purely executive or royal decision, a type 1, request for an appropriation, performative structure does acknowledge the legislature's unique competence to control the country's purse strings. Yet, how relevant is this to the declaring of war? In theory, the four estates could have prevented Charles V from resuming the war against Edward III of England. In practice this seldom happens. So seldom, indeed, that I know of only one case: In 1640, both the Short and Long Parliaments denied Charles I of England new taxes, forcing him to wage the Bishop's War with a feudal levy. Because feudalism had died several centuries beforehand, this work-around failed, provoked the English Civil Wars, and eventually led to the beheading of Charles I. Not the most auspicious example from the executive point of view.

True, in July 1973, the Ninety-third Congress did cut off funding, "to support directly or indirectly combat activities in or over Cambodia, Laos, North Vietnam and South Vietnam or off the shores of Cambodia, Laos, North Vietnam and South Vietnam by United States forces" (Pub. L. No. 93–50, 87 Stat. 129). But, it must be recalled, by the summer of 1973, all American combat forces had left South Vietnam. Needless to say, it is not politically difficult to end funding for troops who no longer need the funds because they have returned home and are no longer engaged in "combat activities." The trick is to do it before the beginning of or during the course of "combat activity," as the Short and Long Parliaments did in 1640, without starting a civil war. Thus, if one could demonstrate that the "power of the purse" had been exercised somewhere in the world more frequently than once in five hundred years, the political value of this type 1, request for an appropriation, performative structure might be seen to be as great as John Yoo (2005) thinks it is. Until then, one must recognize this apparently mixed type as basically the declaring of war in the executive mode – decision-order-announce – notwithstanding the politically astute "grace and favour" detour through the legislature for an appropriation and new taxes. Again, this procedure advances the rule of men, and not law.

A MIXED DECISION, TYPE 2, REQUEST FOR AUTHORIZATION

At the president's request, the Congress has made seven authorizations to use the armed forces between 1955 and 2002 (Elsea and Grimmett 2006). Dwight Eisenhower made two requests, one for the Formosan crisis in 1955 and another in 1957 for a general increase in military and economic assistance to the Middle East as an area threatened by "communist aggression";

Lyndon Johnson made one request in 1964 for the wars in Southeast Asia, the infamous Gulf of Tonkin Resolution; George H. W. Bush also made one request in 1991 for the Persian Gulf War; and George W. Bush made two requests, once on the heels of 11 September 2001 for the terrorist attack and once in 2002 for the 2003 invasion of Iraq.

Interestingly, the 1957 Promotion of Peace and Stability in the Middle East resolution was not really an authorization of the use of the armed forces; its purpose was to increase military assistance to the region (Pub. L. No. 85–7, 71 Stat. 5). That leaves six resolutions that, despite their merely precatory and hortatory status, might be taken as functionally equivalent to a proce-durally perfect declaration of war, and, therefore, in some sense functionally equivalent to the discharge of the Congress's constitutional duty to declare war. However, the near-total irrelevance of the Congress to the president's actual decision to use the armed forces seriously undermines any possible equivalency. As an example of their dysfunctional, "grace and favour" per-formative structure, consider the 102nd Congress's "Authorization for Use of Military Force against Iraq Resolution" for the Persian Gulf War, 1990–1 (Pub. L. No. 102–1, 105 Stat. 3).

To recall, Saddam Hussein invaded Kuwait on 2 August 1990. Relying upon the precedent set by President Truman in June 1950, President George H. W. Bush spoke first through the voice of the United Nations Security Council, which passed its first demand "that Iraq withdraw immediately and unconditionally" from Kuwait that same day, on Thursday, 2 August 1990 (Res. 660 (1990)). On Wednesday, 8 August 1990, President George H. W. Bush ordered and announced the beginning of *Operation Desert Shield*, the movement of American troops to the Persian Gulf. The American forces were soon joined by troops from a wide coalition of other nations. On Thursday, 29 November 1990, three weeks after the midterm congressional elections, a fact not without political significance, the Security Council authorized "the use of all necessary means," unless Iraq implemented the previous eleven resolutions calling on it to withdraw from Kuwait "on or before Tuesday, 15 January 1991" (Res. 678 (1990)). Once the United Nations ultimatum had been issued, the stage was set for the climax.

From the congressional perspective, the climax occurred not at the moment that President George H. W. Bush exercised his "inherent power to commit our armed forces to battle" on Thursday, 17 January 1991, for the initial air attack for *Operation Desert Storm*. Rather, it was the moment he exercised his "grace and favour" power on Tuesday, 8 January 1991, to "convene and give information" to the 102nd Congress. The "information given" was, of course, that he had now made his decision and, hence, desired a hortatory and precatory "authorization to use the armed forces" from the "cooperative" 102nd Congress. "Such an action," the "solicitous" president wrote in his request, "would underline that the United States stands with the international community and on the side of law and decency; it also would help dispel any belief that may exist in the minds of Iraq's leaders that the United States lacks the necessary unity to act decisively in response to Iraq's continued aggression against Kuwait" (Bush 1992, 14). And, indeed, the congressional resolution would do all of these things. What it would not do is fulfill the constitutional duty of the 102nd Congress to declare war.

With only seven days to go before the United Nations deadline, the leadership of the newly elected 102nd Congress scheduled an unusual Saturday session. On Saturday, 12 January 1991, the draft resolution was introduced in the House and passed the same day in both the House (two hundred fifty to one hundred eighty-three) and the Senate (by unanimous consent); it was approved by the president on Monday, 14 January 1991. A "solicitous" president and a "cooperative" Congress had beaten the United Nations deadline with a day to spare (*ibid.* 497). Holding both the Security Council and the congressional "authorizations" in hand, President George H. W. Bush exercised his "inherent power to commit our armed forces to battle" by announcing the start of the air portion of Operation Desert Storm on Thursday, 17 January 1991. He announced the commencement of ground operations on Sunday, 24 February 1991, and the end of combat operations on Wednesday, 27 February 1991.

Again, what is most interesting about this sequence of "grace and favour" events is not the politics, the fact that the timing of the request put the 102nd Congress under all but irresistible pressure. The politics is too easily understood. For, as Ulysses S. Grant observed with regard to President Polk's stampeding of the Twenty-ninth Congress in 1846, "Experience proves that the man who obstructs a war in which his nation is engaged, no matter whether right or wrong, occupies no enviable place in life or history. Better for him, individually, to advocate 'war, pestilence, and famine,' than to act as obstructionist to a war already begun" (Grant 1990, 50).

Rather, what is interesting is the fact that President George H. W. Bush waited until he had actually made up his mind to initiate armed hostilities before requesting congressional "authorization." Before the new year, one must assume that the president believed that the diplomatic pressure emanating from the Security Council might still force Saddam Hussein to withdraw from Kuwait. After all, international opinion, the depth and breadth of the coalition President George H. W. Bush had assembled, and the size of the armed forces drawn up in northeast Saudi Arabia were, literally, overwhelming. Under these circumstances, it was reasonable to assume that armed hostilities could be avoided and, hence, any need for a congressional "authorization." By the beginning of the new year, if not before the November midterm elections, it was no doubt clear in President George H. W. Bush's mind that diplomatic pressure would fail. If armed hostilities were inevitable, then a congressional resolution would be useful, as he said in his letter of request, the icing on the cake of Security Council Resolution 678.

That none of this has anything at all to do with the congressional power to declare war is only to say that a mixed decision, type 2, request for authorization is exactly the same "grace and favour" ploy as a mixed decision, type 1, request for an appropriation. The only difference is the substitution of an extraconstitutional precatory and hortatory resolution for an exercise of the "power of the purse." On the positive side, one can again note that requesting an "authorization," like requesting an "appropriation," does acknowledge the raw existence of the legislature. The king or dictatorial president is not totally contemptuous of his legislature, showing at least an inclination to "solicit congressional support" from a "cooperative" Congress, demonstrating that he does not want "to keep Congress unnecessarily in the dark."

Yet, on the negative side, one is still dealing with the executive manner of "decide," "order," "announce." In outline, 1) the dictatorial president decides the question of war or peace in his privy council. His decision becomes known and manifest to his privy council in a personal and private performative speech act. This then leads 2) to a public speech act, a "request" from the executive to the legislature for an "authorizing" resolution. Since the request is invariably granted, this means that 3) the legislature performs another series of public, collective speech acts to resolve the resolution. Subsequently, with legislative "authorization" in hand, the dictatorial president returns to his privy council and 4) decides on the precise moment to open armed hostilities. His decision, again, becomes known and manifest to his privy council in a personal and private performative speech act. Next, 5) the dictatorial president issues official military "orders" detailing the precise moment to open armed hostilities. His decision becomes known and manifest to his privy council in a personal and private performative speech act. When all is ready, 6) the dictatorial president makes an official, public "announcement" on the precise moment to open armed hostilities.

As with the permission slip your mother signed authorizing your elementary school teacher to take you on a field trip, concerns are raised if "authorization" is not sought and obtained; yet, what harm is really done if "authorization" is neither sought nor obtained? One must conclude, in the end, that the mixed decision types 1 and 2 are essentially identical to the purely executive or royal decision, because of their essentially decide-order-announce performative structure. Still, seeking your mother's authorization before going on a field trip with your school class does make everyone feel better. Once again, this procedure advances the rule of men, and not law.

A MIXED DECISION, TYPE 3, U.S. CONGRESS, STANDING
COMMITTEE ORGANIZATION (1812, 1917, 1941)

It is perhaps with greater irony than hypocrisy that James Madison was the president who developed the management procedures described here. As already discussed in Chapter 2, Madison's problem was that the old-time Jeffersonians in the Congress refused to take the initiative and vindicate the nation's rights by declaring war against either side during the wars of the French Revolution and empire. As early as 1798, during the Adams administration, they had beaten back the Federalist attempt to declare war against France. At that time, the Jeffersonians had substituted *An Act to Declare the Treaties Heretofore Concluded with France, No Longer Obligatory on the United States of 1798* for a proposed Federalist declaration of war. They subsequently limited the American response to French sponsored pirates in the Caribbean to a *Quasi-War* under the congressional power to grant letters of marque and reprisal. Again, in 1807, during the Jefferson administration, when the HMS *Leopard* fired upon the USS *Chesapeake* inside Chesapeake Bay, killing three, wounding eighteen, and arresting four as deserters from the Royal Navy, the response of the Jeffersonians was not to declare war against Great Britain for the affront, but to pass the Embargo Act of 1807. However, by 1811, both the country and the Congress had changed significantly. Both had more than doubled in size, and the new western states had joined with the southern states to foster a more bellicose sentiment. This led to the election of a group of representatives known as the War Hawks led by Henry Clay of Kentucky.

To recall, presidential management of the Twelfth Congress was nearly total. Not only had President Madison taken the initial decision for enmity and against amity in August 1811 while vacationing at Montpelier, but he also provided the indispensable aid and assistance for Speaker Henry Clay and the War Hawks through the constant attentions of his secretary of state, James Monroe, and, finally, he had the State Department draft the actual declaration. When this careful management was combined with control of the relevant committees, opposition to the declaration by the old-time Jeffersonians was quixotic at best, as congressional opposition to presidential desires for wars since 1812 demonstrates over and over again.

As might be imagined with all this maneuvering, the type 3 performative structure is by far the most complex and cumbersome of the possible performative structures. In outline, 1) the president decides the question of war or peace. His decision becomes known and manifest to his privy council in a personal and private performative speech act. 2) He next "convenes and gives information" to the Congress, concluding with a public speech act, a "request" from the executive to the legislature for a declaration of war. 3) He, then, "orders" the Department of State to draft an unreasoned, absolute declaration of war. 4) The State Department does so, and the draft resolution is "introduced" by tradition into the House of Representatives. 5) In 1812 and 1917, the State Department draft was debated in committee and on the floor in both chambers, although this is not a necessary requirement. The debate was omitted entirely in 1941, as already noted. 6) A "vote" is quickly and efficiently taken on the final resolution, which leads 7) to presidential "approval," thereby producing 8) a procedurally perfect, unreasoned, absolute declaration of war.

In theory, this performative structure could produce a fully reasoned conditional declaration of war, but no president has every thought this necessary, and, hence, the State Department has never drafted one. Again, in theory, the members of Congress could substitute their own reasoned declarations for the State Department draft, but no one has every ventured the suggestion. Also in theory, the members of Congress could vote down the president's request, but this is unimaginable, because it is impossible to imagine a "solicitous" president who would submit a request for a congressional declaration of war unless he was absolutely certain it would be passed by a "cooperative" Congress. After all, under type 3, it is a dictatorial president, through his "grace and favour" powers, who controls the exercise of the congressional power to declare war, not the members of the Congress.

Still, it must be remarked, this mixed decision: type 3 performative structure does track the letter of the Constitution. Unfortunately, though, the spirit is missing, because, as just noted, a dictatorial president controls the process, especially the crystallizing moment when the decision for enmity and against amity is actually made. The unalterable fact remains that the Congress decides nothing; it only "cooperates" when "convened and given information" so as to "declare" a decision already taken by the president. No town crier has ever done better.

Further, one should not forget that it is only the lack of a standing military establishment large enough to meet the needs of a world war that forced Presidents Madison, Wilson, and Roosevelt to request a declaration of war from their respective Congresses. Still, on the positive side, three presidents have in the past acknowledged the letter of the Constitution, if not its spirit. In this way, the Congress has been permitted to play a supporting role on three occasions. Yet, the congressional "role" remains rather more that of a town crier, a "grace and favour" indulgence on the part of a "solicitous" president, allowing "cooperative" Congress to associate itself with his majesty. Perhaps this counts for something. Yet, in the end, this procedure only advances the rule of men, and not of law.

A MIXED DECISION, TYPE 4, U.S. CONGRESS, STANDING COMMITTEE ORGANIZATION (1898)

Between 11 and 18 April 1898, the Fifty-fifth Congress 1) drafted a conditional, reasoned declaration of war; 2) debated it in committee and on the floor in both chambers; 3) amended it in the Senate; and 4) debated and voted on the final resolution. This led on Tuesday, 19 April 1898, 5) to a presidential "approval," thereby producing a procedurally perfect collective congressional decision in the form of a solemn, reasoned, conditional declaration of war. 6) President McKinley then turned that conditional declaration into an ultimatum by adding an (unreasonable) forty-eight-hour deadline for Spain to accept the conditions found in the resolving clause – independence for Cuba. When Spain failed to meet President McKinley's ultimatum, President McKinley, acting as executive agent for the Fifty-fifth Congress, officially "ordered" military operations to begin. Once the war had become absolute, the Fifty-fifth Congress again went back to work on Monday, 25 April 1898, and 1) voted and passed, without debate in either chamber, an agreed upon solemn, absolute, unreasoned declaration of war. This led once more to 2) presidential approval, thereby producing a second collective congressional declaration in the form of said solemn, unreasoned, absolute declaration of war.

The 1898 declarations were not "grace and favours" indulgences on the part of a "solicitous" president toward a "cooperative" Congress. Indeed, whatever the substantive justice of the war against Spain, it was fought on the authority of the constitutionally recognized declarer of war in the name of the people of the United States. True, the conditional declaration did not represent a sincere effort at conflict resolution, but, for the first and only time in American history, it did create an organic, coherent ends-means/ideal-in-process relationship between the Fifty-fifth Congress and President McKinley as commander in chief.

It is tempting, therefore, to speculate that this is the way article I, section 8, clause 11, is supposed to work, as both the letter and the spirit of the Constitution have been met, if not exceeded. However, as already noted, a number of excellent reasons exist for thinking that this tempting interpretation is little more than idle speculation. In the first place, the performative structure of 1898 is a failed structure in the sense that it has never been repeated. It therefore represents a one-time anomaly that cannot be reproduced because it has, in fact, not been reproduced in more than a hundred years. In the second place, while President McKinley did step back and allow the Fifty-fifth Congress to draft, debate, amend, and vote on the conditional declaration, he did not do so until he was sure he could no longer hold the line against public opinion. His management of the process was very much more hidden than that of Madison, Wilson, or Roosevelt, but he never lost control completely. Indeed, the most significant difference was the fact that President McKinley did not order the State Department to draft the declaration. Yet, one might ask whether this "most significant" difference is of any substantial importance. Leaning to the side of caution, this procedure still advances the rule of men more than it advances the rule of law. The "games" the Fifty-fifth Congress played in 1898 also reinforce this cautious conclusion.

A PURELY LEGISLATIVE DECISION: COMMITTEE OF THE WHOLE ORGANIZATION

Protests against British policy in North America began at least as early as the Stamp Act Congress of October 1765. They continued through 1774 with the First Continental Congress, which drafted and voted on six different documents of protest, including "The Bill of Rights [and] a List of Grievances" and a "Petition to the King." These efforts to settle the issues separating the Crown from its subjects in North America, however, failed. A Second Continental Congress was convened on Wednesday, 10 May 1775, to pursue the matter. This Congress drafted and voted on eight additional documents, including "A Declaration [of] ... Causes and Necessity..." written by Thomas Jefferson and "The Olive Branch Petition." Any one or all of these documents from 1765 through 1776 could be considered an imperfect, reasoned, conditional declaration of war. That is, the efforts of the colonists to resolve the conflict without resort to an absolute declaration of war were extensive.

In addition to these official documents from continentwide congresses, during the decade between 1765 and 1775, numerous documents of protest were drafted by the individual colonial legislatures, and even more numerous private pamphlets were published on the question, including Thomas Paine's seminal *Common Sense* of Monday, 1 January 1776.

Even after the British raid on Lexington and Concord on Wednesday, 19 April 1775, and the subsequent battles of 1775 and early 1776, few were the colonists who advocated an absolute declaration of war, a demand for independence. Sentiment remained strong that resolution of the conflict was still possible short of an absolute break: that the imperfect, unsolemn war then in progress did not yet bar the road to reconciliation. The question of absolute war or peace, however, came to a head on Friday, 7 June 1776, when Richard Henry Lee introduced three Virginia resolutions, seconded by John Adams of Massachusetts, stipulating:

> That these United Colonies are, and of Right ought to be, Free and Independent
> States, that they are absolved from all allegiance to the British Crown, and that all

Political connection between them and the State of Great Britain is, and ought to be, totally dissolved.

That it is expedient forthwith to take the most effectual measures for forming foreign Alliances.

That a plan of confederation be prepared and transmitted to the respective Colonies for their consideration and approbation. (Maier 1997, 41)

Pressing business delayed discussion of the resolutions until the next morning. The resolutions were taken up and debated in the committee of the whole over three days. Because Sunday was the day of rest, on Tuesday, 11 June 1776, the three resolutions were tabled while the delegates considered the matter further. Yet, in anticipation of eventual passage, three ad hoc committees were appointed – one "to prepare the declaration," one "to prepare and digest the form of a confederation to be entered into between these colonies," and one "to prepare a plan of treaties to be proposed to foreign powers" (*Journals of the Continental Congress* 1904–37, V:431). To prepare the declaration, a Committee of Five was appointed, composed of Benjamin Franklin, John Adams, Roger Sherman, Robert R. Livingston, and Thomas Jefferson. As the junior member, Jefferson was given the task of actually composing the draft. Crucially, by the time Jefferson sat down to write, he saw his job as more one of summarizing and collating the previous eleven years of protests and petitions than of original composition, as he wrote to Henry Lee in a letter dated Sunday, 8 May 1825 (Ford 1905, 12:409; see Wills 1979, 68–72). The "lobbying" for votes to pass Lee's resolutions continued during the month Jefferson was drafting and eventually had success. The ad hoc committee reported back on Friday, 28 June 1776. On Monday, 1 July 1776, the first Virginia resolution was taken up in the committee-of-the-whole again and approved the next day. The committee's draft declaration was now introduced, debated, amended, and voted on Thursday, 4 July 1776.

In outline, this committee-of-the-whole procedure begins 1) when a member of the assembly introduces a resolution, which is seconded. 2) This leads to a general debate and vote on the resolution. 3) If it is passed at that time or if it is likely to pass later, an ad hoc committee is appointed to draft a fully reasoned declaration of war. 4a) If it is passed in step 3), the ad hoc drafting committee reports back to the assembly, which takes up the draft, debating and amending it as a committee of the whole. 4b) If the resolution was tabled in step 3), the resolution is taken up again, debated, and voted up or down. 4c) If the resolution is passed in step 4b), the ad hoc drafting committee reports back to the assembly, which takes up its draft, debating and amending it as a committee-of-the-whole. 5) A final vote is taken on the agreed upon text, which, if passed, is a public communication.

Critically, from introduction to final vote, the entire process is both public and collective. The process was "collective" in an obvious way. Yet, to be clear, it was "public" not in the sense of being out in the open for all to see. For, it must be recalled, the Second Continental Congress met behind closed doors. Yet, crucially, its secret debates and votes took place before the assembled delegates. At no point was the process dominated and determined by the private decision of a single individual, a king or dictatorial president. Consequently, the reciprocal, mutually reinforcing relationship between collective procedures and collective speech acts found in the committee-of-the-whole procedures leads inexorably to the rule of law, and not men. Or, to approach the same issue from its other extreme, proper procedures are what separate mob rule (ochloarchy) from the rule of law. Both a kangaroo court and a jury trial are examples of collective or social decision making. The only difference is the improper procedures of the one and the proper procedures and decorum of the other. The formal or procedural justice of the jury trial largely vouchsafes the quality of the substantive justice meted out by the jury. The improper, unrecognized procedures of a kangaroo court all but guarantee the substantive injustice of the lynching meted out by the mob.

To be sure, private decisions have not been eliminated. But they have been tamed by pushing them off center stage and making them a matter of secondary, largely speculative concern. Why an individual member voted yea or nay is a subjective question that is largely unknowable and of relatively little concern. That he voted is an objective matter of fact, eminently knowable, and a matter of the greatest concern. As a result, the rule of law derives from the relatively objective, collective decision making found in courts and legislatures, whereas the rule of men derives from the private decisions of kings and dictatorial presidents acting in the executive manner. Unfortunately, how this relatively objective collective purely legislative decision procedure might be incorporated into the Constitution of the United States is less than clear. The task is to figure out either how to smuggle a corporate body organized as a committee of the whole into the Constitution itself or how to make it an appendage to the Congress. This challenge is taken up in the next two chapters.

PART III

WHAT ARE THE SOLUTIONS?

8 A Constitutional Amendment

The Congress shall have power ... to declare war, grant letters of marque and reprisal, and make rules concerning captures on land and water;. ...

(article I, section 8, clause 11)

The Congress, whenever two-thirds of both houses shall deem it necessary, shall propose amendments to this constitution, or, on the application of the legislatures of two-thirds of the several states, shall call a convention for proposing amendments, which, in either case, shall be valid to all intents and purposes, as part of this constitution, when ratified by the legislatures of three-fourths of the several states, or by conventions in three-fourths thereof, as the one or the other mode of ratification may be proposed by the Congress.

(article V)

Stated baldly, the Congress has not, cannot, and never will declare war in any meaningful or appropriate manner. It is organizationally, morally, and politically incapable of even dreaming of discharging its constitutional responsibilities in this area. A superficial diagnosis would identify the source of this failure not as a fundamental constitutional flaw, but as lack of congressional initiative in the face of an "imperial presidency." This shallow view leads to the suggestion that the Congress could regain the initiative if only it could regain control over the drafting of the declaration and, hence, control over the question of war or peace. In the next chapter, I take up this suggestion, outlining a way for the Congress to regain the initiative to draft its own declarations, and, hence, to decide the question of war or peace independently of the president. Yet, it must be said, this suggestion is basically a work-around, a way of patching up a fundamental flaw in the Constitution. For political reasons, the work-around may be easier to implement than a constitutional amendment, and a patch is better than nothing, but, to be frank, fundamental flaws require fundamental solutions.

A more penetrating diagnosis, however, would acknowledge that the Federal Convention stacked the deck against the Congress when it failed to assign the power to decide the question of war or peace most explicitly and unambiguously to them. Then, fatally, an increase in size and workload forced the Congress to invent the modern standing-committee system. As a result, the Congress is simply not organized "to declare war." Following up on that last thought, it is perhaps useful to go back to the beginning and work one's way slowly to a truly constitutional solution.

SOCIAL ORDERS AND DEMOCRACY

Just how radical and revolutionary the Constitution of the United States was in 1787 is exceptionally difficult to appreciate. After more than two hundred years of service in good times and bad, it feels like a comfortable old shoe. But revolutionary and radical it was. In the first place, it was a written constitution, the first written constitutions for a sovereign nation-state in history. Previously, national constitutions had evolved slowly over time as well-worn customs matured into hollowed traditions, which were recorded here and there, if at all, from time to time. Despite the title of Walter Bagehot's *The English Constitution* (1963 [1864]), his great volume is not a constitution. Indeed, whatever virtues and authority it does possess, it possesses them only on the principle of *faute de meilleur*. If England had a written constitution, Bagehot would not have had to write his tome. In the second place, the Constitution of the United States was not sanctioned by the ancestral gods. Instead, as one can read on the reverse side of the Great Seal, it was a *Novus Ordo Seclorum*, a new order of the ages, and *Annuit Cœptis*, he (god or providence) approves (our) beginnings. Providence approved, but it did not ordain, sanction, consecrate, or establish it, as the gods or godlike forebears had for all previous governments. The United States does not trace its foundation to the Sun God, or to the Trojans, or to Rome. The president does not possess the Mandate of Heaven. Consequently, in the third place, the foundation of the United States was an act of self-enactment, a performative speech act that reconstituted thirteen states as a nation and that nation as a nation-state, as the preamble makes clear:

> WE, the People of the United States, in order to form a more perfect union, establish justice, insure domestic tranquility, provide for the common defence, promote the general welfare, and secure the blessings of liberty to ourselves and our posterity, do ordain and establish this Constitution for the United States of America.

Again, it was neither the ancestral gods nor forefathers out of memory who had crafted and handed down the constitution. Nor was it an all-powerful sovereign king who graciously favored his subjects with the document. Radically and without precedent, the "people" of that time and place spoke collectively as a corporate body to "ordain and establish this Constitution for [not "of"] the United States of America." The performative verbs are critical. This was not a mystical "social contract" with an unknown party of the first part promising to provide goods and services. This was a fully conscious self-enactment by a "*sovereign* people," an ordination and an establishment so as "to assume among the Powers of the Earth, the separate and equal Station to which the Laws of Nature and of Nature's God entitle them."

But not only did the "sovereign people" consciously constitute themselves as a nation-state in 1789, they unknowingly constituted themselves as the first "*democratic* republic" in history – unknowingly, because the last thing the Founders in Philadelphia wanted to do was create a democracy. They intended to found a republic, which is precisely what they did, but a "democracy," never. Consequently, the abhorrent adjective is nowhere found in the document. Indeed, the Founders knew from their classical training that *demokratia* was really a synonym for *ochlokratia*, mob rule. Yet, times change. At the time, in 1789, a property qualification to vote protected and reinforced the antidemocratic character of the Constitution. It excluded all but the "right" people from voting and all but a select wealthy few from public life. But the property qualification quickly fell by the wayside. By the 1830s, the effective elimination of the property qualification led to more and more citizens voting. With this inexorable increase in the franchise, politics became more and more popular and democratic, despite the antidemocratic republican character of the Constitution. Meanwhile, the term "democracy" was unexpectedly rehabilitated by the French Revolution. Swept up by their enthusiasm for that revolution, the Jeffersonian Republicans established a national system of "Democratic Societies" during 1793 and 1794. Not incidentally, these clubs proved most useful in defeating Federalist candidates (Brant 1941–61, 3:417–20). In retaliation, the Federalists soon began calling Jefferson's party the "Democratic" Republicans. Since Jefferson's election as president in 1800, however, the now-domesticated adjective has stuck, and the revolutionary antidemocratic republican Constitution of 1789 has unwittingly fostered a "democratic" politics, leading to a fundamental tension between America's participatory politics and its antidemocratic, republican mode of government.

Still, the changing fortunes of the adjective "democratic" and an expanding franchise are not the heart of the matter. No democratic republic had ever before been possible because no large and extensive independent nation without social orders had ever existed before. This absence of social orders is, therefore, the heart of "'democracy' construed as an ideal." Thus, while social classes most certainly existed in 1787 America, social orders did not. The existence of slavery was an embarrassment easily ignored and dismissed as a dying anomaly.

Consider the matter further: Aristotle famously saw constitutional theory as a branch of arithmetic. Greek city-states were ruled by either the one, the few, or the many. After the number of the rulers had been counted, the city's constitution more or less followed as a natural consequence of the number: monarchy, aristocracy, or democracy. With regard to the many, however, the crucial point is not participation; Greek society was composed of too many nonparticipating slaves, women, and resident foreigners. Rather, what makes for a "democeacy" is the fact that all citizens possessed a political personality. Citizenship alone qualified an individual both for membership in the assembly and for holding public offices, including deciding trials at law. In contrast, in the Roman Republic and all subsequent republics until 1789, citizenship alone did not produce a political personality. It was only the first requirement. In addition, each citizen belonged to one of several social orders. This dual principle of citizenship and corporate membership meant that individuals qua individuals did not exist as political actors. Only when embedded in a recognized social order did an individual citizen acquire a political personality and qualify for a rigidly restricted range of offices and voting opportunities. Thus, in republican Rome, without elevation to the Senate by the Senate, no plebe or *equites* (knights) would ever think of participating in senatorial offices or debates, any more than a senator would think of participating in the *comitia plebes tributa*.

Prior to 1787, therefore, the most fundamental constitutional question was how to map a constellation of social orders onto the primary functions of any government, for example:

> THE republic of St. Gall [Switzerland] is a league and a half in circumference, and contains nine thousand souls. ... This happy and prosperous, though diminutive republic, has its grand council of ninety persons, its little council of twenty-four, and three burgomasters. The little council consists of the three burgomasters, nine senators, and twelve tribunes. The grand council consists of all the little council, and eleven persons from each tribe; for the city is divided into the society of the nobles, and six tribes of the artisans, of whom the weavers are the principal. Besides these there are, the chamber of justice, the chamber of five, and some others. (Adams 1850–6, IV:342)

What had grown over time out of the social and economic landscape of St. Gall was less a rational division of the executive, legislative, and judicial functions than a complex balancing and counterbalancing of the raw political power of the "six tribes of the artisans" and the "nobles." Individual citizens qua individual citizens played no role, had no vote.

Montesquieu, of course, devoted his *De L'Esprit des Loix* to the disentangling of this fundamental dualism. Closer to home, though, is John Adams's laboriously eccentric, but erudite, analysis entitled *A Defence of the Constitutions of Government of the United States of America, against the Attack of M. Turgot, in his Letter to Dr. Price, 22 March, 1778* (1850–6, IV). Writing in London while serving as the American minister to the Court of St. James, Adams began his pamphlet on 4 October 1786, eight months before the Federal Convention met in Philadelphia (and, hence, the 's' on "Constitutions," which refers to the state constitutions) and did not finish it until 26 December 1787, three months after the convention finished its work. As a result, Adams's work did not influence the Framers in Philadelphia. Its importance, therefore, lies not in its influence, but, as with Montesquieu, in its antiquarian analysis of a problem that no longer existed (Manicas 1989, 85).

In summary, Adams's *Defence* wrestles with the dynamic between social orders and governmental functions in all the republics of history, each one of which he lists and describes, as with the St. Gall example. He concludes that the wisdom of past ages demonstrates that, in order to keep domestic peace, a constitution had to "balance" six different "powers" of two different types. The first type of "power" was the raw political power inherent in the three orders of society, which he identified, in a most eccentric manner, as the Aristotelian the one (the first magistrate), the few (the aristocracy), and the many (the people). The second type of "power" was the power inherent in each of the three functions of government – the executive, the legislative, and the judicial. According to Adams, whenever one social order gained control over more than one governmental function, thereby upsetting this six-legged "balance," this "imbalance" sooner or later led to oppression and a loss of liberty (Adams 1850–6, IV:381; see also Montesquieu 1914, XI, 6).

As one can imagine, trying to balance all the permutations and combinations of these six variables – three social orders against three governmental functions – is a daunting proposition. According to Adams, only the English constitution had achieved it, and then only partially. As with all Gordian knots, however, the solution is not to try to disentangle the complexity, as Montesquieu, Adams, and others attempted, but to slice through it with a single stroke. The Framers in Philadelphia did just this while Adams was laboring on his pamphlet in London. Blessed with a raw colonial society of several classes, but no politically potent social orders, as in St. Gall, the Framers were able to take seriously, if somewhat ironically given the existence of slavery, the old Stoic principle "that all Men are created equal." Pushing this logic, they concluded that all citizens with sufficient wealth and property were also created equal and could participate equally in political life. This cut the traditional problem in half, reducing the variables from six to three. A radical frontier individualism solved Adams's problem of social orders and made America the first republic in history with the potential for a "democratic" politics. Membership in a social order would no longer be required to participate in politics. Citizenship alone would qualify one as a political actor. Abraham Lincoln could now rise from log cabin to White House.

WHY THREE FUNCTIONS?

Unfortunately, solving one problem only reveals other equally confounding issues that need to be considered. Eliminating social orders from the equation still left the problem of governmental functions. In particular, governmental functions are innumerable. No written constitution can include all of them. Therefore, which are important enough to be spoken of and which may be left aside? With regard to the raw number of crucial governmental functions with which writers of a constitution must deal, three was the consensus number in 1787. And, indeed, three is an excellent number. Like the Three Bears' porridge, three is not too limiting, nor too expansive; it appears to be just right. John Locke, Montesquieu, John Adams, and the Framers all agreed on this point.

But, if three is the right number, what are the principal functions? Montesquieu (most of the time), Adams, and the Framers all agreed that the three functions were legislative, executive, and judicial. But two earlier theorists, Jean Bodin and John Locke, dissented. Bodin found four, while Locke agreed that the number was three, but preferred dividing the sovereigns' functions differently, into the legislative, the executive, and the fœderative. The bone of contention, here, is how to fit a nation's foreign affairs and wartime functions into the peacetime functions of republican government of divided powers. Monarchies have no problem here, since the monarch handles all functions – peacetime and wartime, foreign and domestic, legislative and executive, judicial as well. In the divided government of a republic, however, the nation's foreign affairs and war powers just do not fit into a scheme built on the number three. They appear lost as orphans wandering among the government's peacetime functions.

In his 1576 *The Six Bookes of a Commomweale*, Bodin argued that primary governmental functions were the four. Working from a list of more than one hundred and fifty regalian rights, his Chapter X, *Of the true markes of Soueraigntie*, lists the following as the first marks:

1) Legislative: "This then is the first and chiefth marke of Soueraignty, to be of power to giue laws and commaund to all in generall" (Bodin 1962, 162 [161]).
2) Fœderative: "to denounce warre, or treat of peace, one of the greatest points of soueraigne maiestie" (*ibid.* 163 [162]).
3) Executive: "The third marke of Soueraigne maiestie is to be of power to create and appoint magistrats, ... especially the principall officers, which are not vnder the commaund of other magistrats" (*ibid.* 166).

4) Judicial: "But now let vs speak of the fourth marke of Soueraignetie, that is to wit, of the *Last Appeal,* which is and always hath beene one of the most principall rights of soueraignetie" (*ibid.* 168).

In 1690, more than a hundred years later, John Locke's *Second Treatise* treated the question of governmental functions in Chapter XII, *Of the Legislative, Executive, and Federative Power of the Common-wealth.* Since the legislative function is not an issue, consider the confusion that surrounds the executive and the fœderative:

> Sec. 146. This [fœderative power] therefore contains the power of war and peace, leagues and alliances, and all the transactions, with all persons and communities without the common-wealth, and may be called fœderative, if any one pleases. So the thing be understood, I am indifferent as to the name.

> Sec. 147. These two powers, executive and fœderative, though they be really distinct in themselves, yet one comprehending the execution of the municipal laws of the society within its self, upon all that are parts of it; the other the management of the security and interest of the public without, with all those that it may receive benefit or damage from, yet they are always almost united. And though this fœderative power in the well or ill management of it be of great moment to the common-wealth, yet it is much less capable to be directed by antecedent, standing, positive laws, than the executive; and so must necessarily be left to the prudence and wisdom of those, whose hands it is in, to be managed for the public good: for the laws that concern subjects one amongst another, being to direct their actions, may well enough precede them. But what is to be done in reference to foreigners, depending much upon their actions, and the variation of designs and interests, must be left in great part to the prudence of those, who have this power committed to them, to be managed by the best of their skill, for the advantage of the common-wealth. (Locke 1764 [1690], XII)

The "three" functions, according to Locke, can be looked at two different ways. When looked at in terms of the location at which the function is exercised (i.e., at home or abroad), one gets:

I. Domestic affairs
   A. Legislative
   B. Executive (i.e., "the municipal laws of the society within its self")
II. Foreign affairs
   A. Fœderative (i.e., "the power of war and peace, leagues and alliances")

When looked at in terms of which institution is exercising the function (i.e., the king or the Parliament), one gets:

I. The king
   A. Executive (i.e., domestic affairs)
   B. Fœderative (i.e., foreign affairs)

II. Parliament
    A. Legislative (i.e., domestic affairs)

One of course sees what Locke is trying to say, but has he really answered
the question? Perhaps James Madison's critique of Locke's chapter XIV,
Of Prerogative, is apposite to explain Locke's dual system: "The [Locke's]
chapter on prerogatives shows, how much the reason of the philosopher was
clouded by the royalism of the Englishman" (1900–10, 144, n. 1). Locke's
royalist imperative to shoehorn the unified powers of a monarchy into a government of divided powers clearly does little to clarify which are and which
are not the primary functions of a divided government. In order to preserve
the king's prerogatives, notably his power to declare war and make treaties,
Locke has created a less than satisfactory system. Just how unsatisfactory
Locke's system is is indicated by how closely it resembles the dictatorial system President James Madison created in 1812.

    In 1748, fifty-eight years later, the baron de Montesquieu finds Locke's
system less than comprehensible. In his *De L'Esprit des Loix*, he divides
governmental functions most frequently into three, using also the familiar
peacetime arrangement of legislative, executive, and judicial in a general,
undefined sort of way. However, in book XI, section 6, *Of the Constitution
of England*, Montesquieu decides to have Locke's cake and to eat it too.
But instead of these two sets adding up to six functions, Montesquieu finds
only four.

    The first set consists of the legislative and two different executive func-
tions, the second of which is really the judicial, whereas the first is actually
Locke's fœderative:

> In every government there are three sorts of power: the legislative; the executive
> in respect to things dependent on the law of nations; and the executive in regard
> to matters that depend on the civil law. By virtue of the first [i.e., legislative], the
> prince or magistrate enacts temporary or perpetual laws, and amends or abro-
> gates those that have been already enacted. By the second [i.e., fœderative], he
> makes peace or war, sends or receives embassies, establishes the public security,
> and provides against invasions. By the third [i.e., judicial], he punishes criminals,
> or determines the disputes that arise between individuals. The latter we shall
> call the judiciary power, and the other simply the executive power of the state.
> (Montesquieu 1914, XI, 6)

But, a few sentences on, Montesquieu concludes, as Adams would thirty-
eight years later, that the greatest threat to the peacetime stability of a republic occurred when one social order controlled more than one of the peacetime
governmental functions. To express this conclusion, he drops the "executive
as fœderative" and reverts to the more familiar peacetime arrangement of
legislative, executive, and judicial:

> There would be an end of everything, were the same man or the same body, whether of the nobles or of the people, to exercise those three powers, that of enacting laws [i.e., legislative], that of executing the public resolutions [i.e., executive], and of trying the causes of individuals [i.e., judicial]. (*ibid.*)

Montesquieu, of course, was not drafting a constitution; *De L'Esprit des Loix* is a descriptive work, not a manual for writing constitutions. Still, what he has done without quite saying so is to suggest that his compatriot, Bodin, was right all along. The primary governmental functions are really four, and not three:

I. Primary governmental functions
    A. Legislative (i.e., enacting laws)
    B. Executive (i.e., executing public resolutions)
    C. Fœderative (i.e., conducting foreign and military affairs)
    D. Judicial (i.e., trying the causes of individuals)

Curiously, all this indecision about how to fit Locke's fœderative power into a government of three peacetime branches disappears as soon as one turns from a fully sovereign national government to a colonial government. Colonial status simply means that the primary governmental functions are all peacetime functions: executive, legislative, and judicial. True, a royal governor commands a small militia or home guard, but he does not negotiate treaties, declare war, or conduct foreign affairs. These are all matters handled by the fully sovereign metropolitan government. Consequently, a colony can easily be defined as a jurisdiction with some measure of home rule, but no control over foreign and military affairs. In contrast, a fully sovereign nation-state exercises Locke's foreign affairs and wartime fœderative powers in addition to the peacetime executive, legislative, and judicial functions.

Needless to say, the American experience for two hundred years before 1787 was of colonial government composed of three branches – a governor appointed from London either by the proprietor or by the king, a locally elected legislature, and a locally appointed judiciary. Subsequent to the Second Continental Congress's call of 19 May 1776 for the rebellious colonies to constitute themselves as independent states, little changed in the functional structure of the new state governments. For all practical purposes, they remained colonial governments. The local judiciaries and legislatures were already in place. The only change was the substitution of a locally elected governor for a London appointed governor. Foreign and military affairs were still handled by others, the Second Continental Congress during the war and the Confederal Congress after 1781.

This revolutionary situation, however, created a strange sort of double vicious circle. Spinning clockwise, the Second Continental Congress was "sovereign" because it exercised Locke's fœderative powers. In this sense, the thirteen new states were not "sovereign" but continued as "colonies." Now, the Continental Congress managed their foreign and military affairs. Spinning counterclockwise, though, the Second Continental Congress was not "sovereign" because it was entirely dependent on the thirteen "sovereign" states. They had constituted it and supplied much of its military and financial needs. If the states had withdrawn their delegates or stopped supplying it with money, the Second Continental Congress would have simply ceased to exist. In this sense, the thirteen states were "sovereign" because the Second Continental Congress's very existence and life's blood depended upon them. The ambiguity was all but paralyzing. In sum, by outsourcing their fœderative powers to the Second Continental Congress, and later to the Confederal Congress, the states split and dislocated "sovereignty."

But notice how the Federal Convention resolved the issue of split sovereignty. While all of the debate centered on how to reconcile the Virginia and New Jersey Plans, the basic three-branch colonial structure was never questioned. All the delegates were familiar with it; it was working well in each of the states, and it appeared to solve the perceived problems found in the Articles of Confederation. As soon as the Federal Convention had enumerated the powers to be exercised by each peacetime branch of the new government, its work was done. Instead of questioning this "colonial" structure and revisiting the confusion over the number of primary governmental functions – whether they were three or four – the Founders kept the three-branch "colonial" structure and scattered the foreign affairs and wartime fœderative functions that "depend on the law of nations" between the legislative and executive branches in the following manner:

Article I:

Sec. 5 (3) Each House shall keep a Journal of its Proceedings, and from time to time publish the same, excepting such Parts as may in their Judgment require Secrecy;

Sec. 8 (1) The Congress shall have Power To lay and collect Taxes, Duties, Imposts and Excises, to pay the Debts and provide for the common Defence. . . .

* * *

(10) To define and punish Piracies and Felonies committed on the high Seas, and Offences against the Law of Nations;

(11) To declare War, grant Letters of Marque and Reprisal, and make Rules concerning Captures on Land and Water;

(12) To raise and support Armies, but no Appropriation of Money to that Use shall be for a longer Term than two Years;

(13) To provide and maintain a Navy;

(14) To make Rules for the Government and Regulation of the land and naval Forces;

(15) To provide for calling forth the Militia to execute the Laws of the Union, suppress Insurrections and repel Invasions;

(16) To provide for organizing, arming, and disciplining, the Militia, and for governing such Part of them as may be employed in the Service of the United States, reserving to the States respectively, the Appointment of the Officers, and the Authority of training the Militia according to the discipline prescribed by Congress;

(17) To exercise exclusive Legislation in all Cases whatsoever, ...for the Erection of Forts, Magazines, Arsenals, dock-Yards, and other needful Buildings;

Sec. 10 (1) No State shall enter into any Treaty, Alliance, or Confederation; grant Letters of Marque and Reprisal;

* * *

(3) No State shall, without the Consent of Congress, lay any Duty of Tonnage, keep Troops, or Ships of War in time of Peace, enter into any Agreement or Compact with another State, or with a foreign Power, or engage in War, unless actually invaded, or in such imminent Danger as will not admit of delay.

Article II:

Sec. 2 (1) The President shall be Commander in Chief of the Army and Navy of the United States, and of the Militia of the several States, when called into the actual Service of the United States;

(2) He shall have Power, by and with the Advice and Consent of the Senate, to make Treaties, provided two thirds of the Senators present concur; and he shall nominate, and by and with the Advice and Consent of the Senate, shall appoint Ambassadors,

Sec. 3 ... he shall receive Ambassadors and other public Ministers; he shall take Care that the Laws be faithfully executed, and shall Commission all the Officers of the United States.

Article IV:

Sec. 4 The United States shall guarantee to every State in this Union a Republican Form of Government, and shall protect each of them against Invasion; and on Application of the Legislature, or of the Executive (when the Legislature cannot be convened), against domestic Violence.

What the Federal Convention did structurally was to leave undisturbed the peacetime "colonial" status of the thirteen states by keeping Locke's fœderative powers secure at the national level, on the one hand, while, on the other hand, restructuring the Articles of Confederation as a three-branch "colonial" government with fœderative powers. More precisely, because "colonial" governments do not engage in foreign and military affairs, this *Novus Ordo* organized and distributed the primary governmental functions according to two "colonial" principles, 1) the needs of domestic government and 2) the needs of peacetime government, thereby ignoring the need to accord the powers of war and peace an independent status. Thus, all of the many clauses *not* listed deal with various aspects of domestic affairs, whereas all of the fœderative clauses listed deal with those aspects of foreign and military affairs that occur normally and naturally within and among nations during times of peace: raising and supporting armies; providing and maintaining a navy; organizing, arming, and disciplining the militia; erecting forts, magazines, arsenals, dock-yards, and other needful buildings; appointing and receiving ambassadors; and such like.

With the single exception of the first two infinitive phrases found in Article I, section 8, clause 11, "To declare War, grant Letters of Marque and Reprisal," all the other clauses of the Constitution operate and function during times of peace as integral parts of the domestic landscape. True, all these clauses are "dual-use" clauses, operating during time of war as well as during time of peace. Yet, uniquely among all the articles, clauses, and phrases of the Constitution, the two phrases "To declare War, grant Letters of Marque and Reprisal" do not and cannot operate or function during times of peace. These two phrases operate and function only during time of war, exclusively, because their performance terminates the state and condition of peace by declaring the existence of the state and condition of either public or private war, either conditionally or absolutely.

Once this anomaly is noticed, the tension, if not the contradiction, in asking the Congress to declare war emerges, for both organizational and functional reasons, as summarized in Figure 8. In the first place, as was discussed in Chapter 4, the U.S. Congress is incapable of declaring war for well-understood organizational reasons. Presidential leadership and agenda setting are absolutely necessary in order to surmount the exorbitant transaction costs, the extreme difficulty in coordinating shared interests, and the exceptional collective action problems of the five-hundred-thirty-five member, bicameral, majority-rule Congress.

In the second place, and of greater importance from a constitutional perspective, organizational dysfunction only exacerbates functional dysfunction. The Congress is, after all, a legislature. Therefore, it should function as a legislature. A legislature, as Locke, Montesquieu, and all others agree, is dedicated to enacting "antecedent, standing, positive laws,... that concern subjects one amongst another, being to direct their actions." Neither a declaration of war nor a letter of marque and reprisal can meet either of these two criteria. Both concern foreigners. Nor can they operate as "an antecedent, standing, positive law," as the annual declaration of the Lacedaemonian ephors against the helots demonstrates. Thus, four, not three, is the correct number of primary governmental functions for fully sovereign nation-states. A solidly constituted, fully sovereign republic must be constructed upon four pillars, and not three. Only partially sovereign colonial governments are constituted upon three pillars.

Not incidentally, this insight captures faithfully the ends-means/ideal-in-process relationship between the declarer of war and the commander of the diplomatic, economic, or military means. For, in practice, no presidential

Second Continental Congress	United States Congress
+ unicameral + committee of the whole + 44–50 members + foreign affairs (i.e., waging war)	+ bicameral + standing committee + 535 members + domestic affairs

Organizational Impediments

Second Continental Congress	United States Congress
+ moderate transaction costs + moderate difficulty coordinating shared interests + moderate collective action problems	+ exacerbated transaction costs + exacerbated difficulty coordinating shared interests + exacerbated collective action problems

Functional Abilities

Second Continental Congress	United States Congress
fœderative powers + the power of war and peace + the making of leagues and alliances	legislative powers + enacting antecedent laws regulating relations among citizens fœderative powers + declaring war + ratifying treaties

Figure 8. Contrasting Organizational and Functional Abilities.

government can function during peacetime unless a "cooperative" Congress takes its lead from a "solicitous" president who "convenes and gives it information" on the important peacetime issues of the day. But war is not peace, and the "nature" of war requires the declarer of war to decide the question of war or peace independently of the commander. Thus, the fourth pillar of a fully sovereign republic is a Council on War and Peace, although a very much more politically correct name is probably needed: as Locke said, "So the thing be understood, I am indifferent as to the name."

A CONSTITUTIONAL AMENDMENT

Sect. 1. The fœderative power of the United States shall be vested in a Council on War and Peace.

Sect. 2. The fœderative power shall extend to the ratification of treaties, on behalf of the nation, by majority vote; to the undivided and unshared power to decide the question of public war, both domestic and foreign, on behalf of the nation, by majority vote, and to declare and publish same; and to the undivided and unshared power to decide the question of private war, both secret and open, on behalf of the nation, by majority vote, by means of a grant of a letter of marque or reprisal, and to publish same, either immediately or with delay to preserve secrecy.

Sect. 3. The aforesaid power to ratify treaties shall be exercised in accordance with the Circular 175[1] process to distinguish executive agreements from treaties. Only acknowledged treaties shall go forward to the Council on War and Peace for ratification. In case of disagreement over whether an international instrument is a treaty or an executive agreement, the opinion of the Council on War and Peace shall be binding on the executive branch.

Sect. 4. The aforesaid power to decide and declare public war, both domestic and foreign, on behalf of the nation, shall include the imposition of diplomatic, economic, or military sanctions.

The aforesaid power to decide and declare public war, both domestic and foreign, on behalf of the nation, shall be exercised in accordance with Hague Convention III of 1907, both conditionally and absolutely, with a text modeled on the Declaration of Independence. The text shall not take the style of a resolution.

When made conditionally, the public declaration shall indict the gravamina as well as declare the nation's preferred peace terms. The decision to affix an ultimatum to a conditional declaration of war is an executive decision of the president.

When made absolutely, the public declaration shall indict the gravamina, declare the nation's preferred peace terms as well as denounce the termination of the state and condition of peace and declare the unfortunate, but necessary, existence of the state and condition of war.

An unreasoned, absolute, public declaration is appropriate when negotiations over the preferred peace terms previously declared conditionally have failed in the estimation of the Council on War and Peace.

An unreasoned, absolute, public declaration is appropriate when the nation is in such imminent danger as will not admit of delay, or when novel circumstances arise suddenly such that no time exists for the Council on War and Peace to deliberate more extensively.

In cases where either imminent danger or novel circumstances require an unreasoned, absolute, public declaration, the responsibility of the Council on War and Peace to make a fully reasoned, public declaration of war is not lessened. A fully reasoned, absolute, public declaration is still required as soon as time and circumstances permit to ensure that the President as Commander-in-Chief has not exceeded his command authority to employ diplomatic, economic, or military sanctions when not called for.

Sect. 5. The aforesaid power to decide upon and grant authority to the President for private war by means of a letter of marque or reprisal shall be exercised through

---

[1] The Circular 175 process is explained in the next chapter.

carefully circumscribed grants in terms of geographic extent, time, and the means employed.

Sect. 6. The purpose of public declarations for public war or of grants of a letter of marque or reprisal for private war is to express that it is the best and most prudent judgment of the Council on War and Peace, with the president's approval, that the gravamina indicted combined with the declaration of peace, when declared conditionally, and the denunciation and declaration of war, when declared absolutely, constitute true *casus belli*.

Sect. 7. The intention of this amendment is, on the one hand, to make procedurally imperfect declarations or authorizations of public war by either the Congress or president illegitimate, illegal, and unconstitutional; and, on the other hand, to make procedurally imperfect presidential or congressional finding or commissions for private war illegitimate, illegal, and unconstitutional.

Sect. 8. The Council on War and Peace may seek injunctive relief in the Appellate Court against either the Congress or the President for infringing, by means of unconstitutional declarations or authorizations of public war or grants for private war, the Council's right to decide and declare public war or to grant a letter of marque or reprisal for private war.

Sect. 9. The Council on War and Peace may submit a petition for impeachment of the President to the House of Representatives for the waging of a procedurally imperfect public or private war without a procedurally perfect public declaration for public war or a grant for private war from the Council on War and Peace.

Sect. 10. The Council on War and Peace of the United States shall be no greater than fifty Councilors, chosen by the legislatures of the several States, for eight years; and each Councilor shall have one vote. Should the number of States exceed fifty, the votes of the legislatures of two or more States shall be combined to elect one Councilor, preserving the fifty member limit on the number of Councilors.

No person shall be a Councilor who shall not have attained to the age of forty years, and been nine years a citizen of the United States, and who shall, when elected, be an inhabitant of that State or States from which he shall be chosen.

The Council on War and Peace should represent a mix of diplomatic, political, and military experience and expertise.

No Councilor may receive confidential or secret information that is material to a decision for public war. The work of the Council on War and Peace with regard to declarations of public war shall be confined to publically available documents and testimony.

Exceptionally, Councilors may receive confidential or secret information material to the granting of a secret letter of marque or reprisal, when absolutely unavoidable.

Sect. 11. Immediately after they shall be assembled in consequence of the first election, the Councilors shall be divided as equally as may be into four classes. The seats of the Councilors of the first class shall be vacated at the expiration of the second year, of the second class at the expiration of the fourth year, of the third class at the expiration of the sixth year, and of the fourth class at the expiration of the eighth year, so that one-fourth may be chosen every second year; and if vacancies happen by resignation, or otherwise, during the recess of the Legislature or Legislatures of the State or States that elected the Councilor, the Executive or Executives of the States may make temporary appointments until the next meeting of the Legislature or Legislatures, which shall then fill such vacancies. Councilors shall be eligible for reelection to multiple terms.

Sect. 12. The times, places and manner of holding elections for Councilors, shall be prescribed by the Legislature or Legislatures thereof; but the United States Congress may at any time by law make or alter such regulations, except as to the places of choosing Councilors.

The Council on War and Peace shall assemble at least once in every year, as prescribed by law.

Sect. 13. The Council on War and Peace shall be the judge of the elections, returns, and qualifications of its own members, and a majority shall constitute a quorum to do business; but a smaller number may adjourn from day to day, and may be authorized to compel the attendance of absent members, in such manner, and under such penalties as law may provide.

The Council on War and Peace shall choose its own officers.

The Council on War and Peace may determine the rules of its proceedings, punish its members for disorderly behavior, and, with the concurrence of two-thirds, expel a member.

The Council on War and Peace shall keep a journal of its proceedings, and from time to time publish the same; and the yeas and nays of the members on any question shall be entered on the journal.

Sect. 14. The councilors shall receive a compensation for their services, to be ascertained by law, and paid out of the treasury of the United States. They shall in all cases, except treason, felony and breach of the peace, be privileged from arrest during their attendance at the session, and in going to and returning from the same; and for any speech or debate in the Council on War and Peace, they shall not be questioned in any other place.

No Councilor shall, during the time for which he was elected, be appointed to any civil or military office under the authority of the United States, which shall have been created, or the emoluments whereof shall have been increased during such time; and no person holding any office under the United States, shall be a member during his continuance in office.

Sect. 15. Every declaration of war or letter of marque or reprisal which shall have passed the Council on War and Peace, shall, before it become a law, be presented to the President of the United States; if he approve he shall sign it, but if not he shall return it, with his objections to that Council on War and Peace, who shall enter the objections at large on their journal, and proceed to reconsider it.

The Council on War and Peace may not override a presidential negative. It may, after mature consideration, present a revised declaration of war or letter of marque or reprisal to the President for his approval.

If any declaration of war or letter of marque or reprisal shall not be returned by the President within ten days (Sundays excepted) after it shall have been presented to him, the same shall be a law, in like manner as if he had signed it, unless the Council on War and Peace by their adjournment prevent its return, in which case it shall not be a law.

The question that the amendment is designed to answer is how to ensure both the rule of law and the republican character of the government in its foreign affairs, especially during times of war: how to prevent a peacetime president from becoming a wartime dictator by declaring war on his own authority, as kings and emperors always have. The irony in this is that the basic "nature" of war itself is violated whenever kings and dictatorial presidents both declare the desired ends and command the operational means, as they have for more than five thousand years. Only by dividing the declaring of the desired ends from the commanding of operational means can war be made rationally coherent, instrumental, and "subject to reason alone," according to both Madison and Clausewitz (Clausewitz 1976, 89).

The primary function of the amendment, then, is to ensure the rule of law by establishing the proper relationship between the "government" and the "commander" in foreign affairs. This is accomplished by ensuring that the ratification of treaties and the decision for war or peace are made by a corporate speaker in the procedurally perfect manner of all corporate speech acts. This enables the declarer to establish a coherent, organic Clausewitzian ends-means/ideal-in-process relationship between the "government" and the "commander." Furthermore, since the corporate speaker is mandated to make fully reasoned, solemn, conditional, and absolute declarations of war, the full potential of the declaration to facilitate conflict resolution is unlocked.

At a more pragmatic level, the purpose of the amendment is to take the decision for war or peace away from the president, where it now lies, and keep it away. This is accomplished by establishing an institution whose very integrity and existence depends upon its making sure that neither the president nor the Congress infringes upon its powers to decide the question of war or peace, to declare war, to grant letters of marque and reprisal, and to ratify treaties. An active, independent, and jealous institution would now exist to sustain the rule of law and to eliminate the present constitutional ambiguity. One and only one department of government, the Council on War and Peace, would decide the question of war or peace, declare war, grant letters of marque or reprisal, and ratify treaties, appealing to the courts whenever either the president or the Congress attempted to infringe its powers.

In this regard, the pragmatic purpose of the amendment is the same as that of the *collegium fetialis* in early republican Rome or the judiciary in the Constitution. In both cases, an institution was established 1) to accomplish a specialized task that requires a particular knowledge, experience, and skill and 2) to create a corps of experts. For the *fetiales*, their special knowledge, experience, and skill lay in the negotiation of treaties and conditional declarations of war, the diplomatic skills of a foreign service. For the judiciary, their special knowledge, experience, and skill constitute the link that connects the general to the specific, the law to the case. Over time, both the *collegium fetialis* and the judiciary create a body of systematized experience and precedent that maps out the relationship of general legal principles to specific situations of fact. As a result, decisions are, more frequently than not, grounded upon the well-considered experience of many similar cases. Perspective and depth inform the decision, and not simply the gut reactions of a single official.

Equally important, both the *collegium fetialis* and the judiciary have created a corps of experienced experts versed in the application of their respective bodies of systemized experience. Lessons learned in one generation are not lost because a dedicated corps of experts – the judiciary for the law, the *collegium fetialis* for war – existed possessing the required institutional memory.

And, finally, in all logic, the responsibility to ratify treaties cannot be withheld from the Council on War and Peace. As with the *collegium fetialis* in republican Rome, the logic of including the treaty-ratification power is entirely natural and obvious. Bodin conjoined the two in his second mark of sovereignty, "to denounce warre, or treat of peace." Locke did the same with his fœderative power, which "contains the power of war and peace, leagues and alliances, and all the transactions, with all persons and communities without the common-wealth," as did Montesquieu with his second power, which makes "peace or war, sends or receives embassies, establishes the public security, and provides against invasions." To separate the power to treat for peace from the power to declare war does not make much sense. The body that articulates the nation's initial peace terms/war aims is the only body qualified to accept or reject the final – no doubt much changed – conditions found in the eventual peace treaty

In addition, such a change would relieve the Senate of the burden of giving its "advice and consent" to treaties, without losing a check on the president. Instead of an overburdened and distracted Senate discharging this fœderative function, a specialized branch would now do so. Thus relieved, the Senate could devote more time to the peacetime aspects of foreign affairs, especially to its exercise of the "power of the purse" with regard to foreign affairs. Such a change would further rationalize the structure of the Constitution and make that structure more solid and durable.

By way of commentary, sections 1 to 5 are exceptionally narrowly drawn. They do not include the legislative power to "make rules concerning captures on land and water," which remains with the Congress. Equally important, the Congress retains the "power of the purse."

Section 4 lists three cases in which an absolute declaration of war is called for: 1) situations as in 1898 when a conditional declaration has already been made, 2) situations as in the 1941 surprise attack on Pearl Harbor by Imperial Japan, or 3) situations as in 1983 when Ronald Reagan invaded Grenada after the unexpected murder of the prime minister.

Despite how grossly unfair it is to the reader, section 5 also elaborates the full potential of the power "to grant Letters of Marque and Reprisal." Unfortunately, to explain how and why the Council on War and Peace should establish a coherent, organic ends-means/ideal-in-process relationship for what were once called "private" wars but are now called "secret" or "covert" wars would take another book. I, therefore, take the liberty to point out the potential, allowing for others to fill in the blanks (e.g., Lobel 1995; Sidak 2005).

Sections 6 and 7 cover the purpose and intention of the amendment. Section 6 states explicitly that the purpose is to respect the speech act character of declaring war and granting a letter of marque or reprisal. It requires that procedurally perfect, fully reasoned declarations of war be drafted, debated, amended, and voted up or down. Section 7 states explicitly that any imperfect presidential or congressional declarations are illegal, illegitimate, and unconstitutional. Presidential findings or commissions for private war are also condemned.

Sections 8 and 9 allow the council both to defend its own powers and to enforce the ban on unconstitutionally declared war. The ability to appeal to the courts and to submit a bill of impeachment is vital because the council does not possess the "power of the purse," which is what gives the Congress its ability to defend itself against the president on issues other than war.

Section 10, the council is limited to fifty members on the model of the Second Continental Congress. Fifty-six members eventually signed the Declaration of Independence, but of course not all the members were present at all the debates all the time, and six to twelve were absent at any one time (Hazleton 1970 [1906], Ch XI; Wills 1979, 341; Jillson and Wilson 1994, 10, 117). Thus, on the basis of the experience of the Second Continental Congress, fifty appears to be a good number for the group that drafts, debates, and votes solemn declarations of war. Still, for reasons of group dynamics, to alleviate the still present transaction costs, coordination of shared interests, and collective action problems, a smaller number might be better. For example, the fifteen-member United Nations Security Conucil might provide an alternative model. Under chapters VI and VII, it discharges essentially fœderative powers in a highly successful manner.

Councilors would be elected by state legislatures, the way senators were elected before the ratification of the Seventeenth Amendment in 1913, although one might consider appointment by the president and confirmation by the Senate as an alternative. One assumes that "favorite sons" with wide experience, toward the end of their careers and reasonably well known to the members of a state legislature, would be chosen. Popular election is not an option because funding statewide campaigns would be impractical. How would they be financed? Who would donate money to a candidate whose only campaign promise was not to send fathers and sons, mothers and daughters, into harm's way, except when it was truly necessary?

The age minimum of forty years is to ensure that experienced, and presumably wise, people would be chosen.

Since two of the primary functions of the council are to facilitate the initial steps toward conflict resolution and to ensure the establishment of a Clausewitzian coherent and organic ends-means/ideal-in-process relationship with the president as commander in chief, no need exists for the council to possess classified information for the declaring of public war. Classified information may be useful for determining when to open armed hostilities, but not for the declaring of public war, most notably conditional declarations. Should any doubt on this point exist, the tragic experience of George W. Bush should suffice. The "people" should never be asked to support a war on the basis of "secret" intelligence. The fissure that separates the amity of peace from the enmity of war is always public knowledge; it is never secret. Naturally, confidential information is needed to grant a letter of marque or reprisal for a secret private war. But this should be the exceptional case, to be avoided as far as possible. Secret operations seldom come to any good, as the Bay of Pigs operation demonstrates.

Sections 11–14 deal with administrative matters. Section 15 provides for a presidential negative on the council's declarations, but no override. If the president vetoes a declaration, then the declaration is clearly neither timely nor prudent. The imprudence of venturing upon a war that is opposed by the commander should be obvious. That the Athenian Assembly appointed Nicias one of the commanders of the Sicilian expedition after he had voiced strong misgivings should be demonstration enough (Thucydides 1982, VI, 8–25). Of greater consequence, though, presidential disapproval means that the council has failed to establish a coherent, organic Clausewitzian ends-means/ideal-in-process relationship with him. Under such circumstances, the council must reevaluate its thinking and its position to take into account the president's objections.

Since the Congress also retains its "power of the purse," the ability of the Council on War and Peace to declare war or grant a letter of marque or reprisal is restrained by a double check: the president's veto and the Congress's refusal to fund the enterprise.

9 A Congressional Work-Around

The Congress shall have power ... to declare war, grant letters of marque and reprisal, and make rules concerning captures on land and water.

> (article I, section 8, clause 11)

Each House may determine the rules of its proceedings.

> (article I, section 5, clause 2)

Short of an amendment to the Constitution, how might the Congress regain the initiative to decide on and draft its own declarations of war? For, he who controls the drafting largely controls the decision for war or peace. The answer, of course, is to enable the Congress to set its own agenda independently of the president. Not, of course, in all matters, most especially, not in terms of its peacetime lawmaking. For its peacetime lawmaking, presidential agenda setting and leadership are absolutely essential for two reasons: first, because of the need for close executive-legislative coordination and, second, for the purpose of overcoming the inherent problems of any large, majority-rule organization characterized by extremely high transaction costs, great difficulty in coordinating shared interests, and large collective action problems. Without strong leadership from the nation's chief executive, the passing of appropriate and timely peacetime legislation would be impossible, as more than two hundred years of congressional history demonstrates. But war is not peace, and a declaration of war is not like an earmark for a "bridge to nowhere." Different rules and procedures need to apply to the wartime and peacetime duties of the Congress.

More properly, the structural problem is to understand how and why the change from a committee-of-the-whole to a standing-committee organization created two insuperable barriers to the Congress's initiating a procedurally perfect, fully reasoned declaration of war. The first barrier is related to quality – the inability of members to gain the required expertise. The second relates to quantity – the sheer number of members and the volume of their workload. The relationship between the two barriers is inverse: as quantity increases quality decreases. This makes it virtually impossible for the Congress to take the initiative to draft, debate, and vote its own fully reasoned declarations of war, as the Second Continental Congress did.

THE COMMITTEE-OF-THE-WHOLE SYSTEM

By way of introduction, it is important to remember that the modern standing-committee system is a nineteenth-century American invention. Previously, all legislative bodies had operated on a committee-of-the-whole system, from the Roman *comitia* to the Major Council of Venice to the Grand Council of St. Gall. Not surprisingly, then, all the colonial legislatures were small bodies organized on the committee-of-the-whole system, as were the First and Second Continental Congresses, which consisted of fifty-six delegates, not all of whom were present at any one time. The same was true of the Confederal Congress. Standing committees were, of course, not unknown, but their functions were executive, not legislative. For example, to manage the conduct of the revolution, the Second Continental Congress had appointed fifteen standing committees with executive functions by 1776, Committees on Cannon, Clothing, Medicine, and Secret Correspondence, among others (*Journals of the Continental Congress* 1904–37, 6:1061–8). What is unprecedented is the modern American invention of nonexecutive standing committees, of a legislature systematically organized so that most of its work is done in a set of preestablished, permanent legislative committees of limited membership and determinate jurisdiction (Jillson and Wilson 1994, 23).

The difference between a committee-of-the-whole and a standing-committee regime is, perhaps, best seen in the architecture of their respective legislative halls. Legislative halls constructed before 1800 for committee-of-the-whole regimes are all large and do not have adjacent committee meeting rooms or private offices for the members. Examples include the State House in Philadelphia, where the Continental Congresses met, and the enormous, ornate hall of the Major Council in the Doge's Palace in Venice, which is surrounded by even more ornate smaller chambers for meetings of the republic's executive committees. The doge's private apartment is also housed in the palace. Another example is St. Stephen's Chapel, where the House of Commons met until Westminster Palace was destroyed by fire in 1834. A vaulted Gothic chapel easily accommodates large assemblies that always meet as a single group but cannot accommodate numerous small committee meetings. And, where would one put a large number of private offices in a Gothic chapel?

Legislative halls constructed after 1800, such as the rebuilt Westminster, surround large meeting chambers with members' offices and meeting rooms. As the number of members and committees increases, large adjacent office buildings are also constructed, such as at the Capitol in Washington, with its surrounding office complexes for the members of the House and Senate and their staff. The noble families that composed the Venetian Major Council would no doubt be envious. They had to stand during sessions and had no meeting rooms, no private offices, no staff, but, then, no committee meetings to attend, either.

If the physical difference between a committee-of-the-whole and a standing-committee regime is best seen in the architecture of their respective legislative halls, the practical political difference turns on whether one views the new standing committees positively or negatively. Viewing them positively, one emphasizes legislative action and efficiency:

> The old system of discussion in Committee of the Whole, under slight control, was wrecked by its cumbersome procedures. The transfer of responsibility from Committee of the Whole to a substantial number of standing committees and the consequent subdivision of labor and opportunity for specialization of members' interests and competence made the House, under [Henry] Clay's direction, an effective instrument of action. (White 1951, 56; Jillson and Wilson 1994).

Viewing them negatively, one emphasizes, as Thomas Jefferson did, the need for full and extensive deliberation, the need to preclude precipitous action, or the need to prevent special interest legislation. In Dumas Malone's paraphrase:

> If he [Jefferson] were to view the procedures of Congress today, however, he would probably be disturbed by one major departure from the recommendations he based on the time-honored practices of the House of Commons. He laid great emphasis on the committee of the whole house, as his party did in the 1790's. The idea was that matters of general concern should be considered by the whole body in the first place, under conditions which permitted everybody to speak. Only after the sense of the meeting had been made manifest should an important measure be referred to a small special committee for the working out of details. His desire to guard the interests of minorities by means of ordered procedures was supplemented by his concern that the legislature serve the general good against particular interests. He wanted Congress to be a genuinely deliberative body, not a register of decisions reached by small groups working behind the curtain. In the House of Representatives, which had not formally approved his *Manual* [*of Parliamentary Practice for the Use of the Senate of the United States* (1801)], the period following the War of 1812, was marked by a decline in the importance of the committee of the whole and the rise of the standing committees. This trend may have increased

legislative effectiveness, but these committees could be appointed by Speakers to serve special interests. Henry Clay packed the committee on manufactures with pro-tariff advocates [and the Committee on Foreign Relations with pro-war advocates in 1811–12]. Nothing comparable to this specialization occurred in the House of Commons for a couple of generations, if indeed it ever did, and one may assume that Jefferson would approve of the present procedures in Parliament more than of the rigid system of standing committees in the American Congress. (1948–81, 3:457)

At the risk of offending Thomas Jefferson, the simple fact of the matter is that, whereas a committee-of-the-whole system is entirely appropriate for the simplicity of an agricultural society, its inefficiency immediately condemns it in the ever-growing complexity of an industrial society.

The great irony of this condemnation, however, is that the shift from the committee-of-the-whole to the standing-committee system little affected the proper functioning of all the congressional functions and powers, except the mandate to declare war and grant letters of marque or reprisal. That is only to say more precisely that the standing-committee system offers many benefits for the management of the innumerable peacetime duties of the Congress in an increasingly complex modern society, but none for its single wartime duty.

A QUESTION OF QUANTITY

Before beginning, two initial points must be made: First, the Senate, until well into the nineteenth century, was too small and politically too insignificant to be of any concern. Laws were initiated and passed in the House, while the Senate reviewed and agreed to them. It is, therefore, to the House that one must look for the organizational change analyzed here; later, as the Senate became larger and more politically active, it too would forsake Jefferson's *Manual* and its committee-of-the-whole structure and adopt the standing-committee organization of the House, with all the consequences thereto.

Second, although the changes and their effects on the Congress would not be complete until the end of the nineteenth century, they were sufficiently manifest by 1812 to allow President James Madison, Speaker of the House Henry Clay, and the War Hawks to set the precedents that would transfer the decision for war or peace to a "solicitous" president and the drafting of congressional declarations to the State Department, leaving a "cooperative" Congress with the role of town crier, a story already told in Chapter 2. Thus, the critical period during which the Congress lost its power to decide and declare war occurred during the interval between 1789 and 1812. What then occurred during this critical thirty-three-year interval?

Much happened. For, 1789 not only marks a revolution in the constitution of republican government, it also marks – more or less – the beginning of the Industrial Revolution, one of the less anticipated consequences of which was to transform radically the internal organization of the Congress. Basically, the world became very much more complicated; the country grew very much larger; the representatives in the House became very much more numerous; and the traditional committee-of-the-whole organization broke down under the accumulated stress to be replaced in fits and starts by the modern standing-committee organization of today.

Recall just how complicated the world suddenly became at the end of the eighteenth century: In 1764, James Hargreaves invented the spinning jenny. By 1779, Samuel Crompton's much improved spinning mule sharply increased productivity. This was followed in 1785 by Edmund Cartwright's mechanical loom and in 1793 by Eli Whitney's cotton gin. James Watt's first steam engine was installed in 1776. Robert Fulton's steamboat appeared on the Hudson River in 1807, and George Stephenson's first steam locomotive chugged along on its rails at four miles per hour in 1814. Samuel Morse's telegraph was just over the horizon. As Alexander Hamilton announced in his 5 December 1791 *Report of the Secretary of Treasury on the subject of manufactures*, "The expediency of encouraging manufactures in the United States, which was not long since deemed very questionable, appears at this time to be pretty generally admitted" (Hamilton 1961–87, 10:230).

Not only was the world changing rapidly and radically, the country was doubling in population and size before the ink was dry on the Constitution, before its radical innovations could be tested and adjusted. In the twenty years between 1790 and 1810, the country's population went from 3,929,214 to 7,239,881 (U.S. Census Bureau 2009); the country's size doubled and reached the Pacific Ocean with the purchase of the Louisiana Territory in 1803, and five more states joined by 1812 (Vermont in 1791, Kentucky in 1792, Tennessee in 1796, Ohio in 1803, and Louisiana in 1812). In response to all this doubling, the House of Representatives also more than doubled from sixty-five members in 1789 to a hundred and forty-three in 1811. As the country continued to grow and the Industrial Revolution spread, the number of representatives would more than double again by 1873 to two hundred and ninety-two, before stabilizing in 1913 at four hundred and thirty-five. Under the pressure of all these changes and growth, the workload of the members also grew exponentially. How were an ever-larger number of representatives to keep up with an ever-changing world that imposed an ever-growing workload?

The answer was obvious enough: just follow "the old rule of procuring dispatch by dividing the labor," as Representative Nathaniel Macon from North Carolina reminded his colleagues during the debate on Tuesday, 12 November

1811, to organize the select committees for the Twelfth Congress (*Annals of Congress*, 12th Cong., 1st sess., 340). Instead of a hundred and forty-three members trying to comprehend every nuance of each piece of legislation in an unwieldy committee of the whole, a small committee could do the heavy lifting and report back its results. Still, "procuring dispatch" proved to be a double-edged sword. On the positive side, this increase in congressional efficiency facilitated closer executive-legislative coordination. As Joseph Cooper observed, "What occurred, both before and even more after 1810, was the establishment of close relations between department heads and committees charged with subjects of major interest to them" (1965, 60). On the negative side, establishing close relations with committee members also facilitated a presidential strategy of "divide and conquer." If the small committee could be captured, its report could be manipulated to produce the desired executive result. For example, the Department of State could draft the Committee on Foreign Relations declaration of war. As Cooper continues:

> In their effort to dominate these committees and use them as instruments of its will the executive admitted them into its confidence. This augmented the prestige of these committees, ... and their members. Because their members were vastly better informed than other members and because they were regarded as spokesmen for the Administration, the House began to look up to these committees and to rely on them. (*ibid.*)

Despite its greater efficiency, the adoption of a standing-committee system got off to a slow and rough start. On Wednesday, 26 October 1791, the second day of the First Session of the Second Congress, in the House, a resolution was "laid on the table contemplating the appointment of a Committee of Contested Elections." Representative Samuel Livermore of New Hampshire immediately protested: "He totally disapproved of the idea of delegating to a committee this power of judging [a contested election], expressly given to them by the Constitution. Such a transfer of power, he conceived, would be as unconstitutional as to delegate Legislative authority" (*Annals of Congress*, 2nd Cong., 1st sess., 144–5). The compromise finally agreed to was that the House Committee of Contested Elections "should examine the evidences brought forward, arrange them, and lay then in order before the House for their information; but then he [Alexander White of Virginia] insisted on the necessity of letting the determination depend upon a vote of the House" (*ibid.*, 145). The template for the yet-to-be standing-committee system was now in the record. Two years later, on Monday, 2 December 1793, the first day of the First Session of the Third Congress, just after resolving to appoint two chaplains, the House resolved to appoint, not just a Committee on Elections, but a *standing* Committee on Elections. This committee, then, became the first of all the twenty-four standing committees that manage the mountain of congressional business in the House today (*Annals of Congress*, 3d Cong., 1st sess., 134).

From this halting beginning, by 4 November 1811, the Monday on which the Twelfth Congress first met, the House was operating under a complex system of four different types of committees. Much business was still conducted as a committee of the whole. In addition, standing committees, ad hoc committees, and select committees divided the labor to procure dispatch and to facilitate presidential leadership and agenda setting.

The standing committees were nine by the time of the Twelfth Congress: 1) the Committee on Elections, of course; 2) the Committee of Accounts; 3) the Committee of Claims; 4) the Committee of Commerce and Manufactures; 5) the Committee for the District of Columbia; 6) the Committee on the Post Office and Post Roads, 7) the Committee on the Public Lands, 8) the Committee of Revisal and Unfinished Business; and 9) the Committee of Ways and Means (*Annals of Congress*, 12th Cong., 1st sess., 332–4). The names of the committees are important. They show the trends in the congressional workload. They indicate on what the members were spending most of their time and energy; what was of most concern to their constituents. Notably, the bulk of the members' time and energy was not devoted to foreign, military, or naval affairs, as was the case for the members of the Second Continental Congress in 1776. In 1812, most of the members' time and energy was devoted to domestic, peacetime issues, claims by their constituents of one sort or another.

The ad hoc committees were too numerous to count. The procedure for their establishment was on a motion:

> On motion of Mr. Gold, a committee was appointed to inquire into the expediency of providing by law for the more convenient taking of recognisances of bail and affidavits in cases depending in the respective Courts of United States; with leave to report a bill. – Mr. Gold, Mr. Milnor, and Mr. Ridgely, were appointed the committee. (*Annals of Congress*, 12th Cong., 1st sess., 344)

Notice the subtle shift. "[T]he expediency of providing by law for the more convenient taking of recognisances of bail and affidavits" was not first "considered by the whole body," as Jefferson recommended. Nor was "the sense of the whole meeting" made manifest before a committee was appointed to report a bill. Instead, dispatch was procured by shunting the "inquiry" and drafting responsibilities off to an ad hoc committee without a general discussion. The whole House was no longer either involved or in charge, its attention and interests having been fractured and divided, unlike the Second Continental Congress in 1776, whose whole attention and interest were always and entirely focused on the war. True, Representative Thomas Ruggles Gold's "inquiry" was not of the moment and importance of the

Declaration of Independence, but importance and moment are not the issues here; procedures are.

Naturally, after an ad hoc committee had completed its work, it of course reported back to the committee of the whole, "Mr. [Benjamin] Tallmadge, from the committee appointed on the petition of Abraham Whipple, presented a bill for relief of Abraham Whipple; which was read and committed to a Committee of the Whole on Friday next" (*ibid.*). As is to be expected, the questions submitted to these ad hoc committees dealt entirely with the domestic and peacetime concerns of the members' constituents.

Select committees were of two kinds: those that dealt with topics deemed too important for ad hoc committees and those that arose out of the president's Annual Message. An example of the former is:

> Mr. [George] Poindexter presented a petition of sundry inhabitants of the Mississippi Territory, praying that the said Territory may be made into a separate State and admitted into the Union. – Referred to a select committee.
>
> Mr. Poindexter, Mr. Grundy, Mr. Ormsby, Mr. Lacock, Mr. Wilson, Mr. Widgery, and Mr. Crittenden, were appointed the committee. (*ibid.*)

Again, notice the subtle shift from an inefficient initial consideration of the petition by the committee of the whole to gain "the sense of the meeting" before the appointment of a select committee and the very much more efficient immediate shunting of the petition to a select committee. Also, this first type of select committee dealt with the domestic and peacetime issues that concerned the members' constituents most directly.

The latter type of select committee is very much more relevant to the inability of the Congress to declare war. On Tuesday, 5 November 1811, the second day of the session, President James Madison's Annual Message was read in both Chambers. While many topics were discussed – Indian affairs, manufactures, the Spanish colonies in South America, which were then declaring their independence, and smuggling and taxation – more than a quarter of the address concerned Anglo-American relations and the need to augment the army, the navy, and the production of small arms and cannon. In light of Madison's August 1811 decision to declare war against Great Britain, this is not unexpected. Yet, the only passage that might be construed as a call to arms is less than ringing:

> With this evidence of hostile inflexibility [by Britain], in trampling on rights which no independent nation can relinquish, Congress will feel the duty of putting the United States into an armor and an attitude demanded by the crisis, and corresponding with the national spirit and expectations. (*ibid.*, 13)

The following week, on Tuesday, 12 November 1811, "the House resolved itself into a Committee of the Whole on the state of the Union, in order to take into consideration the Message of the President of the United States, at the opening of the session" (*ibid.*, 334–5). By the end of the day, in a stunning example of presidential agenda setting, the House had divided the president's message into nine tasks and referred three of those tasks to standing committees and the remaining six to select committees, which it then appointed: 1) the select Committee on Foreign Relations, 2) the select Committee on Indian Affairs, 3) the select Committee on Military Affairs, 4) the select Committee on Naval Affairs, 5) the select Committee on Small Arms and Cannon, and 6) the select Committee on Spanish-American Colonies. Needless to say, Henry Clay used his prerogative as Speaker of the House to appoint War Hawks to the key committees: Foreign Relations, Military Affairs, and Naval Affairs (*ibid.*, 342–3).

The importance of the establishment of these key select committees is not that President Madison, with Speaker Clay's able assistance, was able to pack them, important as that may be. Nor does it lie in the way in which the president was setting the congressional agenda. By 1811, all recognized the vital need for presidential leadership and agenda setting. Rather, the importance is, on the one hand, how the select committees had subtly changed the whole dynamic of the legislative process, and, on the other hand, how standing/ select committee system deprived the members of the needed expertise to draft, debate, and vote on fully reasoned declarations of war.

A CHANGED DYNAMIC

As Jefferson would have noted, on 12 November 1811, before the appointment of the select committees, a general discussion of the president's Annual Message took place. However, the discussion was not focused on any specific resolutions or on determining "the sense of the meeting." Rather, it emphasized agenda co-option. Instead of creating an independent congressional agenda, the discussion centered on adopting the president's legislative agenda and appointing the members to either the standing or the select committees required to implement his agenda. Most pointedly, on the question of war or peace, no general discussion took place in the committee of the whole to ascertain the sense of the House. Consider the difference between 1776 and 1811–2: On Friday, 7 June 1776, Richard Henry Lee had introduced the three Virginia resolutions. Before any of the ad hoc committees was appointed, a general debate occurred over three days among the fewer than fifty delegates then present. This general debate ascertained the sense of the meeting, which, not surprisingly, was ambivalent. The members were not yet for independence, but they were not completely against it either. Whether for or against, the three Virginia resolutions had clearly defined the question and enabled a general debate. More, the general debate was not over. In the interim, however, an ad hoc committee was appointed for each resolution on Tuesday, 11 June 1776, and instructed to report later with more detailed language. A month later, on Monday, 1 July 1776, the committee of the whole took up again the resolution on independence and approved it, still in general terms. Only after "the sense of the meeting had been made manifest" by the vote on premise of the resolution did the Second Continental Congress then address itself to the detailed language of the draft Declaration of Independence, which it debated and amended for three days, taking its final vote on Thursday, 4 July 1776.

On 12 November 1811, the sense of the meeting was not made manifest. The somewhat fewer than one hundred and forty-three members of the House present that day were not asked to debate President Madison's August decision to declare war against Great Britain. Few of the members and none of the public knew of it. Instead, the House was asked to establish a select Committee on Foreign Relations that would consider "the duty of putting the United States into an armor and an attitude demanded by the crisis, and corresponding with the national spirit and expectations," whatever that means. Seven months later, on 1 June 1812, when a "solicitous" President Madison sent a second message explicitly requesting a declaration of war against Britain to this "cooperative" Congress, the deal was already done. The State Department had already written the committee's war manifesto and declaration of war, and the very select Committee on Foreign Relations had long since decided to report its recommendation for war and against peace. The question when the House resolved to sit as a committee of the whole on 4 June 1812 was not so much whether war was desirable or undesirable but, critically, whether to accept the best judgment of the select Committee on Foreign Relations and the president or to oppose their best judgment. The subtle displacement of the question is not insignificant. The interjection of the select committee turned the legislative process on its head: "The ultimate result was that by 1825 the role of the committee of the whole had been transformed from that of initial decider of the principles of important subjects to that of reviewer of the recommendations and plans of smaller committees" (Cooper 1965, 62).

Whereas the Second Continental Congress, as a corporate body, clearly and unequivocally initiated the question of war or peace and then decided for war and against peace as a committee of the whole in 1776, the Twelfth Congress did not do the same in 1812. Instead, President James Madison initiated and made the decision in August 1811, while relaxing at home on vacation. His decision was next adopted by the very select Committee on Foreign Relations and, finally, endorsed by the House and Senate. More, because the Twelfth Congress did not draft, debate, or vote on its own declaration, but passed the unreasoned, absolute declaration written by the State Department, it unlocked none of the conflict resolution potential of a conditional declaration; nor did it establish an organic ends-means/ideal-in-process relationship with President Madison as commander in chief. All it did was to endorse the Committee on Foreign Relation's endorsement of President Madison's August decision. This double endorsement cannot possibly be the meaning of a *congressional* power to declare war. An "endorsement" is not a "declaration."

Once again, it must be emphasized, this displacement of the final vote from the issue itself to the acceptance or rejection of the dual recommendation of the president and the modern standing committees has had few, if any, deleterious effects on all the other peacetime powers and functions of the Congress. Indeed, the increased efficiency of the standing-committee system has made it possible for the Congress to meet its peacetime responsibilities despite the ever-growing complexity of modern societies.

To drive this point home, consider another similar and very successful procedural adjustment: Many have argued that the stunning increase in international executive agreements since World War II is but another example of how the "imperial presidency" circumvents the clear dictates of the Constitution, the need for Senate "advice and consent" on treaties in this case. Yet, upon closer examination, the use of executive agreements is seen to be an effective adaptation by both the president and the Senate Foreign Relations Committee to the unimagined increase in the quantity and technical detail of international agreements since World War II. Working cooperatively through the Circular 175 (C-175) procedure, the Senate Foreign Relations Committee staff and the Office of the Assistant Legal Adviser for Treaty Affairs in the State Department have thoroughly streamlined and modernized the process, institutionalizing the decision as to which international agreements will go forward as treaties for "advice and consent" and which will not (Krutz and Peake, 2009).

Still, for all of its success in adapting to the peacetime needs of modern society, the standing-committee system has failed entirely to meet the constitutional need for someone other than the president to decide the question of war or peace and to declare war. This is because war is not peace, and the ways of peace are not the ways of war. More than two hundred years of American history demonstrate that the modern standing-committee system frustrates all attempts of the Congress to exercise its power to decide and declare war. Instead of the Congress's deciding the question, the president does, as kings and emperors always have.

A QUESTION OF QUALITY: A DEGRADATION OF EXPERTISE

But it is not just the subtle displacement of the question that frustrates the Congress's ability to declare war. It is also the lack of expertise. For, an increase in quantity inevitably leads to a decrease in quality. The comparison, again, is between the Second Continental Congress and the post-1812 Congresses.

Unquestionably, the members of the Second Continental Congress were highly qualified experts on the question at hand, on the causes of the conflict between Great Britain and its North American colonies. If one were looking for the most knowledgeable and experienced experts on this conflict in 1776, the fifty or so delegates gathered at the State House in Philadelphia would be the people one was looking for. Unlike the members of Lord North's government in London, who were constantly distracted by other matters, the fifty or so men gathered at the State House had been intently focused upon British-American relations for more than a decade, since at least 1765 and the Stamp Act Congress. Several, such as Benjamin Franklin, had served in London as agents for their colonies. The delegates knew both sides of the issue, inside and out. When time came to indict and denounce the casus belli, no other group in the world was better prepared to discharge the responsibility.

In contrast, since 1789, how many members of the U.S. Congress have had either the inclination or, of supreme importance, the time to study, to learn, and truly to understand the casus belli of any of America's many wars? How many members could claim the depth of thought and understanding that informed the members of the Second Continental Congress in 1776? How many members were truly qualified to indict the gravamina, denounce them, and articulate the peace terms that would resolve the conflict at hand?

The answer, of course, is none. Since 1789, the U.S. Congress has been like Lord North's government in London, constantly distracted by other matters, by the ever-expanding complexity of its peacetime responsibilities. The issue, therefore, is not the indolence of the members. Rather, it is their constant distraction, the insatiable demands of their domestic peacetime duties. As an extreme example, what little time most of the members of the Congress gave to the impending world war between 1933, when Hitler took power, and 7 December 1941 was devoted to vociferously opposing any American involvement and passionately advocating "America First" policies. Then, suddenly, on 8 December 1941, all but one member voted for war against Imperial Japan, their precipitous vote that day resulting, not from years of thoughtful deliberation and debate, as in 1776, but from sudden shock and angry outrage at the attack on Pearl Harbor.

But how can the members develop the expertise? How can the members develop the special knowledge, experience, and skill needed to indict the gravamina as well as to propose meaningful peace terms, when the standing-committee system systematically pushes them in the opposite direction? For example, while Representative Gold and his ad hoc committee were inquiring into the expediency of providing by law for the more convenient taking of recognisances of bail and affidavits in cases depending in the respective courts of the United States; and Representative Tallmadge and his ad hoc committee were presenting a bill for relief of Abraham Whipple; and Representative Poindexter and his select committee were evaluating a petition of sundry inhabitants of the Mississippi Territory, praying that the said territory might be made into a separate state and admitted into the Union; and the other members were overwhelmed by attending committee meetings on the domestic concerns and business of their constituents, the Committee on Foreign Relations had already reached agreement with President Madison on the question of war or peace.

Instead of thoughtful deliberation, as Jefferson advocated, what the standing-committee system fosters is the "opportunity for specialization of members' interests and competence" in the specific area of the committee's jurisdiction. This means that, at best, only the members of the House and Senate committees on foreign relations, perhaps, armed services, also, will have the opportunity to develop the required knowledge, experience, and skill to declare war to a level somewhat comparable to that of the members of the Second Continental Congress. This is clearly inadequate if the *Congress*, the whole Congress, is to discharge its responsibility to declare war.

To probe this problem more fully, consider by analogy the following counterfactual: Imagine that Article III establishing the judiciary had not been written. Imagine that the argument was made in 1787 that the Congress should adjudicate the law as well as legislate it, because he who makes the law best understands the laws he makes. All arguments about congressional intent are eliminated if the Congress interprets the laws it has made. In 1787, this was not an entirely fanciful hypothesis. The Congress met for six months or less; that left the members unemployed for half a year or more. Why not employ them full time? The members would meet at the Capitol for four or five months a year to legislate and then scatter to their home districts to adjudicate for the balance of the year. In the eighteenth century, the workloads of both the courts and the Congress were not overwhelming or prohibitive.

But, if the hypothesis was not entirely fanciful in 1787, it soon became so. Under current workloads, with the Congress sitting twelve months a year, how would this fanciful hypothetical work? In the afternoon, after the members had provided constituent services, reconciled conflicting interests, overseen the executive departments, and voted on funding for "bridges to nowhere" – not to mention raising several thousands of dollars for their upcoming campaign – they would retire to hear court cases. Even on the assumption that the members had the required legal expertise, would they have the time?

But this is precisely what the members are asked to do with regard to the congressional power to declare war and grant letters of marque or reprisal.

Needless to say, it cannot be done, as more than two hundred years of congressional history demonstrate conclusively. Consequently, the best solution is to amend the Constitution, as was advocated in the previous chapter. Should that prove politically impossible, a second best solution lies in a further division of labor, in smuggling a corporate body organized as a committee of the whole into the Congress as an appendage. But, critically, the division of labor is not for the purpose of procuring dispatch. Quite the contrary: this appendage is for procuring deliberation by a small body of experts, a nonpartisan body with the leisure, interest, and desire to acquire a level of knowledge, experience, and skill equivalent to that of the members of the Second Continental Congress in 1776. Again, the best way to do this is to establish a fourth pillar of government through a constitutional amendment to establish a Council on War and Peace, as argued in the last chapter. However, should that prove too difficult politically, a congressional work-around is also possible, if very much inferior.

THE NATIONAL WAR POWERS COMMISSION REPORT OF 2008

In 2008, the former Secretaries of State James Baker and Warren Christopher chaired a commission that proposed a draft law, entitled *War Powers Consultation Act of 2009* (*National War Powers Commission Report* 2008). The intent here was to remedy all the sins of omission and commission found in the War Powers Resolution of 1973 by building a robust system of congressional and presidential "consultation." Although some thought the commission's scholarship was thin (Fisher 2008), the basic problem with the proposal, of course, was that it offered the problem yet again as the solution:

> Section 2. Purpose. The purpose of this [proposed] Act is to describe a constructive and practical way in which the judgment of both the President and Congress can be brought to bear when deciding whether the United States should engage in significant armed conflict. (National War Powers Commission Report 2008, 43–4)

One can perhaps be excused for wondering how the commission's desire for "the judgment of both the President and Congress [to] be brought to bear" differs from the 1973 War Powers Resolution's call for "the collective judgment of both the Congress and the President." Likewise, one wonders what separates the commission's call for "consultation" on "significant armed conflict" from the 1973 resolution's "introduction of United States Armed Forces into hostilities, or into situations where imminent involvement in hostilities." The shift from "hostilities" and "imminent involvement in hostilities" to "significant armed conflict" was perhaps an improvement; yet, distinguishing between "significant" and "insignificant armed conflicts" would appear to present exactly the same problems as distinguishing between "imminent" and "not-imminent hostilities." Most significantly, though, like the 1973 resolution, the commission's proposal does not explicitly mandate that the Congress actually declare war, as the Constitution mandates. "Statutory authorizations" are fully acceptable in the eyes of the National Commission.

What the commission hoped for was that, if gentlemen would only act as gentlemen, robust "consultation" by a "solicitous" president with a "cooperative" Congress would soon produce a meeting of minds:

> This [proposed] Act is not meant to define, circumscribe, or enhance the constitutional war powers of either the Executive or Legislative Branches of government, and neither branch by supporting or complying with this Act shall in any way limit or prejudice its right or ability to assert its constitutional war powers or its right or ability to question or challenge the constitutional war powers of the other branch. (*ibid.*, 44)

Beyond doubt, the proposed "consultations" would not "in any way limit or prejudice its right or ability to assert its constitutional war powers or its right or ability to question or challenge the constitutional war powers of the other branch." At the same time, "This Act is [clearly] not meant to define, ... or enhance" the ability of the Congress to declare war.

Yet, despite itself, the proposed draft law does offer some interesting language, most especially its proposed "Joint Congressional Consultation Committee." However, to take advantage of this interesting language, the proposal has to be stood on its head and turned inside out. First, one has to redefine the issue away from facilitating more collegial "consultation" to finding a way for the Congress, and the Congress alone, actually to decide and declare war and grant letters of marque or reprisal on every occasion, not just when the president makes a request by "convening and giving it information." Second, one has to render illegitimate procedurally imperfect declarations of war by either the president or the Congress. And, third, one has to recognize how the standing-committee organization of the bicameral Congress frustrates the ability of the Congress simply to draft on its own initiative declarations of war and grant letters of marque or reprisal in the first place. For, the problem has always been finding a way for the Congress to decide the question of war or peace by picking up a pencil and writing words on the sheet of paper, as Thomas Jefferson did for the unicameral Second Continental Congress.

This last point means that the work-around has to take the "Council on War and Peace" amendment proposed in the last chapter and insert it into a proposed joint committee, now renamed the "Joint Drafting Committee." In this way, the inability of the Congress to draft its own declarations without the aid and assistance of a "solicitous" president and the Department of State is overcome. Once the Congress possesses its own independent "Joint Drafting Committee," it then possesses both an independent initiative and a body with the stature and expertise needed to draft fully reasoned declarations of war modeled on the Declaration of Independence.

A JOINT DRAFTING COMMITTEE

A JOINT RESOLUTION TO ESTABLISH A JOINT CONGRESSIONAL DRAFTING COMMITTEE OF 20XX

WHEREAS, Article I, section 8, clause 11 of the Constitution empowers the Congress alone to effect, establish, and create the state and condition of public war by declaring war solemnly and of private war by granting letters of marque or reprisal; and

WHEREAS, Article I, section 8, clause 11 of the Constitution does not condition this sole power with any qualification whatsoever, such as exercising this congressional power as "the collective judgment of both the Congress and the President," as is suggested in the preamble of the War Powers Resolution of 1973; and,

WHEREAS, despite the silence of Article I, section 8, clause 11 of the Constitution, the procedurally imperfect declaring of public war by either the Congress or the president undermines the republican and democratic character of the nation and its Constitution, just as executive findings or authorizations of private war undermines the congressional power to grant letters of marque or reprisal. Consequently, procedurally imperfect acts by either the Congress or the president must be considered illegitimate and unconstitutional; and,

WHEREAS, in accordance with Hague Convention III, *Relative to the Opening of Hostilities*, one of the larger purposes of the congressional power to declare war and grant letters of marque or reprisal is to take the first necessary steps toward resolving a conflict. This is achieved in the case of public war by declaring war conditionally before declaring war absolutely with fully reasoned declarations. This is achieved in the case of private war by carefully circumscribing the commissions granted in letters of marque or reprisal; and,

WHEREAS, the proper relationship between the congressional powers found in Article I, section 8, clause 11 of the Constitution and the presidential powers as commander-in-chief found in Article II, section 2, clause 1 of the Constitution is that of a coherent, organic ends-means/ideal-in-process relationship, wherein the congressional declaration of public war or its grant of letters of marque or reprisal for private war articulates the nation's political desires or purposes, while the operational control of the diplomatic, economic, or military means rests with the president as commander-in-chief.

NOW THEREFORE BE IT RESOLVED:

Section 1. Short Title.

The War Powers Resolution of 1973, Pub. L. No. 93–148, is hereby repealed. This Resolution shall be cited as the Joint Congressional Drafting Committee Resolution of 20XX.

Section 2. Purpose and Intention.

2(A). The purpose of this resolution is to establish a joint committee of the Congress dedicated solely to the preparation and drafting of fully reasoned, conditional and absolute declarations of public war and carefully circumscribed letters of marque or reprisal for private war.

2(B) The intention of this resolution is to make procedurally imperfect declarations of public war by either the Congress or president illegitimate, illegal, and unconstitutional, as well as making procedurally imperfect executive findings or authorizations for private war illegitimate, illegal, and unconstitutional.

Section 3. Definitions.

3(A). The "Joint Congressional Drafting Committee" consists of:
(i) The Speaker of the U.S. House of Representatives and the Majority Leader of the Senate;
(ii) The Minority Leaders of the House of Representatives and the Senate.

3(B). The Chairmanship and Vice Chairmanship of the Joint Congressional Drafting Committee shall alternate between the Speaker of the House of Representatives and the Majority Leader of the Senate, with the former serving as the Chairman in each odd-numbered Congress and the latter serving as the Chairman in each even-numbered Congress.

Section 4. Staffing.

4(A). The Joint Congressional Drafting Committee shall have two staffs:
(i) The support staff consists of administrative, clerical, and research assistants as needed.
(ii) The Special staff consists of no greater than fifty members.
(iii) Qualifications for service on the Special staff are:
    (a) to have attained to the age of forty years, and
    (b) to have been nine years a citizen of the United States.
(iv) The Special staff is chosen by the members of the Senate and House of Representatives by secret ballot from a slate recommended by the Joint Congressional Drafting Committee,
    (a) for eight years, and
    (b) representing a mix of diplomatic, political, and military experience and expertise.
(v) Immediately after they are assembled in consequence of the first election, the Special staff shall be divided as equally as may be into four classes.
    (a) The seats of the first class shall be vacated at the expiration of the second year,
    (b) of the second class at the expiration of the fourth year,
    (c) of the third class at the expiration of the sixth year, and
    (d) of the fourth class at the expiration of the eighth year,
    (e) so that one-fourth may be chosen every second year; and
    (f) if vacancies happen by resignation, or otherwise, a special election by the members of the Senate and House of Representatives voting by secret ballot from a slate recommended by the Joint Drafting Committee shall be held, which shall then fill such vacancies for the remainder of the Special staff member's term.
(vi) The Special staff assembles at least once in every year at the same time as the Congress.

(vii) A majority of the Special staff constitutes a quorum to do business;
    (a) but a smaller number may adjourn from day to day, and
    (b) may compel the attendance of absent members, in such manner, and under such penalties as law may provide.
(viii) The Special staff chooses its own officers.
 (ix) The Special staff determines the rules of its proceedings,
    (a) punishes its members for disorderly behavior, and,
    (b) with the concurrence of two-thirds, expels a member.
 (x) Each Special staff shall have one vote.
 (xi) The Special staff keeps a journal of its proceedings, and from time to time publishes the same; and the yeas and nays of the members on any question shall be entered on the journal.
(xii) They shall in all cases, except treason, felony and breach of the peace, be privileged from arrest during their attendance at the session, and in going to and returning from the same; and for any speech or debate in their meetings, they shall not be questioned in any other place.
(xiii) The Special staff receives no confidential or secret information material to the declaring of public war.
    (a) The work of the Special staff relative to the declaring of public war is confined to publically available documents and testimony.
(xiv) Exceptionally, the Special staff may receives confidential or secret information material to the granting of letters of marque or reprisal for secret private wars.
    (a) Normally, the work of the Special staff relative to the granting of letters of marque or reprisal shall be confined to publically available documents and testimony.

4(B). The Special staff receives compensation equal to the greater as between the Senate or the House of Representatives.
 (i) No Special staff, during the time for which he is elected, is appointed to any civil or military office under the authority of the United States,
    (a) which shall have been created, or the emoluments whereof shall have been increased during such time; and
    (b) no person holding any office under the United States, shall be a member during his continuance in office.

Section 5. Duties of the Special Staff.

5(A). The duties of the Special staff are
 (i) to draft, debate, amend, and vote fully reasoned declarations of public war for both
    (a) domestic and
    (b) foreign wars, and
 (ii) to draft, debate, amend, and vote carefully circumscribed letters of marque or reprisal for private war.
(iii) For declarations of public war, the draft will be a bill, modeled on the Declaration of Independence. The text shall not take the style of a resolution.

(5B). The duties found in 5(A) are exercised in accordance with Hague Convention III of 1907 both

    (i) conditionally by
        (a) indicting the gravamina as well as
        (b) declaring the nation's preferred peace terms or
    (ii) absolutely by
        (a) indicting the gravamina
        (b) declaring the nation's preferred peace terms
        (c) denouncing the termination of the state and condition of peace and
        (d) declaring the existence of the state and condition of war as well.
  (iii) An unreasoned absolute, public declaration of war is appropriate,
        (a) when negotiations over the preferred peace terms declared conditionally have failed in the estimation of the Special staff, or
        (b) when the nation is in such imminent danger as will not admit of delay, or
        (c) when novel circumstances arise suddenly.
  (iv) In cases where either imminent danger or novel circumstances require an unreasoned, absolute, public declaration, the responsibility of the Joint Drafting Committee to make a fully reasoned, public declaration of war is not lessened. A fully reasoned, absolute, public declaration is still required as soon as time and circumstances permit to ensure that the President as Commander in Chief has not exceeded his command authority to employ diplomatic, economic, or military sanctions when not called for.
  (v) The decision to affix an ultimatum to a conditional declaration of war is an executive decision of the president.

5(C). The draft declarations of public war or the draft grants of letters of marque or reprisal for private war passed by the Special staff represent the best and most prudent judgment of the Special staff that
    (i) the gravamina indicted
    (ii) combined with the declaration of peace constitute true *casus belli.*

5(D).The Special staff may recommend that the Joint Congressional Drafting Committee seek injunctive relief in the Appellate Court against the president
    (i) whenever a presidential declaration infringes upon the congressional right to declare public war, or
    (ii) whenever a presidential act or finding infringes upon the congressional right to grant letters of marque or reprisal for private war.

5(E). The Special staff may submit a petition for the impeachment of the president to the Joint Congressional Drafting Committee for the waging of either public or private war unconstitutionally.

Section 6. Congressional Approval or Disapproval.

6(A). Once the Special staff have drafted, debated, amended, and voted either a fully reasoned declaration of public war, or a letter of marque or reprisal for private war,
    (i) the Chairman and Vice Chairman of the Joint Congressional Drafting Committee shall introduce identical versions of the Special staff's draft in the Senate and House of Representatives as a bill, calling for approval without amendment.
    (ii) Voting shall be by secret ballot. The clerks of each House shall collect and tally the ballot slips from the members before announcing the totals for and against.

The ballots will remain secret in the care of the clerks for five years at which time the clerks will publish the names of the persons voting for and against the draft declaration or letter of marque or reprisal and shall entered the names and votes on the journal of each House respectively.

6(B). Once introduced, the Special Staff's bill may be called up by any Senator or Representative, shall be highly privileged, shall become the pending business of both Houses, shall be voted on within 5 calendar days thereafter, and shall not be susceptible to intervening motions, except that each House may adjourn from day to day.

(i) If the bill is approved, it is presented to the president for his approval or disapproval.

(ii) If the bill is disapproved by the president, the bill dies; no attempt shall be made to override a presidential disapproval. The bill is returned to the Special staff of the Joint Drafting Committee, with his objections, for review and revision.

6(C). The Special staff's bill is debated in both Houses without amendment out of respect for the acknowledged stature and expertise of the Special staff.

(i) A vote of approval by either House represents the members' best and most prudent judgment that
  (a) the gravamina indicted
  (b) combined with the declaration of peace constitute true *casus belli*.

(ii) A vote of disapproval by either House represents the members' best and most prudent judgment that
  (a) the gravamina indicted
  (b) combined with the declaration of peace do not constitute true *casus belli*.

Section 7. Severability.
If any provision of this Resolution is held invalid, the remainder of the Act shall not be affected thereby.

By way of a few brief comments, the heart of the "Joint Drafting Committee" proposal is the election of the fifty distinguished individuals to a "Special Staff" by the members of the Senate and House for eight-year terms. In this way, the Special Staff are similar to the Roman *collegium fetialis*. They would also receive the same pay and benefits as the senators and representatives. This of course establishes them as both equivalent to and independent of the senators and representatives. The two other essential provisions are 1) that no amendments are allowed from the senators and representatives and 2) that the senators and representatives vote by secret ballot. True, Thomas Jefferson's committee draft was immeasurably improved by amendments and changes in style and substance made during the committee-of-the-whole debate in the Second Continental Congress. Unfortunately, more than two hundred years prove that the senators and representatives lack the knowledge, experience, skill, and interest either to draft or to amend declarations of war. The members are most skilled at playing political games, as in 1898 or 1914, not at either drafting or amending declarations of war. In contrast, the delegates to the Second Continental Congress possessed the knowledge, experience, skill, and interest to make substantive changes to Jefferson's draft. Simply put, no evidence exists at all that any amendment ever made by the members of the U.S. Congress has ever enhanced a congressional declaration, whereas much evidence exists that every amendment ever made by the Congress has weakened or obfuscated the congressional declarations. Declaring war is not – or, at least, should not be – an exercise in congressional gamesmanship.

Likewise, it is absolutely essential that the senators and representatives vote their consciences, and not their fears of political retribution. When the "Special Staff" presents a draft declaration of war, emotions will often be running high and retaliation for voting the "wrong" way is inevitable, unless the senators and representatives are protected by a secret ballot. No senator or representative should fear the fate of Senators Wayne Morse of Oregon and Ernest Gruening of Alaska for their opposition to the 1964 Gulf of Tonkin Resolution. Both lost their next election. Sadly, to repeat, Ulysses S. Grant was very much too correct when he observed that "experience proves that the man who obstructs a war in which his nation is engaged, no matter whether right or wrong, occupies no enviable place in life or history. Better for him, individually, to advocate 'war, pestilence, and famine,' than to act as obstructionist to a war already begun" (Grant 1990, 50). Yet, it is precisely the restrained and thoughtful votes of members such as Senators Morse and Gruening in 1964 or Representative Jeannett Rankin of Montana in 1941, who are most needed when a vote on a declaration of war is taken. A secret ballot is absolutely essential. Conscience, not fear, must drive the congressional vote.

And, finally, the proposed Joint Drafting Committee is clearly a workaround, a way of patching up a fundamental constitutional flaw. A fundamental constitutional defect requires a fundamental constitutional amendment, as argued in the previous chapter. But a patch is better than doing nothing, better than allowing the president to continue to declare war as kings have always done. The rule of law requires no less.

PART IV

WHAT IS THE THEORY?

10 *Bellum Justum et Pium*
The Rule of Law and Roman "Piety"

A [Roman] slave had bargained money for his freedom, and he gave the money to his owner. The owner died before he manumitted the slave, and in his will he ordered that he be free, and he left him a legacy of his *peculium* [a sum given to a slave by his master to manage on his own]. He [the now freed slave] asked [the jurist] whether or not his patron's heirs were obliged to return the money that he had given to his owner in return for freedom. [The jurist] replied, if after he had received the money, the owner had entered it in his accounts as his money, it immediately ceased to be part of the [slave's] *peculium*; but if, in the meantime, until he manumitted him, he had recorded it as due to the slave, it appeared to be part of the *peculium* and the heirs were bound to restore it to him now that he was free.

(cited in Watson 1993, 67)

The cultural perspective undergirding the jurist's decision is the peculiarly Roman concept that substantive justice depends on "piety." "Piety" for the Romans, of course, did not mean a personal, spiritual relationship to God, as Christians later came to reinterpret the word. For the Romans, it implied a strict adherence to recognized rituals and ceremonies in all situations, both public and private. Consequently, the Roman "religion" was not about personal salvation; nor did it encompass an abstract theological investigation of man's relationship to God. Rather, it was a very practical system of state-sponsored public and private rites that disciplined, ordered, and governed Roman life in the most transparent and predictable way possible. In the case of the freed slave's *peculium*, "impious," unpredictable, subjective sentiments of fairness or equity as between poor slaves versus rich slave owners played no role in the decision. Instead, the "pious" act of transferring an account receivable to income earned ensured both procedural and substantive justice decided on solid, objective, and, hence, uncontroversial grounds. Law ruled, not men.

Both the Romans themselves and other ancient authors attributed Roman success in war and peace to their "religious" virtue, to their exceptional "piety" (see Cicero, *De natura decorum*, 2.3.8 and *De harpispicum responsis*, 9.19; cited in Watson 1993, 78–9). As Augustine later commented, "It would certainly appear proper that the care shown by the worshippers for the gods' rites be matched by the gods' concern for their behavior" (*De civitate Dei*, 2.4; cited in Watson 1993, 66). Several centuries earlier, Polybius, the Greek historian, had recorded:

> 6.56.6 But the quality in which the Roman state is most distinctly superior is, in my opinion, the nature of their religious convictions. 7. I believe that the very thing which among other people is an object of reproach, I mean superstition, is what maintains the Roman state. 8. These matters are clothed in such formalities and are introduced into their public and private life to such an extent that nothing could exceed it. This is a fact that will surprise many. (cited in Watson 1993, 65)

For the ancients, then, Roman "piety" was a practical political virtue. It was the "care" with which the Romans "clothed" or preserved the order and substantive justice of their communal life. It was how they worshipped the rule of law in both their private and public lives. By reducing to a minimum the occurrence of procedurally imperfect, functionally equivalent speech acts, the ever-practical Romans maximized the clarity of their plans and intentions to themselves and to others. Not surprisingly, therefore, the Romans of the republic established a unique system of state-sponsored religious congregations or colleges to perform and maintain the various rites and rituals needed to ensure their continued "piety" and prosperity. For the conduct of their foreign relations, this sodality was the *collegium fetialis*, which was composed of approximately twenty priests who oversaw the rites pertaining to the declaring of war and the sanctification of treaties in accordance with the relevant laws, the *jus fetiale* (*ibid.* 1993).

In accordance with the solemnities of the *jus fetiale*, the Senate and people of Rome could not declare war conditionally until after 1) the Senate had indicted the gravamina and declared its preferred peace terms in a conditional declaration of war and 2) the *collegium fetialis* had vetted both the indictment and the declaration of peace. If they approved of the text, a legation composed of several of the fetiales went to the offending party with the conditional declaration of war to resolve the conflict through negotiations. The negotiations could last for up to thirty-three days. Depending on the outcome of the negotiations, the fetial delegation would return to Rome and a) announce the success of their negotiations and the resolution of the conflict or b) officially denounce the offending party before the Senate for the failure of the negotiations. Only then could the Senate take up the question of an absolute declaration of war, which again had to be vetted by the fetiales before they would return to the offending party to declare absolute war in a ceremonial manner. To be sure, the actual drafting, debating, amending, and voting on the two declarations of war were in the hands of the Senate, as was the actual decision for enmity and against amity. But, the fetiales provided an official and solemn review by a quasi-judicial "religious" body of foreign affairs experts, since they would not form a legation unless they were convinced that both the conditional and absolute declarations were *justum et pium* (Livy 1919, I, xxxii, 13–14; Nussbaum 1952, 679). By extension, if the declarations were *justum et pium*, then the war itself was most probably both *justum et pium*.

Not incidentally, the primary speech act functions of a declaration of war were satisfied by the ritual solemnities surrounding the Senate's declaring of war and the dispatch of the fetial legation. First and foremost, the solemnities forced the Senate to define and constitute its perceived conflict as a specific, well-articulated war. Beginning with the initial debates over the conditional declaration, the Senate was forced by the procedures to clarify its thinking, its reasoning, its explanation of the casus belli. Second, the solemnities established a properly coherent ends-means/ideal-in-process relationship between the Senate and the commander of the legions sent to wage the war. By simply reading the two declarations, the commander knew that he was not a king, but, instead, an executive agent for the Senate and people of Rome. He also knew why he and his army were fighting, the political purpose of the war, and when victory would be achieved or defeat suffered.

And, most important of all, the solemnities provided the Romans with an effective international conflict resolution strategy. As Alan Watson has observed, "The whole purpose of the *ius fetiale* was the preservation of peace among an ethnically and linguistically related group of states that also were faced by hostile neighbors" (1993, 62). Critical to the effectiveness of this conflict-resolution strategy was the clarity of the "pious" speech that accompanies the rule of law. Rome's neighbors were always clear about the state of their relations because procedurally imperfect, functionally equivalent speech acts were exceptionally infrequent. For example, Cato the Elder's repeated *"Carthago delenda est"* (Carthage must be destroyed.) was an influential opinion, not a public policy. Before Rome acted, it spoke ritually and unambiguously and adhered to the rule of law. In modern times, to recall, the outlines of this Roman conflict resolution strategy still find a faint echo in Hague Convention III, *Relative to the Opening of Hostilities*. But of course the armature that once drove this conflict resolution strategy has long since been lost. No longer are kings and dictatorial presidents willing to adhere to the rule of law. Declaring war with procedurally imperfect, functionally equivalent speech acts suits their purposes better. Since the demise of the *jus fetiale*, men rule, not law.

To be sure, the declaring of war and the making of treaties are no longer overseen by a religious *collegium*. The liturgical language of the Romans is strange, indeed. But notice the startling asymmetry: While modern societies still demand that their wars be just, the Romans insisted that their wars be both just and "pious" as well. For example, Cicero remarked in *De Re Publica*, "by means of the fetial rites, ... any war which had not been denounced and indicted should be considered unjust and impious" (1928, II, xvii 31; translation modified.) As a result, for the Romans, unsolemnly declared hostilities were "impious" and, hence, by definition, imprudent, if not entirely illegal and wrong. Just as the solemn and decorous speech acts of procedural justice are a necessary, but not sufficient, condition for substantive justice in the courts of law, so a solemn and decorous declaration of war is a necessary, but not sufficient, condition for substantive justice in war. To short circuit the necessary solemnities and procedures of war produces the same "impious," untoward, and imprudent consequences as short circuiting well-established procedures in the courtroom, the legislature, or the executive, not to speak of the rule of law in general.

Thus, whereas the Romans spoke liturgically of "piety," their goal was a substantive justice well seasoned with prudence through procedurally disciplined discussions, judgments, and decisions taken collectively by the republican institutions of the community. Not incidentally, Thomas Jefferson's preference for the committee-of-the-whole system sprang from this same concern, a concern for procedurally disciplined discussions that led to collective judgments and decisions, or, as he put it, judgments and decisions arrived at "[o]nly after the sense of the meeting had been made manifest." True, with regard to the peacetime duties of the Congress, the endless complexity of postindustrial societies no longer allows for the inefficiencies of the committee-of-the-whole deliberations; yet, with regard to the declaring of war, the procedures of the Second Continental Congress remain the only truly successful model in American history.

The larger point, to repeat, pertains to the role and importance of rituals and procedures and the deleterious effects of procedurally imperfect, functionally equivalent speech acts. For, procedures, such as those found in the Constitution of the United States or in the Roman *jus fetiale*, are not mere rituals. Rather, they provide the necessary tangible institutional structures or the visible machinery through which disciplined and, above all, collective decision making is possible, as is discussed more fully in Chapter 11. Corporate or collective decision making is crucial so as to restrain and resist the subjective emotions, passions, biases, and prejudices of politically powerful individuals, such as dictatorial presidents. When so restrained, the community is protected as it moves systematically to a decision in a court of law, in a legislative chamber, or in an executive bureau. Most pointedly, the constitutional "pieties" of an amended declare war clause provide the visible machinery by which a collective decision concerning both the justice and the prudence of taking up arms can be made. In the absence of proper procedures, imprudent, if not unjust, decisions are more likely because men, and not law, rule.

AN "IMPIOUS" BUSH

To illustrate how "impiety" leads to imprudence, no better negative example can be found since 1945 than the 2003 invasion of Iraq, although the Vietnam saga is another excellent example (Mann 2001). During the autumn of 2002, while President George W. Bush was preparing for an early spring 2003 invasion of Iraq, the members of the 107th Congress were preparing to let power slip "through their fingers," to recall the words of Justice Robert Jackson. Preoccupied with the upcoming midterm election and other congressional business, the members were more than happy to have the White House staff draft a joint resolution "to authorize the use of United States Armed Forces against Iraq." To have the White House draft this functionally equivalent declaration of war was, of course, a break with tradition. Usually, the State Department is asked by the president to write the draft. Whatever the reason for this innovation, the draft was sent to the House of Representatives on Thursday, 19 September 2002; introduced simultaneously into both chambers on Wednesday, 2 October 2002; and passed on Friday, 11 October 2002, nine days after it was introduced and less than three weeks before the midterm elections (White House 2002). In accordance with the Constitution, on Wednesday, 16 October 2002, President George W. Bush approved the resolution his staff had written (Pub. L. No. 107–243, 116 Stat. 1498). The president's "solicitude" in relieving the overbusy and distracted members of the 107th Congress of their constitutional responsibilities to draft, debate, and vote a "pious" declaration of war was much appreciated by the "cooperative" 107th Congress.

Notice how interest and confusion clash in this example: While certainly interesting, the politics of this example are not confusing. They are straightforward and traditional. As is usual, President George W. Bush waited until the members were most vulnerable, until just before the midterm elections, when it was next to impossible for them to deny him his desire. Then, as a "solicitous" president, he "convened and gave information" to a "cooperative" Congress. His father had done the same; Lyndon Johnson, Franklin Roosevelt, James Polk, James Madison, and many other presidents have done the same. Wait for the propitious moment when the members cannot refuse, and then send them the declaration or authorization, as may be the case. What is confusing, as already noted in passing in Chapter 5, is the two-faced or Janus-faced character of the "authorizing" resolution. Viewed from the right-facing face, the joint resolution was entirely proper and "pious" in the double sense that the joint resolution was both a legislative enactment and entirely within the competence of the 107th Congress to pass. After all, the Congress is entirely competent to pass precatory and hortatory "authorizations" on whatever topics it wishes. Authorizing strawberry festivals and praising the Boy Scouts are, after all, the meat and potatoes of workaday congressional politics.

Yet, viewed from the left-facing face, the resolution was also, at the same time, an "impious," functionally equivalent declaration of war. Is this not confusing? "Pious" with respect to itself, the precatory and hortatory joint resolution "authorizing" the use of force is also "impious" with respect to the constitutional requirement that the Congress declare war. This confusion, however, is only confusing. What is important is that the 107th Congress had not just let power slip "through its fingers," but the absence of procedural justice opened the way for imprudence. As on too many previous occasions, individual, private, presidential decision making had replaced public, corporate decision making. A man ruled, not the law.

From a Roman perspective, though, the 107th Congress was not the only branch of the government that fell victim to an imprudence aided and abetted by an "impious" failure to follow proper procedures. George W. Bush as president frequently succumbed to the temptation. Time and again, his actions and decisions were cut from the same "impious" cloth. As a result, most of his trials and troubles can be put down quite simply to his lack of "piety," in the Roman sense, not in the Christian sense.

Had George W. Bush insisted that the 107th Congress declare war "piously" on the authority of the whole nation, as the Constitution mandates, instead of only "authorizing" him to do that which he had already decided to do on his own "inherent" authority as commander in chief, he would have avoided much opprobrium and political pain that later befell him, if not the disaster that the invasion of Iraq became.

Had he observed the "pieties" of the United Nations and secured an unambiguous Security Council resolution in 2003 authorizing "all necessary means" against Iraq, he would have avoided much international controversy over the invasion of Iraq.

Had he observed the "pieties" of the Geneva Convention regarding the status and treatment of prisoners of war or, alternatively, the "pieties" of American law regarding the status and treatment of those arrested for crimes such as terrorism, he would have avoided much opprobrium and controversy over that entirely new and unheard-of category of nonprisoner, the so-called unlawful enemy combatant.

Had he observed the "pieties" of the Convention on Torture, and Other Cruel, Inhuman or Degrading Treatment or Punishment or, alternatively, the relevant American laws and regulations on interrogation practices and methods, he would have avoided much of the opprobrium and controversy over the treatment of the "unlawful enemy combatants" at Guantanamo and assorted detainees and prisoners in Abu Ghraib, in Afghanistan, or in the secret prisons maintained by the Central Intelligence Agency around the world and supplied through "rendition."

Had he observed the "pieties" of the Foreign Intelligence Surveillance Act of 1978 and obtained warrants for the National Security Agency to eavesdrop on American citizens, he would also have avoided much of the opprobrium and controversy on this civil liberties issue.

And, so on and so forth, in each case, the failure to follow the established rules, laws, or procedures renders the action imprudent and suspect, if not entirely illegitimate and illegal, from the outset. The obvious point of this cascade of "impieties" is that Christian piety is no substitute for Roman "piety," in politics, at least. Proper procedure and the rule of law, if not transparency and procedural justice, are more than mere "formalities." They tend to ensure in the most practical terms both prudence and substantive justice, as Polybius observed of the ever-practical Romans.

BUREAUCRATIC PROPRIETY

But, perhaps, it is time to switch from the liturgical language of the Romans to the modern language of bureaucratic management, which many will find more familiar. The switch in language does not, however, change the point. It does not change the way in which procedurally imperfect, functionally equivalent speech acts lead to ambiguity and imprudence, which, in turn, lead to disorder and unpredictability in communal life. For example, consider the official critique of Prime Minister Tony Blair's management of the decision to ally the United Kingdom with the United States for the 2003 invasion of Iraq, a decision that was widely and deeply opposed in Britain. Lord Robin Butler, in testimony before the Commons' Public Administration Select Committee, substituted the English word "informal" for the Latin *pium* but drew a thoroughly Roman conclusion. In his opinion, "the informal nature of much of the Government's decision-making process and the relative lack of established Cabinet Committee machinery" had led to ill-informed decisions (Blick 2005, 50). By "informal," Lord Butler meant precisely what Thomas Jefferson meant, that "wider collective discussion and consideration by the Cabinet [was limited] to the frequent but unscripted occasions when the Prime Minister, Foreign Secretary and Defence Secretary briefed the Cabinet orally" (*ibid.*). By "relative lack of Cabinet Committee machinery,"

Lord Butler meant that "excellent quality papers were written by officials ... [but they] were not discussed in Cabinet or in Cabinet Committee ... [nor] circulated in advance" (*ibid.*). Consequently, Lord Butler concluded "that the informality and circumscribed character of the Government's procedures which we saw in the context of policy making towards Iraq risks reducing the scope for informed collective political judgments [inside the cabinet]" (*ibid.*). Lord Butler was in a unique position to know of this reduced scope for informed collective judgment by the cabinet because he had not only served as cabinet secretary to Prime Minister Blair but had also been charged to write a House of Commons report on the process that led to the invasion (Butler 2004).

If further confirmation were needed, Lord Butler's conclusions were echoed by Lord Richard Wilson, who had also served as cabinet secretary to Prime Minister Blair: "I believe there is a connection between proper process and good government ... the risk is that informality can slide into something more fluid and unstructured, where advice and dissent may either not always be offered or else not be heard" (Blick 2005, 52). In response to these findings, so as to reestablish the "pious" link "between proper process and good government," Prime Minster Blair subsequently restored the established cabinet committee machinery and began to allow minutes to be kept of all cabinet meetings. In passing, one must note that Lord Wilson's observation on how "informality" promotes a certain "sliding" into war recalls Charles Molloy's observation on how unsolemnly declared wars promote a certain "slipping" into war. Neither "slipping" nor "sliding" into war is prudent.

On the other side of the Atlantic, it comes as no surprise to learn that precisely the same charge of "informally" (i.e., "impiously") sliding "into something more fluid and unstructured, where advice and dissent may either not always be offered or else not be heard" has been made against George W. Bush's decision making. The critique in President Bush's case, of course, is very unofficial, as an official inquiry into his decision making on Iraq would be unthinkable (Kessler 2003, A1). Still, as Thomas Ricks, the author of *Fiasco: The American Military Adventure in Iraq* (2006), has observed, "That is one of the things in these [recent] books [about President George W. Bush's conduct of the war in Iraq] – I was struck by the absence of the President. He should be a central figure in decision-making. And again and again, there's never any one key meeting. For example, the actual decision to go to war doesn't seem to ever have been [made at] a meeting in which people formally sat down and said, 'Do we all agree?'" (Koepp and Thompson 2006/7, 162). Ricks's outsider's observation is confirmed by George Tenet, President Bush's director of the Central Intelligence Agency at the time: "One of the great mysteries to me is exactly when the war in Iraq became inevitable" (Tenet 2007, 301; see also Woodward 2004, 258, 261, 368; Metz 2010).

But, perhaps Justice Robert Jackson has once again captured the essence of the matter: "With all its defects, delays and inconveniences, men have discovered no technique for long preserving free government except that the Executive be under the law, and that the law [as well as declarations of war, one might add] be made by parliamentary deliberation" (*Youngstown Co. v. Sawyer*, 343 U.S. 579, 655 (1952)). Thomas Jefferson could not have agreed more.

In conclusion, then, the Roman ideal in both war and peace is to seek, not merely substantive justice, but procedural justice as well. The substance of justice is elusive and illusory when the search is not governed by a prudent "piety." For, one of the principal benefits of proper procedure is the way in which it obstructs the rush to judgment by powerful individuals, such as dictatorial presidents or prime ministers. It does this by requiring an objective, public, and disciplined process, which, in turn, introduces clarity and the expectation of clarity into communal life. The procedurally imperfect, functionally equivalent short cuts taken by dictatorial presidents or prime ministers only confuse and mislead everyone – the enemy, the general public, the president or prime minister himself. In fine, the expectation of a procedural clarity in communal life is but an expectation of the rule of law in politics.

11 The Rule of Law
Searching for Ontology

'Twas brillig, and the slithy troves
Did gyre and gimble in the wabe:
All mimsy were the borogoves
And the mome raths outgrabe.

Jabberwocky
Lewis Carroll

When arms speak, the laws are silent.

Cicero
(1979, *Pro Milone* IV. xi)

So far, the story has been one of the fatally impractical division of the sovereign's war powers that led to congressional incapacity and presidential tyranny. A constitutional amendment to establish a fourth branch of government to exercise the fœderative power then became the obvious solution. This solution was achieved, however, by a simple substitution of positive values for negative values. Once the impractical division is corrected by vesting the fœderative power in a Council on War and Peace, capacity returns; tyranny is overcome, and the rule of law is restored during time of war as well as peace. This process of substitution no doubt provides an excellent solution, but it makes for a very poor explanation of how and why the substitution restores the rule of law. Instead of an explanation, one finds an unsubstantiated claim that the rule of law is superior to the rule of men. The claim is no doubt commonsense; it is surely the firm faith of many. Winston Churchill certainly captured its commonsense essence when, during the Commons debate to amend the Parliament Act of 1911, he took the floor at 3:40 pm on Tuesday, 11 November 1947, and said, "Democracy is the worst form of government except all those other forms that have been tried from time to time" (Churchill 1947, 206–7). True enough, but Churchill has provided a bon mot, a quip, not an explanation.

The lack of an explanation, so far, has been due primarily to an unavoidable negligence concerning the relationship between the material world and man's socially constructed world. Both law itself and the constitutional framework for the rule of law are socially constructed human institutions. Yet, they are created and operate within a complex context of man's material environment, the one impinging upon the other. Unavoidably, however, any study of the congressional incapacity "to declare war" must neglect the material consequences of the infinitive phrase so as to focus narrowly on the speech act, more or less in isolation. In Chapter 5, this isolation was breeched slightly when discussing the four primary functions of declarations of war. But functions are only part of the relationship. A fuller look at the Janus-faced relationship between speech acts and material acts, however, is no longer avoidable for those interested in the rule of law.

UNIVERSAL AFFECTIVITY AND PERFORMATIVITY

Unfortunately, the question is rather narrow, while the topic is extremely broad. Therefore, one must narrow the scope of the discussion, but only after acknowledging its breadth: "Speech" is here taken in the broadest possible sense, to include any languagelike medium of communication – body language, dance, clothing and dress, tattoos, music, images, displays, and so on. Such "speech" is both grammatical and affective. It is grammatical in the double sense that it gives an external, perceptible material structure or shape to that which is communicated and simultaneously possesses an internal structure or patterned regularity, a grammar. It is affective in that it moves or influences its listeners, producing a subjective effect within them. For example, infant babbling is "speech" in this broadest sense. It is a material representation of the infant's mental processes, and it possesses a grammar, if not propositional meaning. It is also very affecting, as every parent and grandparent will testify. Similarly, Lewis Carroll's *Jabberwocky* is also "speech" in this universal, but trivial sense. When recited, it makes material the speaker's mental processes, and it possesses the grammar of English. It is also most affective because it reassures listeners that the borogoves will be exceptionally mimsy whenever it is brillig.

But notice the problem: If speech possesses only a grammar and is only affective in this trivial, because universal and subjective, sense, then speech is just talk, so much gossip, and we live in a postmodern world of relative values where men rule, and not law. In such an untethered subjective world, opinions matter, and the opinions of the rich and powerful matter most. As the Athenian ambassadors told the Melians, in a world of affective speech "the strong do what they can and the weak suffer what they must" (Thucydides 1982, V, 89). In such a world, what one says affects one's social surroundings positively or negatively, in this way or that way, but these subjective affects do not directly and immediately change or transform one's social and material world at a macrolevel. They do not produce immediate social and material effects directly, in and of themselves, and, most certainly, not in large politically significant ways. In order for macrolevel political effects to occur in a world of affective speech, opinions must accumulate over time. That is, if speech possesses only a grammar and is only subjectively affective, then performative speech acts are little more than what Judith Butler calls "performativity." They construct social reality "through a series of acts which are renewed, revised, and consolidated through time" (Butler 1990, 274).

Helpfully, performativity explains the construction of abstract social institutions when seen as objects to be explained to students and others. For example, as an abstract social institution, war can indeed be seen as produced "through a series of acts [by innumerable emperors, king, and dictatorial presidents over the past five thousand years and more] which are renewed, revised, and consolidated through time." Further, one can add that this series of acts conform to a set of constitutive and regulative rules (i.e., a grammar) that shape, define, or construct the abstract social institution of war, as with any other abstract social institution. The problem here is that abstract explanations cannot be lived. No one has ever died in an explanation. In war, people die. "To declare war," therefore, is not simply to affect the world subjectively. It is to create or effect a lived reality; it is to transform one's social and material world radically, changing it from amity to enmity, from peace to war.

Unhelpfully then, performativity is an abstract, contranormative, value-neutral, positive approach to understanding war that does not touch upon the concrete issues of actual wars, wars in which people die. In particular, an abstract contranormative approach cannot illuminate either the primary functions of declarations of war or the relative value of lawful versus unlawful decisions and declarations. From an abstract, positive, contranormative viewpoint, the rule of law is irrelevant. Both procedurally perfect and procedurally imperfect declarations are equally viable ways to "renew, revise, and consolidate" the institution of war, as more than five thousand years of sedimented history demonstrate. The constitutive rules of the abstract institution are adequate for connecting a declaration of war to the material conditions of war over time, but inadequate to distinguish lawfully from unlawfully declared war, as will be seen in a moment. However, since these are among the critical questions at the heart of the rule-of-law issues raised by the congressional incapacity "to declare war," a different approach is needed. An approach is needed that better defines the particular, agentive relationship between the "pious" or "impious" quality of words spoken and their material effects in the world. In order to tackle the issues of performative effect, as opposed to performativity affect, one must become familiar with John Austin's technical vocabulary.

PERFORMATIVE SPEECH ACTS: A TECHNICAL VOCABULARY

> Her Majesty [Queen Elizabeth] was taken by surprise for a moment as the ship moved, but quickly said, "I name this ship Queen Elizabeth and wish success to her and all who sail her." At the same time she released the bottle of wine, which swung and broke against the ship's stem.
>
> The Times
> Wednesday, 28 September 1938 (7)

John Austin, a British analytic philosopher of language, delivered the William James Lectures at Harvard University in 1955. These lectures were subsequently collected into a slender volume with the awkward title *How to Do Things with Words* (1975). The point of both the title and the lectures was the infinitive "to do." Austin pointed out that there exists a class of human acts ("behaviors," if you will) that are "done" with words. That is, the saying of certain prescribed words by certain authorized people in certain defined circumstances is always a necessary, and sometimes a sufficient, condition for bringing the named social reality into existence (*ibid.* 8–9). For example, in order to "name" a ship the *Queen Elizabeth*, an authorized person, Queen Elizabeth, accompanied by her two young daughters, must travel from London to the Glasgow shipyard of John Brown and Company and say, "I name this ship the *Queen Elizabeth*," while smashing a bottle of wine against the ship's bow. Or, to "give and bequeath," a person of sound mind and body must say in his last will and testament, "I give and bequeath my gold watch to my grandson" (*ibid.* 5). That is, to introduce Austin's technical language, in the prescribed context (a bottle of wine at the ready), the prescribed words of an authorized "namer" will possess three characteristics in addition to their grammar and propositional content:

1) *the locution,* or the words or other languagelike signs that are actually spoken, written, or communicated ("I name this ship the *Queen Elizabeth*."),
2) *the illocution,* or the intended social function (to "name") of the locution, and
3) *the perlocution,* or the consequential affects or effects of the illocution (or intention) in the world. (In this case, the creating or effecting of a

new social reality – the association of the name *Queen Elizabeth* with a large steel hull dripping with wine)

Austin's point, of course, is that, above and beyond any affects, the queen's words had an immediate and creative effect. They "did" something, actually, two things. On the one hand, her words were another affective link in the chain of performativity that "renews, revises, and consolidates through time" the abstract social institution of "ship naming." On the other hand, and more relevant to the declaring of war, the queen's words effected, constituted, or created, ab initio, the aesthetic, moral, and legal reality of the RMS *Queen Elizabeth*. Before the smashing of the bottle of wine, a large iron hulk sat in the slipway of John Brown and Company. After the smashing of the bottle of wine, the Cunard Line's RMS *Queen Elizabeth* slid into the waters of the river Clyde, as the immediate creative effect of the queen's performance.

To take another example, a person on an African safari might say, "Look. The rhino is going to charge" (paraphrasing *ibid.* 98). The words spoken are the locution. The locution possesses a grammar, which can be diagrammed (Subject + Predicate), and a propositional meaning (or a semantic structure), which can be ascertained by looking up each word in a dictionary. However and crucially, the locution also possesses a social function. The speaker intended his words to "do" something, affecting or effecting his social situation in a certain way. The listeners decode or come to understand this social function by noting the illocutionary force of the locution. Did the speaker intend his utterance concerning the rhino to be taken as a statement or as a question or, perhaps, as a warning?

As a statement, the intonation would have been flat and would have been appropriate in a context in which the group was observing a rhinoceros at some distance and the speaker wished to affect the others by providing some interesting information. "Look," he might say, "the rhino is going to charge (that lion)." As a question, the intonation would have been rising and would have been appropriate in the same situation, except that the speaker would not have been sure whether the rhino was going to charge or not. Lacking assurance, the speaker would also hope to affect the others, eliciting from them their opinions on the matter. "Look," he might say, "the rhino is going to charge?" As a warning, the intonation would have been excited and would have been appropriate when the rhino was close at hand and moving rapidly toward the speaker and his group. In this case, crucially, the speaker would have wanted to do much more than affect the other members of his group. He would (or, at least, should) have wanted to effect an entirely new behavior – flight – "Look!! The rhino is going to charge!!!" The point, of course, is that the same locution (the same words with the same grammar and the same referential meaning) may have many different social functions or illocutionary purposes, depending upon the context in which it is spoken.

Still, the intentions or illocutionary force of a locution are just so many empty desires until they actually produce consequences in the world. In the case of the charging rhino, if the illocutionary force of the locution was marked as a statement or a question, the speaker may have affected his fellow rhino watchers in several different ways: They may have responded with a comment or two of their own by way of pleasant conversation. Or, they may have developed a certain admiration for the speaker as the one in the group with the sharpest eyes. Or, his comment may have only marked him out as unimaginative, only able to remark upon the obvious. Then, again, nothing may have happened. The listeners may have been unaffected, considering his talk as inconsequential babble. They may have done nothing, not even nod their heads in agreement.

If, however, the illocutionary force of the locution was that of a "warning," much should have happened. Above and beyond any affect the locution may have had, the material effect of panic and helter-skelter running around should have been immediately observed in the group. This scattering of the group represents the perlocutionary or real world effect of the locution taken to possess the illocutionary force of a "warning." The sentence "Look!! The rhino is going to charge!!!" now provides the necessary linguistic initiative to crystallize the moment and to modify or change the group's social reality, its behavior. Once again, it is important to notice that the same locution (the same words with the same grammar and the same referential meaning) may have different consequential effects or perlocutionary results, depending upon the illocutionary force with which it is spoken.

SELF-CONTAINED AND NOT-SELF-CONTAINED SPEECH ACTS

According to John Austin, then, performative speech acts are words that create or effect that which is spoken of in the world, above and beyond any affect that they may produce in the hearts and minds of hearers. His claim is straightforward enough. Yet, one might wonder, create what? How? Where? After some investigation, the universe of performative speech acts appears to divide, first, into two broad classes: 1) those speech acts that are self-contained because their illocutionary force is both necessary and sufficient to effect that which is spoken of and 2) those speech acts that are not self-contained because their illocutionary force is necessary, but not sufficient, to effect that which is spoken of. As one might expect, the latter class subdivides into two valances – positive and negative – on account of the gap between the necessary and the sufficient conditions, as is illustrated in Figure 9.

The first broad class of performative speech acts includes "announcements," "bequests," "bets," and "promises," among others. This class is self-contained

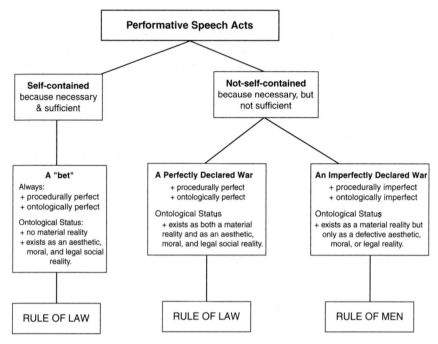

Figure 9. Performative Speech Acts and the Rule of Law.

because its members are without imperfection. Their utterance always produces procedurally and ontologically perfect results, ontologically perfect because procedurally perfect. For example, one can forget a bet; one can welch on a bet; one can even deny a bet was ever made. But the moment the bettor says, "I bet you ..." and the bettee accepts, the new social reality has come fully and completely into existence in all its aesthetic, moral, and legal consequences. Nothing more needs nor can be done. Ontologically, the locution, its necessary illocutionary force, and its sufficient perlocutionary effects have occurred instantaneously and simultaneously and are fully formed with the exchange of words. The bettor and bettee have said what they meant, and, as a result, the "bet" exists. No slippage is possible between word and world. However, it must be remarked, this instantaneous procedural and ontological perfection is possible only because the relevant world is uniquely the speakers' own immaterial social world, an immaterial and social world the bettor and bettee have created with their self-contained speech act.

Unfortunately though, the limited class to which a "bet" belongs does not cover most of man's social world. Most especially, it does not cover declarations of war, which belong to the second, not-self-contained class, those speech acts that are only necessary, but not sufficient, to create that which is spoken of. For example, the superficially redundant legal formula "I give and bequeath ..." illustrates well the contrast between the two broad classes. To "bequeath" is a self-contained, procedurally and ontologically perfect speech act. When one writes, "I give and bequeath ...," the new social reality of the bequest is fully formed, but not the "giving." As with a "bet," the "bequest" now exists in all its necessary illocutionary and sufficient perlocutionary ramifications as an aesthetically, morally, and legally binding "bequest." Again, like a "bet," not receiving the "bequest" does little to diminish the social reality of the bequest itself, its immaterial aesthetic, moral, and legal status. "My grandfather bequeathed his gold watch to me, but my uncle refused to give it to me," describes two different social facts, both of which are equally real, equally clear, and equally unambiguous. The gold watch was indeed "bequeathed" to me as a purely aesthetic, moral, and legal social fact, but it was not "given" to me as a simple material fact. "Bequeathing" is an instance of a self-contained, procedurally and ontologically perfect speech act. "Giving" is an instance of a not-self-contained procedurally perfect, but materially imperfect speech act. The material imperfection is caused by the fact that my uncle has yet to meet his aesthetic, moral, and legal obligations actually to hand over grandfather's gold watch to me. When he does meet these obligations, the sufficient perlocutionary conditions of "giving" will have been met. Word and world will no longer be in conflict. Meanwhile, the perlocutionary effect is in a state of suspension. Because of its material imperfections, the "giving" exists as an immaterial aesthetic, moral, and legal social fact. But it will not and cannot exist as a material fact until the gold watch is handed over.

THE RULE OF MEN: SLIPPING THROUGH THE GAP BETWEEN WORD AND WORLD

> "Then you should say what you mean," the March Hare went on.
>
> "I do," Alice hastily replied; "at least – at least I mean what I say – that is the same thing, you know."
>
> A Mad Tea Party
> Lewis Carroll (1962 88–9)

The performative structure of not-self-contained speech acts, then, is naturally open to exploitation. This exploitation occurs when procedurally imperfect, functionally equivalent speech acts slip through the gap between word and world. The slippage occurs because, as the March Hare tried to explain to Alice, sincerity is a characteristic of dictatorial presidents and the rule of men. Like Alice in Wonderland, dictatorial presidents and their ilk always mean what they say, thinking that that is the same thing as saying what they mean. For example, with the greatest sincerity imaginable, President Harry

Truman and the United Nations Security Council can avoid saying what they mean by simply meaning what they say. Instead of saying that they are declaring war on North Korea in June 1950, President Truman, for his part, can create the material conditions of war by "ordering" American forces to defend South Korea, whereas the United Nations Security Council, for its part, can do the same by "recommending" "that the Members of the United Nations furnish such assistance to the Republic of Korea as may be necessary to repel the armed attack and to restore international peace and security in the area (Res. 83 of 27 June 1950)." The functional equivalence of "ordering" and "recommending" for producing the material condition of war without "declaring" war in a procedurally perfect manner is of inestimable political and public relations value.

The only way to avoid this dictatorial exploitation of the slippage between word and world exhibited by the not-self-contained speech acts is through a rigorous adherence to the rule of law: that is, to a rigorous commitment to saying what one means, and not simply meaning what one says. As the ever-"pious" Romans well knew, the procedural perfection of the locutions ensures the structural integrity of the performance's necessary illocutionary force to produce its sufficient perlocutionary effects. The resulting onto-logical perfection, then, bars the way to procedurally imperfect, functionally equivalent simulacra, or what John Searle, an American philosopher of lan-guage and student of John Austin's, calls "indirect speech acts" (1975).

To unpack the multiple imperfections here, one must ask a version of the chicken and the egg question:

1. Does the world come first, which means that the spoken word simply corresponds with or names that which already exists?
2. Or, does the spoken word come first as the necessary, and sometimes sufficient, condition to bring the world into existence in all socially constructed cases?

John the Evangelist argued for the second: "In the beginning was the Word, and the Word was with God, and the Word was God [the creator]" (John 1:1). John Searle, however, argues for both. In the case of procedurally and ontologically perfect performative speech acts, such as marriage or war, Searle argues undoubtedly correctly that the word comes first. The minis-ter's official "pronouncement" necessarily comes before a couple's material consummation of their marriage; the declarer's procedurally perfect "declara-tion" necessarily comes before the commander's "orders" provide the mate-rial consummation of the declaration. Problems arise, however, when Searle begins to consider functionally equivalent simulacra such as cohabitation or a war declared in a procedurally imperfect manner. In these cases, Searle sug-gests that the problem is entirely different. The problem is one of describing how society deals retroactively with the material consequences of cohabitation or a UN police action. For Searle, these procedurally imperfect, functionally equivalent simulacra look very much like the "brute facts" of physical nature. One day it is not snowing; the next day, it is. One day a couple is not living together; the next day, they are. One day no military operations are occurring; the next day, they are. Society deals with these seemingly "brute facts," Searle argues, by recognizing that some "brute facts" are also "social facts," which need to be assimilated into a society as "institutional facts." To describe this process formally, Searle developed the notation Y *is imposed on X in context C*, or, more frequently, *X counts as Y in context C*, and provides two salient examples:

> War is an exception [to the general need for a procedurally perfect declaration] for the obvious reason that the brute facts – people killing one another on a large scale, for example – usually make official indicators unnecessary. (Searle 1995, 119)

Explaining more fully, Searle continues:

> in typical [i.e., procedurally imperfect declared] wars, the sheer events count as having a certain legal or quasi-legal status that is supposed to impose certain responsibilities and rights on the participants; and in such cases the war is more than a social fact; it is an institutional fact [institutionalized or codified, for example, by the Geneva and Hague conventions]. Furthermore, as with marriage, there are ways in which the institutional status [of common law marriage] is supposed to be imposed. (*ibid.* 89)

Searle concludes his argument with a real world example, pointing out the ironic or, if one prefers, the hypocritical linguistic consequences of the subsequent "imposing" of "institutional status" upon a wild, warlike set of pre-existing "brute facts":

> Thus in the case of the war in Korea, the American authorities at the time were very anxious that it not be called "the Korean War" (it was called "the Korean conflict") because it did not satisfy the legal definition of war; since no war had been legally declared in accordance with the Constitutional provision for a declaration of war. They had a choice: If it was a "war," it was unconstitutional; so it was not a "war"; it was a "United Nations police action," a different status-function altogether. Since the phenomenon did not satisfy the X term for imposing the status-function, the Y term "war" was not applied. By the time of the Vietnam War, these sorts of evasions had been abandoned and the sheer physical and intentional facts warranted the application of the term "war," even though the legal situation was no more that of a declared war than had been the case in Korea. (*ibid.*)

But, of course, war is not an exception, not any more than is marriage. In both cases, the material chicken does not come before the speech act egg. Consider marriage first: The "institutionalization" of cohabitation as a "common law marriage" is possible only because the slippage between word and world allows for retroactive consecration. This slippage means that a couple can reverse the process. They can consummate their marriage in the material world long before it is officially "pronounced" by clergy as an officially sanctioned social fact. Yet, crucially, this procedurally, and, hence, ontologically imperfect simulacrum of marriage is not a "brute fact." It is ab initio a social fact. The necessary, but not sufficient, performative speech act for cohabitation is a procedurally perfect "request" to cohabit made by one of the two. When the other agrees, all that is required to consummate the propositional content of the "request" is for one to move in with the other. Thus, cohabitation is no more of a "brute fact" than marriage. Both are social facts created by performative speech acts – a "request" to cohabit, in the one case, a "pronouncement" of marriage, in the other case. The point of confusion is that, because they are consummated in the same way, cohabitation is also a procedurally imperfect, functionally equivalent simulacrum of marriage. As a result, the couple's status as cohabitants can be either consecrated retroactively via a subsequent official "pronouncement" of marriage or institutionalized proactively via a law defining and instituting "common law marriage." In all cases, though, the necessary speech act egg creating the aesthetic, moral, and legal status of the couple comes before the sufficient material consummation. The process is one of creating new social realities, not of naming existing "brute facts."

With regard to war, one must take note of the silence of the Eighty-first Congress in June 1950 and contrast this silence with the performative speech of the Second Continental Congress in July 1776. In 1776, the Second Continental Congress spoke and declared war in a procedurally perfect manner against Great Britain, thereby establishing an organic, Clausewitzian ends-means/ideal-in-process relationship between it and Commander in Chief Washington as its executive agent. In the first place, Commander in Chief Washington's official "orders" and his public "announcements" of them now functioned clearly and unambiguously to implement or consummate the Second Continental Congress's decision. His "orders" and his public "announcements" of them initiated the material military means needed to achieve the political ends desired by the Second Continental Congress in a coherent manner. In the second place, the primary illocutionary force and the primary perlocutionary effects of Commander in Chief Washington's "orders" and his public "announcements" of them were contained, restrained, and given purpose by the Second Continental Congress's declaration of the ends it desired, independence. And, finally, precisely because Commander in Chief Washington's "orders" and his public "announcements" of them consummated the congressional declaration, no ambiguity could exist about any secondary ancillary effects of his "orders" and his public "announcements." The illocutionary intent of Commander in Chief Washington's "orders" was clearly and unambiguously only for the purpose of consummating and fulfilling the illocutionary intent of the Second Continental Congress's "declaration" – independence. Law, and not a man, clearly ruled.

In contrast, when North Korea invaded South Korea in June 1950, the Eighty-first Congress did not speak. By not speaking, it did not establish an organic or any other relationship with President Truman. Instead, President Truman was set adrift as a free agent, forced both to "declare" the political ends desired in Korea and to "order" the diplomatic, economic, and military means to be employed. Set adrift in this moral and legal vacuum, the second-ary ancillary illocutionary force and perlocutionary effects of his "orders" and his public "announcements" of them would now have to function as if they were a congressional declaration. A man, not law, would clearly rule.

In greater detail, congressional silence meant that both the illocutionary force and the perlocutionary effects of President Truman's "orders" and public "announcements" of his "orders" now had to serve two entirely dif-ferent and incompatible functions. The president's words still carried the pri-mary illocutionary intent of consummating the political ends desired. That is, his "orders" and pubic "announcements" of them functioned primarily to direct military operations on the ground in Korea. Crucially, though, the political ends sought were those of President Truman, and not of the Eighty-first Congress. Consequently, the president's "orders" and public "announcements" of them now had to carry the secondary illocutionary intent of "declaring" war in a procedurally imperfect manner against North Korea. Because the rule of law had been violated, the greatest ambiguity now existed about the illocutionary force of the president's "orders" and public "announcements" of them. Which illocutionary intent did his words carry when he spoke? Were his "orders" and "public announcements" sim-ply intended to discipline the warlike means? Or, were they to declare war indirectly? In fine, President Truman's illocutionary intent was no longer clear and unambiguous precisely because a man, and not law, ruled. He no doubt meant what he said, but he was no longer able to say unambiguously what he meant.

Once again, the speech act egg has come before the material chicken. A necessary, but not sufficient speech act was required to create or establish the material state and condition of war, albeit in a procedurally imperfect man-ner, in an unconstitutional manner. American participation in the Korean War did not begin as "brute facts" in Korea that were later "institutionalized." No, American participation began ab initio as a "social fact" with President Truman's official "orders" and public "announcements" of them, which now carried the secondary ancillary illocutionary force of a procedurally imperfect declaration of war. This complex structure is diagrammed in Figure 10.

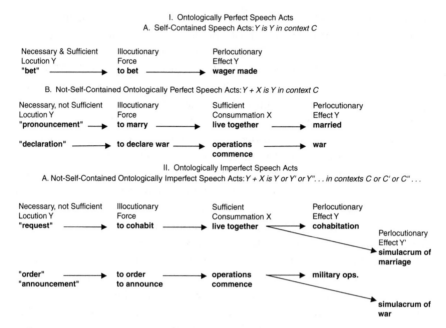

Figure 10. Ontologically Perfect and Imperfect Speech Acts.

In sum, the performative structure of the relationship among locution, illo-cutionary intent, and perlocutionary effect cannot be reduced to a simple naming formula, such as *Υ is imposed on X in context C* or *X counts as Υ in context C*. In order to represent the relationship between the words spoken and the aesthetic, moral, and legal reality so created, a much more com-plex terrain must be mapped. Thus, for an utterance that is self-contained and, therefore, procedurally and ontologically perfect, the notation would be tautological:

$$Υ \text{ is } Υ \text{ in context } C,$$

where *Υ* is both necessary and sufficient to effect the social reality spoken of in *context C*.

This formula captures the fact that such utterances are always ontologically perfect because the locutions are both necessary and sufficient to effect that which is spoken of. The formula is tautological because no slippage between word and world is possible. Consequently, the speaker always says what he means.

For example, by making and accepting a "bet," the bettors initiate and effect a procedurally and ontologically perfect "bet." The perfection of the speech act arises out of the straight-line alignment of the locution, illocution, and perlocution. That is, the bettor's necessary and sufficient locution identifies the illocutionary purpose of the ceremony unambiguously, thereby ensuring that it creates or produces the intended perlocutionary effect – a "bet."

A second example, by making a "bequest," the bequestor initiates and effects an ontologically perfect "bequest." The perfection arises out of the straight-line alignment of the locution, illocution, and perlocution. That is, the necessary and sufficient locution of the person making the bequest identifies the illocutionary purpose of the ceremony unambiguously, thereby ensuring that it creates or produces the intended perlocutionary effect – a "bequest."

In contrast, for a not-self-contained, procedurally perfect utterance, the notation would be:

$$\Upsilon + X \text{ is } \Upsilon \text{ in context } C,$$

where Υ is the necessary, but not sufficient, speech act required to effect the social reality spoken of *in context* C, and X is the sufficient material consummation needed to effect Υ *in context* C.

This formula captures the fact that such utterances are both procedurally and ontologically perfect or complete only after they are consummated. Consequently, the speaker says and does what he actually means.

For example, by "pronouncing" a couple "man and wife," the minister *initiates* and effects the necessary, but not sufficient, collective speech act procedure of an ontologically perfect or complete "marriage." As soon as the couple enacts the sufficient material consummation, the "marriage" will be procedurally and ontologically complete. The completeness arises out of the straight-line alignment of the locution, illocution, and perlocution. That is, the minister's merely necessary locution identifies the illocutionary purpose of the ceremony unambiguously, thereby ensuring that it creates or produces the intended perlocutionary effect – that the couple are indeed "married," and not "cohabiting" – as soon as the couple supply the materially sufficient consummation.

A second example, by "declaring" war in 1776, the Second Continental Congress *initiated* and effected the necessary, but not sufficient, collective speech act procedures of an ontologically perfect or complete "war." As soon as Commander in Chief Washington "ordered" the sufficient material consummation, the "war" was procedurally and ontologically complete. The completeness arose out of the straight-line alignment of the locution, illocution, and perlocution. That is, the Second Continental Congress's merely necessary locution identified the illocutionary purpose of the ceremony unambiguously, thereby ensuring that it created or produced the intended perlocutionary effect – that the nation was indeed at "war" – as soon as Commander in Chief Washington "ordered" the materially sufficient consummation.

And, finally, for a not-self-contained, procedurally imperfect utterance, the notation would be

$$\Upsilon + X \text{ is } \Upsilon \text{ or } \Upsilon' \text{ or } \Upsilon'' \text{ ... } \textit{in contexts } C \textit{ or } C' \textit{ or } C'' ...,$$

1) where Υ is the necessary, but not sufficient, speech act required to effect the social reality spoken of *in context C*, 2) where X is the sufficient material consummation needed to effect Υ, Υ, *or* Υ'... *in context C or C' or C''* ... respectively, and 3) where Υ, Υ'' ... are other functionally equivalent social realities of Υ that are also consummated by X *in contexts C' or C''*. ...

This notation captures the fact that the procedurally and ontologically imperfect utterances Υ' *or* Υ''... are procedurally imperfect, functionally equivalent simulacra with regard to Υ, *in contexts C' or C''*..., as soon as they are consummated. Consequently, the speaker says what he means, but the hearer often misperceives the perlocutionary effect as a procedurally imperfect, functionally equivalent simulacrum of Υ.

For example, by acceding to a "request" to cohabit, a couple initiates and effects a procedurally and ontologically perfect "cohabitation," Υ, but also, simultaneously, a procedurally and ontologically imperfect "marriage," Υ'. The procedural and ontological imperfection of the speech act arises out of the optional alignments of the locution, illocution, and perlocution. The merely necessary locution is a "request" to cohabit containing the illocutionary intent of establishing an intimate relationship of "cohabitation," the perlocutionary consummation of which is achieved when the couple starts living together. Yet, because of 1) the slippage between word and world found in this not-self-contained speech act and 2) the extreme material similarity of "cohabitation" to "marriage," the fact of "cohabitation" is too easily perceived – perhaps, mistaken – for "marriage." "Cohabitation," of course, is not "marriage," not really, unless it continues too long, at which point it becomes "instutionalized" as Υ', a "common law marriage." At least society calls it such, attempting to impose a new name and the rules of procedurally perfect marriage on couples who cohabit too long.

A second example, by issuing a procedurally and ontologically perfect "order" to commence hostile activities and subsequently making a procedurally and ontologically perfect public "announcement" of the "orders," a dictatorial president as commander in chief initiates a procedurally and ontologically perfect or complete "order" and "announcement" of them, Υ, but also simultaneously an ontologically and procedurally imperfect, functionally equivalent simulacrum of a "declaration" of war, Υ'. The imperfection of the "declaration" arises out of the optional alignments of the locution, illocution, and perlocution. The merely necessary locutions are a procedurally and ontologically perfect "order" and the "announcement" of them containing the illocutionary intent of initiating hostile activity, the perlocutionary consummation of which is achieved when diplomatic, economic, or military sanctions are actually imposed. However, because of 1) the slippage between word and world found in these not-self-contained speech acts and 2) the extreme material similarity of imperfectly and perfectly declared war, the fact of hostile sanctions is too easily perceived – perhaps, mistaken – for a procedurally perfect declaration of war, which it is not, at least not aesthetically, morally, or legally.

In fine, Lewis Carroll's Mad Hatter defined the core of rule of law long ago. As the Mad Hatter might say, when a speaker says what he means by carefully aligning his words with his intentions and their consequential effects in the world, the speaker has spoken "piously" with procedural and ontological perfection that accords with the rule of law. When a speaker carelessly misaligns his words, his intentions, and their consequential effects in the world, only meaning what he says, the speaker has spoken "impiously" with procedural and ontological imperfection that accords with the rule of men. Or, as John Austin might have said, when the necessary locution, its illocutionary force, and the sufficient perlocutionary effects are all aligned, the utterance is perfect and in accordance with the rule of law. When the necessary locution and sufficient perlocutionary effect are not aligned with the locution's primary illocutionary force, the utterance is imperfect and not in accordance with the rule of law.

For self-contained procedurally and ontologically perfect speech acts, as a "bet," this alignment is always direct and perfect because the locutions for such speech acts are both necessary and sufficient to "do" that which is spoken of. For not-self-contained speech acts, as a "request" to cohabitate or an "order" and its public "announcement," the alignment is sometimes perfect and sometimes imperfect, depending on whether the speaker conforms to the rule of law or indulges, instead, in the rule of man.

In conclusion, then, what Searle calls "typical wars" (i.e., wars declared in a procedurally imperfect manner) derive their "quasi-legal status" from the "quasi-legal," procedurally imperfect, functionally equivalent secondary illocutionary purposes of "quasi-legal," procedurally imperfect, functionally equivalent locutions. The paternity of this "quasi-legal status" is, therefore, not a process whereby "brute facts" ("the sheer events") are treated as "social facts," which, in turn, are codified as "institutional facts." Rather, their "quasi-legal status" arises, ab initio, in the moment in which the "quasi-legal" "impious" words are spoken. If one desires something more than "quasi-legality," one has only to perform unquestionably legal, procedurally perfect ceremonies, as the "pious" Romans did.

As for the curious the term "police action," it never had official status because it was a spur-of-the-moment ad-lib. It was cut from whole cloth during President Truman's press conference of 29 June 1950. A reporter wondered out loud whether "police action" was the correct term to describe what was happening in Korea, since Truman had been at pains to insist that what was happening was not a war (Truman 1965, 502–6). In response to the suggestion, Truman said, sure, and all the newspapers picked it up. However, "police action" only muddied the waters unnecessarily and, as Searle notes, was never used again.

HOW NOT TO DECLARE WAR: THE INSUFFICIENCY OF THE SUFFICIENT CONSEQUENCES

I was there [in St. Louis]; the plane [President Truman's] came in a minute or two after 2:00 and I got aboard. The first thing the president said to me was, "We're in trouble, I think."

Sunday, 25 June 1950
Secretary of Treasury John Snyder (1975)

The crucial point, however, is that the Korean "War" became the Korean "Conflict," not because of "the sheer events" happening in Korea, nor the "institutionalization" of those "sheer events" via Searle's naming formula *Y is imposed on X in context C*, nor because of what President Truman said and did, but ultimately because of what the Eighty-first Congress failed to say and do. Had the Eighty-first Congress discharged its constitutional responsibility to declare war, as the Second Continental Congress had in 1776, President Truman would not have been set adrift as a free agent, but, instead, would have acted as an executive agent for the Eighty-first Congress. This would have prevented him from saying or doing anything "quasi-legal," anything even marginally outside his constitutional role as commander in chief, as had been the case with Commander in Chief Washington in 1776. For the simple fact stands unchallenged that, had the Eighty-first Congress stood up and made a congressional indictment, denunciation, declaration of peace, and declaration of war, the rule of law would have been respected, in form, if not in substance, and the letter of the Constitution, if not its spirit, would have been followed. Law, not men, would have ruled.

But, of course, that was unimaginable. Who can imagine the Eighty-first or any subsequent Congress discharging its constitutional responsibility to speak? As a result, President Truman pioneered an entirely modern and innovative way to circumvent the Constitution and the rule of law. Instead of one constitutionally mandated authority speaking, the congressional silence was filled in June 1950 in the strangest way by two speakers – President Truman and the brand new, untried United Nations Security Council. Thus, the Korean "event" is an unusually interesting example of how not to declare war because of its magnificent profusion and confusion of illocutionary purposes.

The "sheer event" began at 4:00 am Korean time on Monday, 26 June 1950, or 2:00 pm Washington time on Sunday, 25 June 1950, with the North Korean attack across the thirty-eighth parallel into South Korea. President Truman was at his home in Independence, Missouri, when he learned of the attack. During the course of the afternoon, he flew back to Washington, met with his advisers, and 1) "ordered" the Seventh Fleet to Sasabo, Japan, to await further orders; 2) "ordered" General Douglas MacArthur, commander in chief, Far East, to dispatch a survey mission to Korea and to resupply the urgent needs of the South Korean forces; and 3) "authorized" air and naval action "to prevent the overrunning of Seoul-Kempo-Inchon area in order to insure safe evacuation of US dependents" (Teletype Conference 1950; see also Jessup 1950). Instead of making a public announcement himself, however, Truman decided to speak through the newly established United Nations Security Council, which met that same day in Lake Success, its temporary headquarters, and, invoking its authority under chapter VII (39) of the UN Charter:

> *Determines* that this [North Korean] action [of attacking South Korea on 25 June 1950] constitutes a breach of the peace, and
>
> I. *Calls for* the immediate cessation of hostilities;
>
> II. *Calls upon* the authorities of North Korea to withdraw their armed forces to the thirty-eighth parallel. ...
>
> III. *Calls upon* all Members to render every assistance to the United Nations in the execution of this resolution and to refrain from giving assistance to the North Korean authorities. (Res. 82 of 25 June 1950)

When the North Korean authorities failed to heed the Security Council's "determination" and "call," a more forceful resolution was passed two days later on the eve of the fall of Seoul under chapter VII (42) of the UN Charter. In this resolution, the council

> *Recommends* that the Members of the United Nations furnish such assistance to the Republic of Korea as may be necessary to repel the armed attack and to restore international peace and security in the area. (Res. 83 of 27 June 1950)

That same day, Tuesday, 27 June 1950, responding to the Security Council's "recommendation," President Truman "announced" publicly what he had "ordered" done on 25 June 1950 (Truman 1965, 492).

In the absence of a clear, fully legal declaration from the Eighty-first Congress, what is of interest is the way in which the locutions, their very plastic illocutionary forces, and their several perlocutionary effects do not quite line up as expected. Needless to say, this misalignment has moral, if not deontological, consequences, as John Searle emphasizes (1995, 70–6). In particular, on top of the indirect effects of President Truman's "order" and its "announcement," which produced an "impious" unconstitutional, imperfect declaration of war, notice the confused and confusing illocutionary purposes of the Security Council resolutions as it produced its own imperfect declaration of war.

The first point of concern is the legitimacy of the Security Council to speak. An alliance coordinating body like the Security Council is not sovereign; only the member states are. In this case, only the member states possess both the power (i.e., the armed forces) and the authority (i.e., sovereignty) to declare war in a perfect manner. For the Security Council to declare war in a perfect manner would be both impractical (it possesses no armed force) and a usurpation of the jealously guarded sovereignty of the member states. Thus, the more honest, but less diplomatic, way for the Security Council to have spoken would have been for it to have, first, "determined" that a breach of the peace had occurred and, then,

> Recommend[s] that the Members of the United Nations *declare war in accordance with their respective constitutional processes against the authorities of North Korea* and furnish such assistance to the Republic of Korea as may be necessary to repel the armed attack and to restore international peace and security in the area.

The italic phrase, first, establishes a proper relationship between the Security Council's nonsovereign authority to "determine" and "recommend" and the member states' sovereign authority to declare war in a perfect manner. Second, the italic phrase reaffirms the coordinate principles that govern member state cooperation with the Security Council: namely, that "the Members of the United Nations agree to accept and carry out the decisions of the Security Council in accordance with the present Charter" under chapter V (25), but that, in return, the Security Council agrees to employ the armed forces of the member states only under agreements "subject to ratification by the signatory states in accordance with their respective constitutional processes" under chapter VII (43.3). Needless to say, this condition is echoed in the UN Participation Act of 1945, which stipulates that the agreements between the United States and the United Nations "shall be subject to the approval of the Congress by appropriate Act or joint resolution." (Pub. L. 264, 59 Stat. 619)

But, if an alliance coordinating body like the Security Council is not sovereign, it is, nonetheless, authorized to perform the specific speech acts that it performed. Under chapter VII (39), it is authorized to "determine" whether a breach of the peace had occurred. Under chapter VII (42), it is authorized to "recommend" "action by air, sea, or land forces" whenever it "determines" that a breach of the peace has occurred. Thus, with respect to the *primary/direct* illocutionary force of its procedurally perfect locutions and their *primary/direct* perlocutionary effects, the authority and legitimacy of the Security Council's speech acts cannot be questioned.

Yet, exactly like President Truman's "order" and its public "announcement," neither the *primary/direct* illocutionary purposes nor the *primary/
direct* perlocutionary effects are of concern. Rather, it is the *secondary/indir-
ect* effects. For, the issue turns not on whether the Security Council can
"determine" and "recommend," but, rather, on whether the Security Council
possesses the legitimate authority to produce by indirection a *secondary* illocutionary purpose, with the *secondary* perlocutionary effects that follow on,
as a result of its legitimate authority to "determine" and "recommend."[1] The
convoluted ducking and weaving of the previous sentence identify the precise nature of the problem: How legitimate, one must ask, are the equivocal,
misaligned knock-on effects of the council's "determination" and "recommendation" when compared to the unequivocal, straightforward effects of a
"recommendation" for the member states to declare war "in accordance with
their respective constitutional processes"? Such a "recommendation" would
progress directly from the Security Council's locution to its illocutionary
intent to the predictable perlocutionary effect: a decision by the individual
member states "in accordance with their respective constitutional processes"
to accept or reject the Security Council's "recommendation."

In a more technical language, once spoken, both a "determination" and
a "recommendation" have exhausted their *primary/direct* illocutionary and
perlocutionary consequences. This is the case for a "determination," which
is a self-contained performative speech act; it is the case for a "recommendation," which is a not-self-contained speech act, because its perlocutionary
consequences require the member states to consummate the "recommendation" by acting or not acting upon it. However, the *secondary/indirect*
illocutionary and perlocutionary consequences of the Security Council's
"recommendation" are to effect a simularcum of war, a procedurally imperfect declaration of war against North Korea. This is a derivative illocutionary
purpose that must be deduced from 1) the propositional content of "assistance" and 2) the circumstances that surround the Security Council's determination and recommendation. The "impious" indirection of the process
highlights the "quasi-legal" status of the council's speech acts and, hence,
considerable potential for confusion, error, and mischief.

Aesthetically, morally, and legally, as the March Hare pointed out to
Alice, meaning what one says is not the same as saying what one means. The
Security Council said it was recommending assistance, but it meant to initiate
an imperfectly declared war against North Korea. Since the aesthetic, moral,
and legal coherence and clarity that derive from saying what one means are to

---

[1] Note that the referents to the terms "primary/direct" and "secondary/indirect" are the reverse
of Searle's usage in "Indirect Speech Acts" (1975, 62). Because he views the sincerity condition differently, he sees the "literal" illocutionary act as "secondary" and the "not literal"
illocutionary act as "primary."

be valued over the imprecision of euphemistic (dissembling?) speech, a more honest locution was desirable. Or, at least, it is desirable for those who seek to strengthen the rule of law, and not men.

In defense of the Security Council, however, its euphemistic indirection was and continues to be forced upon it. Superficially, the council is restrained by the 1928 Kellogg-Briand Pact and by article II (4) of the UN Charter, both of which theoretically outlaw war, "renounc[ing] it, as an instrument of national policy," in the case of the Kellogg-Briand Pact or "refrain[ing] ... from the threat or use of force" in the case of the charter. Hence, for the Security Council to recommend that the member states involve themselves in a theoretically illegal activity would have been unseemly in the extreme. Good manners, therefore, excuse the Security Council's indirection. Good manners do not, however, excuse the failure of the Eighty-first Congress to speak during the "events" of June 1950, as the Constitution mandates it to speak. That the Congress failed once again to speak demonstrates yet again the fatal flaw in the Constitution and the need for an appropriate amendment in order to advance the rule of law in war as in peace.

Epilogue

Senator Malcolm Wallop

Succinct and insightful explanations of the power to declare war are few and far between. However, they do exist and can be found, often in the most usual places. For example, who would ever think to pick up the *Congressional Record* and turn to the Senate debate of Wednesday, 24 October 1990? The debate that day concerned an effort to overturn President George H. W. Bush's veto of the Civil Rights Act of 1990, known also as the Kennedy-Hawkins Bill. The vetoed bill was an effort again to outlaw certain discriminatory employment practices that had recently been struck down by the Supreme Court.

For Senator Malcolm Wallop, Republican from Wyoming, however, civil rights was less pressing an issue than the war against Iraq for the liberation of Kuwait. With less than two weeks before the midterm elections, Senator Wallop was greatly frustrated that the 101st Congress had yet to discharge its constitutional duty "to declare war." During a break in the civil rights debate, while negotiations were being conducted on the Senate floor, the Majority Leader, Senator Robert Dole, conceded time to Senator Wallop to voice his concerns.

Senator Wallop began his remarks by recalling the institutional impediments. Iraq had invaded Kuwait three and a half months ago, on 2 August 1990, and no member had yet taken the initiative to introduce a draft declaration:

> Mr. President [of the Senate], it had been my purpose to introduce a joint resolution calling for a declaration of war against the government of Saddam Hussein and Iraq. It is clear to me that despite the gasps of amazement, outrage, and dismay that this action would have caused, its effect might will [*sic*] have been salutary.

Even mentioning such an intention on my part is bound to elicit shock, Mr. President, but hear me out. A declaration of war is not – let me repeat not – a call to combat, but a declaration of national purpose.

War does not necessarily entail the clash of armed forces, but it is a contest of wills and of opposing interests, interests which must be backed up with the moral and material readiness to fight if necessary.

A declaration of war defines the circumstances of basic conflict between states. It may lead to a variety of outcomes, depending on the will and capabilities of the antagonists. But it leaves no doubt in the mind of either side as to the other's purpose. Yet such doubt does exist today with respect to Operation Desert Shield.

After noting the first function of a declaration, how it defines or constitutes a war, Senator Wallop next turned to a declaration's second function, the relationship between the political purposes sought and the success of the operational means employed:

When muddle and confusion hold sway over military operations, then we face far more than a temporary inconvenience. We court disaster. We face the needless deaths of young Americans in faraway places. We risk permanent damage to vital national interests.

In warfare there is a direct relationship – a synergism – between the combatant nation's purposes in the conflcit [*sic*] and the conduct of the war at the operational or tactical level. No military commander can ever be assured of victory. But clear and sound national policies, goals, and overall strategies generally contribute to success on the battlefield. On the other hand, lack of clarity of purpose, with flawed goals and policies, inevitably lead to operational failure and needless loss of life.... This is the issue that I want to address, Mr. President. The same uncertainty and confusion that spelled disaster [for President Reagan] in Lebanon [in 1982–4] are now creeping into our Persian Gulf operation, and hold the same potential for disaster.

Reverting to his first topic, Senator Wallop then dilates on the institutional impediments and laments the lack of seriousness in discussion of the power to declare war:

I believe the founders conferred this power [to declare war in a procedurally perfect manner] on the Congress for a loftier purpose than to instigate a constitutional game of chicken with the executive every time we face a foreign threat.

The power to declare war should not be seen as an impediment to the executive branch; it is a congressional obligation, in the right circumstances. It contributes to victory by ensuring first a clear understanding of the war aims, and of gaining the Nation's commitment to those aims.

The Bush administration appears to differ with the Congress over the interpretation of the constitutional provisions to declare and prosecute a war.... A declaration of war certainly does not oblige him immediately to launch an offensive, or a military action of any kind....

For all these reasons, I believe that a debate on a declaration of war would be the best means to force ourselves to begin thinking more rigorously about our national interests, our policy goals, and our military and diplomatic strategy. Perhaps then Mr. President, our purposes – and the national commitment needed to ensure success – will become clear....

So I feel compelled, Mr. President, to raise the question of a declaration of war. I am not eager to see carnage or bloodshed. On the contrary, I believe that armed conflict must be the last resort, and I hope that we can achieve our aims short of open war. Nor do I wish to raise an impediment to decisive, forceful action by the administration, nor undermine the clear warmaking prerogatives of the President implicit in the Constitution. Nonetheless, someone has to raise these questions – we must know what we are about.

A declaration of war requires passage of a joint resolution in both Houses. Mr. President, sadly, there is not enough time left in this session for the required parliamentary steps to bring it to completion before both houses.

Reverting to his second topic, Senator Wallop reiterates the importance of the relationship between the political purposes sought and the success of the operational means employed:

Precisely what are our military forces in the Persian Gulf supposed to accomplish, and how are they supposed to accomplish it? It is necessary to consider in our own minds the relationship between our ends and our means in this conflict.

Since World War II, few of America's deployments of military forces overseas have been successful. Korea, Vietnam, and our recent involvement in Lebanon turned into national tragedies largely because the President and Congress sent troops in harm's way without even seeking to answer fundamental questions: Whom are we marching off to fight? What is the military objective, which, if achieved would constitute success and allow us to come home with heads held high? Just what are our plans for achieving that objective? What is the endgame?...

... It is possible for democratic nations to fight wars without declaring them, or by calling them by other names – police actions for example – just as it is possible for men and women to live together without declaring marriage, or by calling their cohabitation by other names. But declarations of war, like declarations of marriage, are useful because they force people to ask themselves, "What am I doing?", and, once they understand, to make the sort of commitment that enhances the prospects of securing our long-term interests.

And, finally, he concluded:

But Mr. President, I urge my colleagues to ponder these critical issues and their own responsibilities, as befits the elected leaders of a great and free people, and as called for by our Constitution. We owe it to our military, our allies, and our citizens to define a purpose or to come home. I thank my colleagues for their attention, and yield the floor. (136 *Cong. Rec.* S16, 591, 24 October 1990)

The effort to override President George H. W. Bush's veto of the Civil Rights Act of 1990 failed on a vote of sixty-six yeas to thirty-four nays. No need exists to ask whether Senator Wallop's effort to have the 101st Congress declare war succeeded or not.

Appendix I

Five Congressional Declarations of War and One Appropriations Act

1. FOR THE WAR FOR INDEPENDENCE: AN ABSOLUTE, REASONED, SOLEMNLY PERFECT DECLARATION

The Virginia Resolutions:

> That these United Colonies are, and of Right ought to be, Free and Independent States, that they are absolved from all allegiance to the British Crown, and that all Political connection between them and the State of Great Britain is, and ought to be, totally dissolved.
>
> That it is expedient forthwith to take the most effectual measures for forming foreign Alliances.
>
> That a plan of confederation be prepared and transmitted to the respective Colonies for their consideration and approbation (Maier 1997, 41).

Introduced by Richard Henry Lee of Virginia,
seconded by John Adams of Massachusetts,

Friday, 7 June 1776

> In CONGRESS, July 4, 1776.
>
> A DECLARATION
>
> By the REPRESENTATIVES of the
>
> UNITED STATES OF AMERICA,
>
> In GENERAL CONGRESS assembled.

WHEN in the Course of human Events, it becomes necessary for one People to dissolve the Political Bands which have connected them with another, and to assume among the Powers of the Earth, the separate and equal Station to which the Laws of Nature and of Nature's God entitle them, a decent Respect to the Opinions of Mankind requires that they should declare the causes which impel them to the Separation.

We hold these Truths to be self-evident, that all Men are created equal, that they are endowed by their Creator with certain unalienable Rights, that among these are Life, Liberty, and the Pursuit of Happiness – That to secure these Rights, Governments are instituted among Men, deriving their just Powers from the Consent of the Governed, that whenever any Form of Government becomes destructive of these Ends, it is the Right of the People to alter or to abolish it, and to institute new Government, laying its Foundation on such Principles, and organizing its Powers in such Form, as to them shall seem most likely to effect their Safety and Happiness. Prudence, indeed, will dictate that Governments long established should not be changed for light and transient Causes; and accordingly all Experience hath shewn, that Mankind are more disposed to suffer, while Evils are sufferable, than to right themselves by abolishing the Forms to which they are accustomed. But when a long Train of Abuses and Usurpations, pursuing invariably the same Object, evinces a Design to reduce them under absolute Despotism, it is their Right, it is their Duty, to throw off such Government, and to provide new Guards for their future Security. Such has been the patient Sufferance of these Colonies; and such is now the Necessity which constrains them to alter their former Systems of Government. The History of the present King of Great Britain is a History of repeated injuries and Usurpations, all having in direct Object the Establishment of an absolute Tyranny over these States. To prove this, let Facts be submitted to a candid World.

[indictment]

He has refused his Assent to Laws, the most wholesome and necessary for the public Good.

He has forbidden his Governors to pass Laws of immediate and pressing Importance, unless suspended in their Operation till his Assent should be obtained; and when so suspended, he has utterly neglected to attend to them.

He has refused to pass other Laws for the Accommodation of large Districts of People, unless those People would relinquish the Right of Representation in the Legislature, a Right inestimable to them, and formidable to Tyrants only.

He has called together Legislative Bodies at Places unusual, uncomfortable, and distant from the Depository of their public Records, for the sole Purpose of fatiguing them into Compliance with his Measures.

He has dissolved Representative Houses repeatedly, for opposing with manly Firmness his Invasions on the Rights of the People.

He has refused for a long Time, after such Dissolutions, to cause others to be elected; whereby the Legislative Powers, incapable of Annihilation, have returned to the People at large for their exercise; the State remaining in the mean time exposed to all the Dangers of Invasion from without, and Convulsions within.

He has endeavoured to prevent the Population of these States; for that Purpose obstructing the Laws for Naturalization of Foreigners; refusing to pass others to encourage their Migrations hither, and raising the Conditions of new Appropriations of Lands.

He has obstructed the Administration of Justice, by refusing his Assent to Laws for establishing Judiciary Powers. He has made Judges dependent on his Will alone, for the Tenure of their Offices, and the Amount and Payment of their Salaries.

He has erected a Multitude of new Offices, and sent hither Swarms of Officers to harrass our People, and eat out their Substance.

He has kept among us, in Times of Peace, Standing Armies, without the consent of our Legislatures.

He has affected to render the Military independent of and superior to the Civil Power.

He has combined with others to subject us to a Jurisdiction foreign to our Constitution, and unacknowledged by our Laws; giving his Assent to their Acts of pretended Legislation:

For quartering large Bodies of Armed Troops among us: For protecting them, by a mock Trial, from Punishment for any Murders which they should commit on the Inhabitants of these States:

For cutting off our Trade with all Parts of the World:

For imposing Taxes on us without our Consent:

For depriving us, in many Cases, of the Benefits of Trial by Jury:

For transporting us beyond Seas to be tried for pretended Offences:

For abolishing the free System of English Laws in a neighbouring Province, establishing therein an arbitrary Government, and enlarging its Boundaries, so as to render it at once an Example and fit Instrument for introducing the same absolute Rule into these Colonies:

For taking away our Charters, abolishing our most valuable Laws, and altering fundamentally the Forms of our Governments:

For suspending our own Legislatures, and declaring themselves invested with Power to legislate for us in all Cases whatsoever.

He has abdicated Government here, by declaring us out of his Protection and waging War against us.

He has plundered our Seas, ravaged our Coasts, burnt our Towns, and destroyed the Lives of our People.

He is, at this Time, transporting large Armies of foreign Mercenaries to compleat the Works of Death, Desolation, and Tyranny, already begun with circumstances of Cruelty and Perfidy, scarcely paralleled in the most barbarous Ages, and totally unworthy the Head of a civilized Nation.

He has constrained our fellow Citizens taken Captive on the high Seas to bear Arms against their Country, to become the Executioners of their Friends and Brethren, or to fall themselves by their Hands.

He has excited domestic Insurrections amongst us, and has endeavoured to bring on the Inhabitants of our Frontiers, the merciless Indian Savages, whose known Rule of Warfare, is an undistinguished Destruction, of all Ages, Sexes and Conditions.

In every stage of these Oppressions we have Petitioned for Redress in the most humble Terms: Our repeated Petitions have been answered only by repeated Injury. A Prince, whose Character is thus marked by every act which may define a Tyrant, is unfit to be the Ruler of a free People.

Nor have we been wanting in Attentions to our British Brethren. We have warned them from Time to Time of Attempts by their Legislature to extend an unwarrantable Jurisdiction over us. We have reminded them of the Circumstances of our Emigration and Settlement here. We have appealed to their native Justice and Magnanimity, and we have conjured them by the Ties of our common Kindred to disavow these Usurpations, which, would inevitably interrupt our Connections and Correspondence. They too have been deaf to the Voice of Justice and of Consanguinity.

[denunciation of war]

We must, therefore, acquiesce in the Necessity, which denounces our Separation,

[declaration of war]

and hold them, as we hold the rest of Mankind, Enemies in War, in Peace, Friends.

[declaration of peace terms]

We, therefore, the Representatives of the UNITED STATES OF AMERICA, in General Congress, Assembled, appealing to the Supreme Judge of the World for the Rectitude of our Intentions, do, in the Name, and by Authority of the good People of these Colonies, solemnly Publish and Declare, That these United Colonies are, and of Right out [*sic*] to be, Free and Independent States; that they are absolved from all Allegiance to the British Crown, and that all political Connection between them and the State of Great-Britain, is and ought to be totally dissolved; and that as Free and Independent States, they have full Power to levy War, conclude Peace, contract Alliances, establish Commerce, and to do all other Acts and Things which Independent States may of right do. And for the support of this Declaration, with a firm Reliance on the Protection of divine Providence, we mutually pledge to each other our Lives, our Fortunes, and our sacred Honor.

[no authorization]

2. FOR THE WAR OF 1812: AN ABSOLUTE, UNREASONED, SOLEMNLY PERFECT DECLARATION

Be it enacted by the Senate and House of Representatives of the United States in Congress assembled,

[declaration of war]

That war be and the same is hereby declared to exist between the United Kingdom of Great Britain and Ireland and the dependencies thereof, and the United States of America and their Territories;

[authorization]

and that the President of the United States is hereby authorized to use the whole land and naval force of the United States to carry the same into effect, and to issue to private armed vessels of the United States commissions or letters of marque and general reprisal, in such form as he shall think proper, and under the seal of the United States, against the vessels, goods, and effects, of the Government of the said United Kingdom of Great Britain and Ireland, and the subjects thereof. (Pub. L. No. 12–102, 2 Stat. 755)

3. FOR THE MEXICAN-AMERICAN WAR: AN INFORMAL, ABSOLUTE, UNREASONED DECLARATION

Whether this act counts as a declaration of war or not must be disputed. It is basically an appropriations bill that has had its title changed and a single recital pasted on. Certainly it is functionally equivalent to a formal declaration of war, but, precisely because it is functionally equivalent, good reason exists to discount it as declaration "in form." I have reproduced only a select few sections of the act.

An Act providing for the Prosecution of the Existing War between the United States and the Republic of Mexico

[indictment and denunciation of the enemy?]

Whereas, by the act of the Republic of Mexico, a state of war exists between that Government and the United States:

Be it enacted by the Senate and House of Representatives of the United States of America in Congress assembled,

[authorization]

That, for the purpose of enabling the Government of the United States to prosecute said war to a speedy and successful termination, the President be, and he is hereby, authorized to employ the militia, naval, and military forces of the United States, and to call for and accept the services of any number of volunteers, not exceeding fifty thousand, who may offer their services, either as cavalry, artillery, infantry, or riflemen, to serve twelve months after they shall have arrived at the place of rendezvous, or to the end of the war, unless sooner discharged, according to the time for which they shall have been mustered into service; and that the sum of ten million dollars, out of any moneys in the treasury, or to come into the Treasury, not otherwise appropriated, be, and the same is hereby, appropriated, for the purpose of carrying the provisions of this act into effect.

[appropriation]

Sec. 5. *And be it further enacted,* That the said volunteers so offering their services shall be accepted by the President in companies, battalions, squadrons, and regiments, whose officers shall be appointed in the manner prescribed by law in the several States and Territories to which such companies, battalions, squadrons, and regiments shall respectively belong.

Sec. 6. *And be it further enacted,* That the President of the United States be, and he is hereby, authorized to organize companies so tendering their services into battalions or squadrons, battalions and squadrons into regiments, regiments into brigades, and brigades into divisions, as soon as the number of volunteers shall render such organization, in his judgment, expedient; and the President shall, if necessary, apportion the staff, field, and general officers among the respective States and Territories from which the volunteers shall tender their services, as he may deem proper.

Sec. 9. *And be it further enacted,* That whenever the militia or volunteers are called and received into the service of the United States, under the provisions of this act, they shall have the organization of the army of the United States, and shall have the same pay and allowances; and all mounted privates, non-commissioned officers, musicians and artificers, shall be allowed 40 cents per day for the use and risk of their horses, except of horses actually killed in action; and if any mounted volunteer, private, non-commissioned officer, musician, or artificer, shall not keep himself provided with a serviceable horse, said volunteer shall serve on foot. Approved 13 May 1846. (Pub. L. No. 29–16, 9 Stat. 9)

4. FOR THE SPANISH-AMERICAN WAR: A CONDITIONAL, REASONED, SOLEMNLY PERFECT DECLARATION

House Resolution 233 was introduced in the House on 13 April 1898 but completely revised by the Senate. The original resolution read as follows:

Joint resolution (H. Res. 233) authorizing and directing the President of the United States to intervene to stop the war in Cuba, and for the purpose of establishing a stable and independent government of the people therein.

[indictment and denunciation of the enemy]

Whereas the Government of Spain for three years past has been waging war on the Island of Cuba against a revolution by the inhabitants thereof without making any substantial progress towards the suppression of said revolution, and has conducted the warfare in a manner contrary to the laws of nations by methods inhuman and uncivilized, causing the death by starvation of more than 200,000 innocent noncombatants, the victims being for the most part helpless women and children, inflicting intolerable injury to the commercial interests of the United States, involving the destruction of the lives and property of many of our citizens, entailing the expenditure of millions of money in patrolling our coasts and policing the high seas in order to maintain our neutrality; and Whereas this long series of losses, injuries, and burdens for which Spain is responsible has culminated in the destruction of the United States battle ship Maine in the harbor of Havana and the death of 260 of our seamen;

Resolved by the Senate and the House of Representatives of the United States of America in Congress assembled,

[declaration of peace terms]

That the President is hereby authorized and directed to intervene at once to stop the war in Cuba to the end and with the purpose of securing permanent peace and order there and establishing by the free action of the people thereof a stable and independent government of their own in the Island of Cuba;

[authorization]

and the President is hereby authorized and empowered to use the land and naval forces of the United States to execute the purpose of this resolution (*Cong. Rec.* (House) 18 April 1898, p. 4041, where the Senate amendments are also recorded).

[no declaration of war]

* * *

Joint Resolution For the independence of the people of Cuba, demanding that the Government of Spain relinquish its authority and government in the Island of Cuba, and withdraw its land and naval forces from Cuba and Cuban waters, and directing the President of the United States to use the land and naval forces of the United States to carry these resolutions into effect.

[indictment]

Whereas the abhorrent conditions which have existed for more than three years in the Island of Cuba, so near our own borders, have shocked the moral sense of the people of the United States, have been a disgrace to Christian civilization, culminating, as they have, in the destruction of a United States battleship, with two hundred and sixty of its officers and crew, while on a friendly visit in the Harbor of Havana, and cannot longer be endured, as has been set forth by the President of the United States in his message to Congress of April eleventh, eighteen hundred and ninety-eight, upon which the action of Congress was invited: Therefore,

Resolved by the Senate and the House of Representatives of the United States of America, in Congress assembled, First. That the people of the Island of Cuba are, and of right ought to be free and independent.

[denunciation of the enemy and declaration of peace terms]

Second. That it is the duty of the United States to demand, and the Government of the United States does hereby demand, that the Government of Spain at once relinquish its authority and government in the Island of Cuba, and withdraw its land and naval forces from Cuba and Cuban waters.

[authorization]

Third. That the President of the United States be, and he hereby is, directed and empowered to use the entire land and naval forces of the United States, and to call into the actual service of the United States the militia of the several States to such extent as may be necessary to carry these resolutions into effect.

Fourth. That the United States hereby disclaims any disposition or intention to exercise sovereignty, jurisdiction, or control over said island except for the pacification thereof, and asserts its determination, when that is accomplished, to leave the government and control of the island to its people.

Approved, April 20, 1898. (The Joint Resolution was passed at 1:30 am on 19 April 1898; Pub. Res. No. 55–24, 30 Stat. 738.)

[no declaration of war]

* * *

An Absolute, Unreasoned, Solemnly Perfect Declaration

An Act Declaring that war exists between the United States of America and the Kingdom of Spain.

[no indictment and denunciation of the enemy]

Be it enacted by the Senate and House of Representatives of the United States of America in Congress assembled,

[declaration of war]

First. That war be, and the same is hereby, declared to exist, and that war has existed since the twenty-first day of April, anno Domini eighteen hundred and ninety-eight, including said day, between the United States of America and the Kingdom of Spain.

[authorization]

Second. That the President of the United States be, and he hereby is, directed and empowered to use the entire land and naval forces of the United States, and to call into the actual service of the United States the militia of the several States, to such extent as may be necessary to carry this Act into effect.

[no declaration of peace terms]

Approved, April 25, 1898. (Pub. L. No. 55–189, 30 Stat. 364)

5. FOR WORLD WAR I: AN ABSOLUTE, UNREASONED, SOLEMNLY PERFECT DECLARATION

The State Department's draft as approved by President Woodrow Wilson and submitted to the House leadership on 2 April 1917:

JOINT RESOLUTION, Declaring that a State of War Exists between the Imperial German Government and the Government and People of the United States and Making Provisions to Prosecute the Same.

[indictment and denunciation of the enemy]

Whereas. The recent acts of the Imperial German Government are acts of war against the Government and people of the United States:

Resolved. By the Senate and House of Representatives of the United States of America in Congress assembled,

[declaration of war]

that the state of war between the United States and the Imperial German Government which has thus been thrust upon the United States is hereby formally declared; and

[authorization]

That the President be, and is hereby, authorized and directed to take immediate steps not only to put the country in a thorough state of defense but also to exert all of its power and employ all of its resources to carry on war against the Imperial German Government

[no declaration of peace terms]

and bring the conflict to a successful termination. (*New York Times* 3 April 1917, 1)

After passing in the House, the State Department draft was amended in the Senate and, then, accepted by the House:

Joint Resolution Declaring that a state of war exists between the Imperial German Government and the Government and the People of the United States and making provision to prosecute the same.

[indictment and denunciation of the enemy]

Whereas the Imperial German Government has committed repeated acts of war against the Government and people of the United States of America: Therefore, be it

Resolved by the Senate and House of Representatives of the United States of America in Congress assembled,

[declaration of war]

That the state of war between the United States and the Imperial German Government which has thus been thrust upon the United States is hereby formally declared;

[authorization]

and that the President be, and he is hereby, authorized and directed to employ the entire naval and military forces of the United States and the resources of the Government to carry on war against the Imperial German Government;

[no declaration of peace terms]

and to bring the conflict to a successful termination all the resources of the country are hereby pledged by the Congress of the United States (Approved, April 6, 1917; Pub. Res. No. 65–1, 40 Stat. 1).

The declaration of war against the Imperial and Royal Austro-Hungarian Government (Approved, 7 December 1917. Pub. L. No. 65–1, 40 Stat. 429) is identical with the declaration against the Imperial German Government.

6. FOR WORLD WAR II: AN ABSOLUTE, UNREASONED, SOLEMNLY PERFECT DECLARATION

Declaring that a state of war exists between the Imperial Government of Japan and the Government and the people of the United States and making provisions to prosecute the same:

[indictment and denunciation of the enemy]

Whereas the Imperial Government of Japan has committed unprovoked acts of war against the Government and the people of the United States of America; therefore, be it

Resolved by the Senate and the House of Representatives of the United States of America in Congress assembled,

[declaration of war]

That the state of war between the United States and the Imperial Government of Japan which has thus been thrust upon the United States is hereby formally declared;

[authorization]

and the President is hereby authorized and directed to employ the entire naval and military forces of the United States and the resources of the Government to carry on the war against the Imperial Government of Japan;

[no declaration of peace terms]

and, to bring the conflict to a successful termination, all of the resources of the country are hereby pledged by the Congress of the United States (Pub. L. No. (Pub. L. No. 77–328, 55 Stat. 795; Approved, 8 December 1941, 4:10 pm, EST).

The other five declarations for World War II, which are all but identical to the declaration against Japan, except for the name of the country, are against the Government of Germany (Pub. L. No. 77–331, 55 Stat. 796; Approved, 11 December 1941, 3:05 pm, EST.), against the Government of Italy (Pub. L. No. 77–332, 55 Stat. 797; Approved 11 December 1941 3:06 pm, EST.), against the Government of Bulgaria (Pub. L. No. 77–563, 56 Stat. 307; Approved, 5 June 1942), against the Government of Hungary (Pub. L. No. 77–564, 56 Stat. 307; Approved, 5 June 1942), against the Government of Rumania (Pub. L. No. 77–565, 56 Stat. 307; Approved, 5 June 1942).

Appendix II

The Fœderative Powers in Parliamentary Governments

To begin with the obvious, executive functions in a parliamentary regime are not vested in a single chief executive officer, a president, but in a cabinet. As a result, executive decision making is officially collective. A prime minister may dominate the cabinet, but, in theory, at least, no decision is a purely subjective mental act of a single chief executive officer, as in a presidential regime. All executive decisions result officially from collective discussions and processes. To anticipate, this means that a proto–Council on War and Peace already exists in a parliamentary regime. Equally important, the complex executive-legislative relationship in a parliamentary system is very much more organic and integrated than in a presidential-congressional system. A mechanical separation of these two functions is avoided. As a result, the apparent competition and conflict that characterize presidential regimes are largely absent.

Consider a parliament's organic executive-legislative advantages first: As a large, majority-rule body, a parliament naturally suffers from all of the same problems as large, majority-rule congresses: 1) high transaction costs, 2) difficulty coordinating the members' shared interests, and 3) exorbitant collective action problems. To overcome these inherent tensions, parliamentary regimes require the same firm agenda setting and leadership from the executive as congressional regimes. However, instead of trying to separate the executive from the legislative in a very abstract and artificial way with a single chief executive officer or president, parliamentary regimes fold the executive functions directly into the parliament. The majority party or coalition forms the cabinet. This means that executive functions are melded with legislative functions to produce a more seamless and stable form of government.

Nonetheless, parliamentary governments are not above criticism for the ways in which they treat for peace and decide the question of war or peace.

251

Since 1945, no government anywhere in the world has made a procedurally perfect declaration of war. This means that parliamentary governments are no better on this score than any other since 1945. Before 1939, parliamentary governments made perfect declarations war with the same frequency and in the same way as presidential governments. As to frequency, parliamentary governments employed perfect declarations as infrequently as presidential governments. As to procedures, the cabinet decided the question of war or peace in private and, then, made a public announcement. The public announcement was usually a procedurally imperfect statement in the parliament, but, exceptionally, a procedurally perfect declaration of war was made by the head of state – the president in a parliamentary republic, the king in a constitutional monarchy.

As an example of the exceptional case, on Monday, 8 December 1941, on the same day that Commander in Chief Roosevelt delivered his famous "A Date Which Will Live in Infamy" speech requesting a congressional declaration of war against Japan in Washington, Prime Minister Winston Churchill was addressing Parliament in London:

> As soon as I heard last night that Japan had attacked the United States I felt it necessary that Parliament should be immediately summoned. It is indispensable to our system of government that Parliament should play a full part in all the important acts of state, and at all crucial moments in the conduct of the war, and I am glad to see so many members have been able to be in their places in spite of the shortness of notice.

However, a little further on in his address, we learn that the indispensable part that Parliament played in this important act of state consists entirely of forgathering to listen to the prime minister tell it what he and the cabinet have already done:

> The Cabinet, which met at 12:30 today, therefore authorized an immediate declaration of war upon Japan. Instructions to this effect were sent to His Majesty's Ambassador in Tokyo, and a communication was dispatched to the Japanese Chargé d'Affaires at 1 o'clock today to this effect. (Churchill 1941, 14).

As can be seen, parliamentary regimes have clung to their royal roots and John Locke's conception of the king's fœderative powers. War and the declaring of war are still seen as royal prerogatives, albeit now exercised by the cabinet in the name of the king. The members of parliament are not directly involved. Their role is not that of decision maker, but of primary audience for the public announcement of the cabinet's decision.

In this regard, an interesting recent anomaly is the passage of a resolution "supporting" British participation in the 2003 American led invasion of Iraq. As noted in chapter 10, Prime Minister Tony Blair's decision to join with President George W. Bush in the invasion was most controversial in Britain. The controversy grew to such proportions that the prime minister was forced

to accede to an unprecedented American-style resolution, not of "authorization," but of "support" (United Kingdom 2003). Both the debate and the
resolution were anomalous because this was the first time since the English
Civil War that Parliament had debated either a perfect or an imperfect declaration of war. Crucially, however, the prime minister was able to delay the
debate on the resolution until the day before the invasion. This delay meant
that the members were under enormous pressure not just to maintain party
discipline but to avoid the accusation of "abandoning our troops in the field"
as well. As a result, after ten hours of debate, the House divided in favor of
"support," ayes four hundred twelve, nos one hundred forty-nine, at 10:14
pm on Tuesday, 18 March 2003 (*ibid.*). On the basis of two hundred years
of American history, this is precisely what one would expect. Subsequently,
much talk was heard that a historic precedent had been set, and Clare Short
submitted a private members bill to require authorizing resolutions in the
future (*The Armed Forces (Parliamentary Approval for Participation in
Armed Conflict) Act 2005*). The bill was based loosely on the War Powers
Resolution of 1973. At the end of the day, however, the bill failed.

Another interesting development has occurred since the end of the cold
war in Germany and several neighboring North European countries. These
parliaments have revived the "wel gaaf ensample the good wyse kyng charles
the fythe of that name" (Pisan 1937, I, v). Like the medieval French king
before, they have taken advantage of Parliament's "power of the purse"
to give members the opportunity to express their loyalty and love, for, "O
how is that a proffitable thynge in seygnourye / Royame / or Cyte to haue
true subgettis / & of grete loue" (*ibid.*). Parliamentary loyalty and love are
expressed, of course, by passing the budget for any proposed military operation. For example, section 1 of article 115a [Concept and determination of a
state of defense] of the German Basic Law (*Grundgesetz*) reads:

> The determination that federal territory is being attacked by armed force or that
> such an attack is directly imminent (state of defence) are made by the House of
> Representatives with the consent of the Senate. Such determination are made at the
> request of the Government and require a two-thirds majority of the votes cast, which
> include at least the majority of the members of the House of Representatives.

Obviously, this section was written during the cold war and does not respond
to cases when the federal territory is not being attacked. Such cases arose
shortly after the cold war, initially as a result of ethnic cleansing in the former
Yugoslavia. To respond to such cases, new procedures had to be developed:
After the chancellor and cabinet have reached their decision, the chief secretary
of the Federal Chancellery drafts and sends an official report to the Bundestag
informing it of the decision. The chief secretary's report 1) gives reference to
previous relevant documents; 2) provides the rationale (*Begründung*) for the
proposed operation; 3) summarizes the plan in general terms, including the

types and numbers of forces to be deployed; and 4) concludes with a budget (e.g., Regarding German participation in the NATO Extraction Force for Kosovo, see *Deutscher Bundestag, Drucksache* 14/397 of 2 February 1999). Upon receipt of the report, the Bundestag debates the matter and votes the funds requested. As with Charles V of France, not supporting the chancellor and cabinet's decision by not voting the funds requested is unimaginable.

The critical point, of course, is that the power of the purse is not the power to declare war. The chief secretary's report comes from the chancellor and cabinet after, not before, the question of war or peace has been asked and answered. The practical effect of the letter, then, is as an imperfect declaration of war to announce publicly the chancellor and cabinet's decision. Assuming minimal political competence of the chancellor, his decision would not be taken to the cabinet unless he was sure of approval, and the cabinet's decision would not be taken to the Bundestag unless it was sure of approval in turn. In other words, the procedures are the same "appropriations structure" President James Polk used in 1846 to start the Mexican-American War. The only difference, one hopes, is that the German chancellor would not stoop to misleading the Bundestag to secure passage of the appropriations bill, as President Polk did.

Ironically, if not tragically, when the chief secretary's report is sent, the German chancellor and cabinet are following both the letter and the spirit of the Basic Law. Just as in any constitutional monarchy, the German Basic Law betrays its royal roots by vesting the power to declare war in a perfect manner with the head of state, the president of the Federal Republic:

> Article 115a (5) Where the determination of the existence of a state of defence has been promulgated and where the federal territory is being attacked by armed force, the President may, with the consent of the House of Representatives, issued declarations under international law [i.e., Hague Convention III of 1907] regarding the existence of such state of defence.

As a result, one must acknowledge that law rules, but only in a very formal sense. For, the decision is still being made in private, as in the United States; the members of the Bundestag are not being asked to decide the question or war or peace. They are simply being asked to confirm and support a war that the Chancellor and Cabinet have already decided on and declared imperfectly. The politics of declaring war in Germany may be different than in the United States, but the procedures are essentially the same.

In light of this essential sameness of procedures, the fact that the cabinet represents a proto–Council on War and Peace is most significant. In particular, the cabinet is already characterized by collective decision making. This puts it one step ahead of any presidential regime. The major stumbling block, however, is that exercising the foederative powers of treating for peace and declaring of war is not viewed as special and distinct. Instead, they are viewed as just another agenda item, submerged, if not smothered, as it were, in among a long and busy peacetime agenda. As Lords Butler and Wilson's investigations of British cabinet practices in the prelude to the 2003 invasion of Iraq observed, "wider collective discussion and consideration by the Cabinet [were limited] to the frequent but unscripted occasions when the Prime Minister, Foreign Secretary and Defence Secretary briefed the Cabinet orally.... Excellent quality papers were written by officials ... [but they] were not discussed in Cabinet or in Cabinet Committee ... [nor] circulated in advance" (Blick 2005, 50).

The obvious corrective is to pull the fœderative powers out of the list of peacetime cabinet responsibilities and create a purpose-built institutional home for these wartime powers. Most simply, whenever the cabinet met to discuss either the negotiation or ratification of a treaty or the question of war or peace, it would meet, not as the cabinet, but officially and self-consciously as the Council on War and Peace. To make this change of function clear and distinct, when sitting as the Council on War and Peace, the cabinet could take an additional, special oath. For example, it could swear or affirm a version of Cleisthenes' bouletic oath, "To advise according to the laws [of war and peace] what was best for the people." In addition, the council would be supported by a dedicated professional staff, separate from the cabinet staff. As such, "infrequent oral briefings" would not be permitted. Instead, "excellent quality papers" written by the dedicated and other government staff would be required; they would be circulated and discussed in advance in a council committee, before being debated in the Council on War and Peace. Once it was up and running as an official institution, roll-call votes would be required and published for the final ratification of a treaty or for a declaration of war. Publication of the votes of the members of the council would be required to ensure that both the members and the public understood the seriousness of the council's business. That is, to recall the concluding words of the Declaration of Independence, by his vote, each member of the council took the personal responsibility to "support of this [Treaty or] Declaration, with a firm Reliance on the Protection of divine Providence, we mutually pledge to each other our [political] Lives, our [political] Fortunes, and our sacred Honor."

A more ambitious corrective would be to establish a Council on War and Peace as an entirely new and autonomous institution of, say, ten to twenty members. The core of such an autonomous institution would be the cabinet, all of it or some subsection. To this core would be added the leaders of the opposition. The two parameters for adding the leaders of the opposition would be 1) a formula to ensure that parties constituting two-thirds or, perhaps, three-fourths of the Parliament were represented on the Council on War and Peace and 2) that the members of the opposition did not outnumber the members of the cabinet. The second parameter is needed to ensure that the government of the day has the final say, as is only fitting. The first parameter is needed because the government of the day is not truly fit to decide the question of war or peace to the exclusion of the opposition. The fœderative powers of negotiating and ratifying treaties as well as declaring war engage the whole of the nation in distinctive and special ways that call for more than a decision of the majority party in Parliament. The government of the day, being the majority, is fully competent to decide peacetime matters without opposition support – raising or lowering taxes, building bridges to nowhere, and so on. However, wartime matters are different. Forcing a treaty or a declaration of war through the Council on War and Peace without a single vote from the opposition members is not acceptable. Such a government has forsaken national leadership for partisan hubris. It is a government eager to repeat the American experience in Vietnam and elsewhere.

References

Adams, Henry. 1896–1904. *History of the United States of America.* 9 vols. New York: Charles Scribner's Sons

Adams, John. 1850–6. *The Works of John Adams, Second President of the United States: with A Life of the Author, by his grandson Charles Francis Adams.* Boston: Charles C. Little and James Brown.

Ammon, Harry. 1990. *James Monroe: The Quest for National Identity.* Charlottesville: University Press of Virginia.

Annals of Congress. 1834–56. Washington, DC.

Arnold, Hugh M. 1975. Official Justifications for America's Role in Indo-China, 1949–67. *Asian Affairs* 3 (1) September/October, 31–48.

Austin, J. L. (John Langshaw). 1975. *How to Do Things with Words.* Ed. J. O. Urmsom and Marina Sbisa. Cambridge, MA: Harvard University Press.

Bagehot, Walter. 1963 [1864]. *The English Constitution.* London: Collins.

Blick, Andrew. 2005. *How to Go to War: A Handbook for Democratic Leaders.* London: Politico's Publishers.

Bodin, Jean. 1962. *The Six Bookes of a Commonweale: A facsimile reprint of the English translation of 1606, corrected and supplemented in the light of a new comparison with the French and Latin texts.* Ed. and intro. Kenneth Douglas McRae. Cambridge, MA: Harvard University Press.

Brant, Irving. 1941–61. *James Madison.* 6 vols. Indianapolis, IN: Bobbs-Merrill, Co.

Brigham, Clarence S., ed. 1968 (1911). *British Royal Proclamations Relating to North America, 1603–1783.* New York: Burt Franklin.

Bush, George H. 1990. *Public Papers of the Presidents of the United States: George Bush 1989,* (in Two Books) Book II – July 1 to December 31, 1989. Washington, DC: U.S. Government Printing Office.

1992. *Public Papers of the Presidents of the United States: George Bush 1991,* (in Two Books) Book I – January 1 to June 30, 1991. Washington, DC: U.S. Government Printing Office.

Butler, Judith. 1990. Performative Acts and Gender Constitution: An Essay in Phenomenology and Feminist Theory. In *Performing Feminisms: Feminist Critical Theory and Theatre*. Ed. Sue-Ellen Case. Baltimore: Johns Hopkins University Press.

Butler, Robin. 2004. *Return to An Address of the Honourable the House of Commons Dated 14th July 2004 for the Review of Intelligence on Weapons of Mass Destruction Report of a Committee of Privy Counsellors, Chairman: the Rt. Hon the Lord Butler of Brockwell KG GCB CVO*. http://www.butlerreview.org.uk/report/index.asp. Accessed 11 February 2006.

Cappon, Lester J., ed. 1959. *The Adams-Jefferson Letters: The Complete Correspondence between Thomas Jefferson and Abigail and John Adams*. 2 vols. Chapel Hill: University of North Carolina Press.

Carroll, Lewis. 1962. *Alice's Adventures in Wonderland and Through the Looking-Glass*. New York: Collier Books.

Churchill, Winston. 1941. Text of Prime Minister Churchill's Speech in Commons on Japan's Attack. *New York Times*, 9 December, 14.

Churchill, Winston S. 1947. Speech in the House of Commons, 11 November 1947. *Parliamentary Debates*, Commons, 5th ser., vol. 444.

Cicero, Marcus Tullius. 1928. *De Re Publica, De Legibus*. Trans. Clinton Walker Keyes. Cambridge, MA: Harvard University Press. London: William Heinemann.

1928. *De Officiis*. Trans. Walter Miller. New York: G. P. Putnam's Sons.

1967. *On Moral Obligation: A New Translation of Cicero's "De Officiis."* Trans. John Higginbotham. Berkeley: University of California Press.

1969. *Cicero in Twenty-eight Volumes. XV, Philippics*. Trans. Walter A. Ker, the Loeb Classical Library. Cambridge, MA: Harvard University Press.

1979. *Pro Milone*. Trans. N. H. Watts. Cambridge, MA: Harvard University Press; London: Heinemann.

Clausewitz, Carl von. 1976. *On War*. Ed. and Trans Michael Howard and Peter Paret. Princeton, NJ: Princeton University Press.

Clay, Henry. 1959–84. *The Papers of Henry Clay*. Ed. James H. Hopkins; Assoc. Ed. Mary W. M. Hargreares. Lexington: University of Kentucky Press.

Clinton, William J. 2000. Statement on Signing the Iraq Liberation Act of 1998, October 31, 1998. *Public Papers of the Presidents: William J. Clinton – 1998*, Vol. 2. Washington, DC: U.S. Government Printing Office.

Congressional Record. 1873–. Washington, DC: U.S. Government Printing Office.

Cooper, Joseph. 1965. Jeffersonian Attitudes toward Executive Leadership and Committee Development in the House of Representatives, 1789–1829. *Western Political Quarterly* XVII (1), 45–63.

Department of Commerce. 1921. *Statistical Abstract of the United States, 1920: No. 442, Troops Engaged in War*. Washington, DC: U.S. Government Printing Office.

Duby, Georges. 1990. *The Legend of Bouvines: War, Religion and Culture in the Middle Ages*. Berkeley: University of California Press.

Eagleton, Clyde. 1938. The Form and Function of the Declaration of War. *American Journal of International Law* 32 (1) January, 19–35.

Elsea, Jennifer K. and Richard F. Grimmett. 2006. Declarations of War and Authorizations for the Use of Military Force: Historical Background and Legal Implications, Updated August 11. *CRS Report for Congress*, Order Code RL31133. Washington, DC: Congressional Research Service.

Ely, John Hart. 1993. *War and Responsibility: Constitutional Lessons of Vietnam and Its Aftermath*. Princeton, NJ: Princeton University Press.

Farquhar, A. B. 1908. Intimate Recollections of Grover Cleveland. *Harper's Weekly* 1 August, 15.

Fisher, Louis. 1995. *Presidential War Power*. Lawrence: University Press of Kansas.

Fisher, Louis and David Gray Adler. 1998. The War Powers Resolution: Time to Say Goodbye. *Political Science Quarterly* 113 (1), 1–20.

Fisher, Louis. 2008. The Baker-Christopher War Powers Commission. *Presidential Studies Quarterly* 39 (1) March 128–40.

Ford, Paul Leicester, ed. 1905. *The Works of Thomas Jefferson*, Vols. I–XII New York: G. P. Putnam's Sons.

Foreign Relations of the United States 1861–2003. Department of State: Washington, DC: U.S. Government Printing Office.

Glennon, Michael J. 1995. Too Far Apart: Repeal the War Powers Resolution. *University of Miami Law Review* 50 (1) October, 17–31.

Gold, Gerald, Allan M. Siegal, and Samuel Abt, eds. 1971. *The Pentagon Papers: As Published by the New York Times, Based on Investigative Reporting by Neil Sheehan*. New York: Bantam Books.

Gould, Lewis L. 1982. *The Spanish-American War and President McKinley*. Lawrence: University Press of Kansas.

Grant, Ulysses S. 1990. *Ulysses S. Grant: Memoirs and Selected Letters: Personal Memoirs of U. S. Grant: Selected Letters 1839–1865*. New York: Library of America.

Grimmett, Richard F. 2009. *Instances of Use of United States Armed Forces Abroad, 1798–2008*. Washington, DC: Congressional Research Service, February 2, 2009, RL32170.

Hall, David L. and Roger T. Ames. 1987. *Thinking through Confucius*. Albany: State University of New York Press.

Hallett, Brien. 1998. *The Lost Art of Declaring War*. Urbana: University of Illinois Press.

——— 2008. Declarations of War. In *Encyclopedia of Violence, Peace, and Conflict*, San Diego, CA: Academic Press.

——— 2008a. Just-War Criteria. In *Encyclopedia of Violence, Peace, and Conflict*, Ed. Lester R. Kurtz, 2nd ed. San Diego, CA: Academic Press.

Hamilton, Alexander. 1961–87. *The Papers of Alexander Hamilton*. 27 vols. Ed. Harold C. Syrett. New York: Columbia University Press.

Harbom, Lotta and Peter Wallensteen. 2010. Armed Conflicts, 1946–2009. *Journal of Peace Research*, 47 July 2010, 501–9.

Hatzenbuehler, Ronald L. and Robert L. Ivie. 1983. *Congress Declares War: Rhetoric, Leadership, and Partisanship in the Early Republic*. Kent, OH: Kent State University Press.

Hazleton, John. 1970 [1906]. *The Declaration of Independence: Its History*. New York: Da Capo Press.

Hill, George. 1940–8. *A History of Cyprus.* Cambridge: Cambridge University Press.

Howell, William G. and Jon C. Pevehouse. 2007. *While Danger Gathers: Congressional Checks on Presidential War Powers.* Princeton, NJ: Princeton University Press.

Jefferson, Thomas. 1801. *Manual of Parliamentary Practice for the Use of the Senate of the United States.* Washington, DC: Samuel Harrison Smith.

Jessup, Philip. 1950. Memorandum of conversation, dated Sunday, June 25, 1950, by Philip C. Jessup summarizing a post-dinner meeting among the President and his advisors at Blair House. Truman Presidential Museum and Library http://www.trumanlibrary.org/whistlestop/study_collections/korea/large/week1/kw_4_1.htm. Accessed 27 May 2006.

Jillson, Calvin and Rick K. Wilson. 1994. *Congressional Dynamics: Structure, Coordination, and Choice in the First American Congress, 1774–1789.* Stanford, CA: Stanford University Press.

Journals of the Continental Congress, 1774–1789. 1904–37. Ed. Worthington C. Ford et al. Washington, DC: U.S. Government Printing Office.

Kessler, Glenn. 2003. U.S. Decision on Iraq Has Puzzling Past: Opponents to War Wonder When, How Policy Was Set. *Washington Post,* January 12, A1.

Ketcham, Ralph. 1971. *James Madison: A Biography.* New York: Macmillan.

King, Martin Luther. 1972. The Philosophy of the Student Nonviolent Movement (16 November 1961). In *The Voice of Black America.* Ed. Philip S. Foner. New York: Simon & Schuster.

    1986. *A Testament of Hope: The Essential Writings of Martin Luther King Jr.* Ed. James Melvin Washington. New York: Harper & Row.

Kinnard, Douglas. 1977. *The War Managers.* Hanover, N.H.: University Press of New England.

Kluckhohn, Frank L. 1941. Unity in Congress. *New York Times,* 9 December, p. 1:7.

Koepp, Steve and Mark Thompson. 2006–7. The Real War: What Led to So Many Post 9/11 Fumbles? a Group of Intrepid Authors Gives Us Answers. *Time,* 25 December–1 January, 158–62.

Kriesberg, Louis. 1998. *Constructive Conflict: From Escalation to Resolution.* Lanham, MD: Rowman & Littlefield.

Krutz, Glen S. and Jeffrey S. Peake. 2009. *Treaty Politics and the Rise of Executive Agreements: International Commitments in a System of Shared Power.* Ann Arbor: University of Michigan Press.

Leech, Margaret. 1959. *In the Days of McKinley.* New York: Harper & Row.

Lincoln, Abraham. 1907. *Abraham Lincoln: Complete Works.* Ed. John G. Nicolay and John Hay. New York: Century Co.

Livy. 1919. *Livy in Fourteen Volumes.* Trans. B. O. Foster. Loeb Classical Library. London: William Heinemann.

Lobel, Jules. 1995. "Little Wars" and the Constitution. *University of Miami Law Review* 50 (1) October, 61–79.

Locke, John. 1764 [1690]. *Two Treatises of Government.* London. http://www.constitution.org/jl/2ndtr00.htm. Accessed 7 June 2009.

Madison, James. 1900–10. *The Writings of James Madison*, 9 Vol. Ed. Gaillard Hunt. New York: G. P. Putnam's Sons.

1966. *Notes of Debates in the Federal Convention of 1787 Reported by James Madison*. Ed. Adrienne Koch. Athens: Ohio University Press.

Maier, Pauline. 1997. *American Scripture: Making the Declaration of Independence*. New York: Alfred A. Knopf.

Malone, Dumas. 1948–81. *Jefferson and His Time*. 6 vols. Boston: Little, Brown.

Manicas, Peter T. 1989. *War and Democracy*. Oxford: Basil Blackwell.

Mann, Robert. 2001. *A Grand Delusion: America's Descent into Vietnam*. New York: Basic Books.

McElroy, Robert. 1923. *Grover Cleveland: The Man and the Statesman: An Authorized Biography*. 2 vols. New York: Harper and Brothers.

Metz, Steven. 2010. *Decisionmaking in Operation Iraqi Freedom: Removing Saddam Hussein by Force*. Carlisle, PA: Strategic Studies Institute.

Moe, Terry and William G. Howell. 1999. Unilateral Action and Presidential Power: A Theory. *Presidential Studies Quarterly* 29 (4) December, 850–72.

Molloy, Charles. 1672. *De Jure Maritimo or Treatise of Affairs Maritime and of Commerce*, 2 vol. London.

Monroe, James. 1960. *James Monroe Papers 1960*. Presidential Papers Microfilm. Washington, DC: Library of Congress (Microfilm S91026).

Montesquieu, Charles de Secondat, baron de. 1914. *The Spirit of the Laws*. Trans. Thomas Nugent; revised by J. V. Prichard. London: G. Bell & Sons, Ltd.

Moss, Kenneth B. 2008. *Undeclared War and the Future of U.S. Foreign Policy*. Baltimore: Johns Hopkins University Press.

The National War Powers Commission Report. 2008. Charlottesville: Miller Center of Public Affairs, University of Virginia. (Chaired by James Baker III and Warren Christopher) http://millercenter.org/policy/commissions/warpowers. Accessed 4 August 2008.

Nelson, W. Dale. 1990. Bush's Hitler Analogy Disputed. *Seattle Times*, 2 November. http://community.seattletimes.nwsource.com/archive/?date=19901102&slug =1101861. Accessed 11 November 2009.

Nevins, Allan. 1932. *Grover Cleveland: A Study in Courage*. New York: Dodd, Mead and Co.

Nussbaum, Arthur. 1952. The Significance of Roman Law in the History of International Law. *University of Pennsylvania Law Review* 100 (5), 678–87.

Office of the Secretary of Defense, Defense Manpower Data Center, Statistical Information and Analysis Division. N.D. *Principal Wars in Which the United States Participated, U.S. Military Personnel Serving and Casualties* a/. http:// siadapp.dmdc.osd.mil/personnel/CASUALTY/WCPRINCIPAL.pdf. Accessed 9 September 2009.

Paine, Thomas. 1989. *Political Writings*. Ed. Bruce Kuklick. New York: Cambridge University Press.

Pisan, Christine de. 1937. *The Book of Fayttes of Armes and of Chyualrye (Le Livre des Faits d'Armes et de Chevalerie)*. Trans. William Caxton (1489); Ed. A. T. P. Byles. Published by the Early English Text Society. London: Humphrey Milford, Oxford: Oxford University Press.

Polk, James. 1846. Proclamation. *The Times* [of London], 29 May, 6.

Pritchard, James B., ed. 1955. Gilgamesh and Agga. In *Ancient Near Eastern Texts, Relating to the Old Testament*, 2nd ed., corrected and enlarged. Princeton, NJ: Princeton University Press.

Reagan, Ronald. 1982. Letter to the Speaker of the House and the President Pro Tempore of the Senate on the Deployment of United States Forces in Beirut, Lebanon, August 24, 1982. *The Public Papers of President Ronald W. Reagan*. Ronald Reagan Presidential Library. http://www.reagan.utexas.edu/archives/speeches/1982/82482e.htm. Accessed 19 July 2010.

1982a. Letter to the Speaker of the House and the President Pro Tempore of the Senate Reporting on United States Participation in the Multinational Force in Lebanon, September 29, 1982. *The Public Papers of President Ronald W. Reagan*. Ronald Reagan Presidential Library. http://www.reagan.utexas.edu/archives/speeches/1982/92982e.htm. Accessed 19 July 2010.

1983. Letter to the Speaker of the House and the President Pro Tempore of the Senate Reporting on United States Participation in the Multinational Force in Lebanon, August 30, 1983. *The Public Papers of President Ronald W. Reagan*. Ronald Reagan Presidential Library. http://www.reagan.utexas.edu/archives/speeches/1983/83083a.htm. Accessed 19 July 2010.

1983a. Statement on Signing the Multinational Force in Lebanon Resolution, October 12, 1983. *The Public Papers of President Ronald W. Reagan*. Ronald Reagan Presidential Library. http://www.reagan.utexas.edu/archives/speeches/1983/101283c.htm. Accessed 19 July 2010.

1984. Letter to the Speaker of the House and the President Pro Tempore of the Senate on the Termination of United States Participation in the Multinational Force in Lebanon, March 30, 1984. *The Public Papers of President Ronald W. Reagan*. Ronald Reagan Presidential Library. http://www.reagan.utexas.edu/archives/speeches/1984/33084f.htm. Accessed 19 July 2010.

Ricks, Thomas. 2006. *Fiasco: The American Military Adventure in Iraq*. New York: Penguin Press.

Rousseau, Jean-Jacques. 1950. *The Social Contract and Discourses*. Trans. G. D. H. Cole. New York: E. P. Dutton.

Schlesinger, Arthur M., Jr. 1973. *The Imperial Presidency*. Boston: Houghton Mifflin.

Searle, John. 1975. Indirect Speech Acts. In *Syntax and Semantics*. Vol. 3: *Speech Acts*. Ed. P. Cole and J. L. Morgan. New York: Academic Press.

1995. *The Construction of Social Reality*. New York: Free Press.

Sidak, J. Gregory. 1991. "To Declare War." *Duke Law Journal* 41 (1), 27–121.

2005. The Quasi War Cases – and Their Relevance to Whether "Letters of Marque and Reprisal" Constrain Presidential War Powers. *Harvard Journal of Public Policy* 28 (2) Spring, 466–500.

Snyder, John. 1975. Truman Library Institute conference comment, May. [*The Korean War: A 25-year Perspective* Regents Press of Kansas, 1976)] http://www.trumanlibrary.org/whistlestop/study_collections/korea/large/korea62550.htm. Accessed 1 December 2007.

Tacitus. 1970. *Dialogus, Agricola, Germanica*. Trans. Maurice Hutton. Loeb Classical Library. Cambridge, MA: Harvard University Press.

Teletype Conference. 1950. Teletype Conference, dated June 25, 1950, among Commander in Chief, Far East, Douglas MacArthur, the secretaries of the Army and Air Force, Frank Pace, Jr., and Thomas Fineletter, and other U.S. military officials. Truman Presidential Museum and Library http://www.trumanlibrary. org/whistlestop/study_collections/korea/large/week1/kw_7_1.htm. Accessed 27 May 2006.

Tenet, George. 2007. *At the Center of the Storm: My Years at the CIA*. New York: HarperCollins.

Thucydides. 1982. *The Peloponnesian War: The Crawley Translation*. Revised by T. E. Wick. New York: Modern Library.

Trask, David F. 1981. *The War with Spain in 1898*. New York: Macmillan.

Truman, Harry S. 1965. *Public Papers of the Presidents of the United States: Harry S. Truman, January 1 to December 31, 1950*. Washington, DC: U.S. Government Printing Office.

United Kingdom. 2003. *Parliamentary Debates*, Commons: http://www.publications. parliament.uk/pa/cm200203/cmhansrd/cm030318/debtext/30318-06. htm#30318-06_head1. Accessed 20 May 2003.

U.S. Census Bureau. 2009. *Statistical Abstract of the United States*. http://www.census.gov/prod/2008pubs/09statab/pop.pdf. Accessed 2 June 2009.

Vitoria, Francisco de. 1934 (1532). *De Jure Belli*. In James Brown Scott, *The Spanish Origins of International Law: Francisco de Vitoria and His Law of Nations*. Oxford: Clarendon Press and London: Humphrey Milford.

Watson, Alan. 1993 *International Law in Archaic Rome: War and Religion*. Baltimore: Johns Hopkins University Press.

White House. 2002. *White House Discussion Draft of September 19, 2002, Joint Resolution To authorize the use of United States Armed Forces against Iraq*. http:// usinfo.state.gov/topical/pol/terror/02091914.htm. Accessed 24 September 2002.

White, Leonard D. 1951. *The Jeffersonians: A Study in Administrative History 1801–1829*. New York: Macmillian.

Wills, Garry. 1979. *Inventing America: Jefferson's Declaration of Independence*. New York: Vintage Books.

Wilson, Woodrow. 1966–93. *The Papers of Woodrow Wilson*. 69 vols. Ed. Arthur S. Link et al. Princeton, NJ: Princeton University Press.

World Islamic Front Statement. 1998. Jihad against Jews and Crusaders. http://www. fas.org/irp/world/para/docs/980223-fatwa.htm. Accessed 6 August 2007.

Wright, Quincy. 1932. When Does War Exist? *American Journal of International Law* 26 (2) April, 362–8.

Woodward, Bob. 2004. *Plan of Attack*. New York: Simon & Schuster.

Wormuth, Francis D. and Edwin B. Firmage. 1989. *To Chain the Dog of War: The War Power of Congress in History and Law*. Urbana: University of Illinois Press.

Yoo, John. 2005. *The Powers of War and Peace: The Constitution and Foreign Affairs after 9/11*. Chicago, IL: University of Chicago Press.

Index